BRINCH HANSEN ON PASCAL COMPILERS

PER BRINCH HANSEN

PRENTICE-HALL, INC., Englewood Cliffs, New Jersey 07632

Library of Congress Cataloging in Publication Data

Brinch Hansen, Per (date)
Brinch Hansen on Pascal compilers.

Bibliography: p.
Includes index.
1. PASCAL (Computer program language) 2. Compiling
(Electronic computers) I. Title.
QA76.73.P2B75 1985 001.64'2 84-26586
ISBN 0-13-083098-4

Editorial/production supervision: *Kathryn Gollin Marshak*
Cover design: *Ben Santora*
Manufacturing buyer: *Gordon Osbourne*

To my teacher
Konrad Jahn

Printed in the United States of America

10 9 8 7 6 5 4 3 2

ISBN 0-13-083098-4 01

PRENTICE-HALL INTERNATIONAL (UK) LIMITED, *London*
PRENTICE-HALL OF AUSTRALIA PTY. LIMITED, *Sydney*
EDITORA PRENTICE-HALL DO BRASIL, LTDA., *Rio de Janeiro*
PRENTICE-HALL CANADA INC., *Toronto*
PRENTICE-HALL HISPANOAMERICANA, S.A., *Mexico*
PRENTICE-HALL OF INDIA PRIVATE LIMITED, *New Delhi*
PRENTICE-HALL OF JAPAN, INC., *Tokyo*
PRENTICE-HALL OF SOUTHEAST ASIA PTE. LTD., *Singapore*
WHITEHALL BOOKS LIMITED, *Wellington, New Zealand*

CONTENTS

ALGORITHMS

The following is a list of the algorithms described in the text. The format of the list is illustrated by the following example:

5.13 BlockBody [2] *91*

This entry refers to Algorithm 5.13, which is the second version of a procedure named BlockBody. The procedure appears on page 91.

PREFACE

This is a book about compilers for beginners. To get the most out of it you should know Pascal and have access to a computer with a Pascal compiler.

While emphasizing *practical methods*, the book

- Concentrates on a single Pascal compiler.
- Discusses all the compilation phases in depth.
- Uses the recursive-descent method of compilation.
- Shows you how to test a compiler systematically.
- Explains how you make Pascal code portable.
- Presents performance figures for the compiler.
- Includes the program text of the compiler.
- Describes a compiler project in detail.
- Suggests further reading.

You can use any Pascal compiler for the project, including the Pascal* compiler that I developed for the *IBM Personal Computer* and the *Compaq Portable Computer* (see the information on Software Distribution at the end of the book).

The text and the project are designed for an undergraduate compiler course. I assume that you understand Pascal and know how to use sets, pointers, and variant records.

Every chapter deals with a major compilation task: lexical analysis, syntax analysis, scope analysis, type analysis, and code generation. While writing the book, I programmed and tested the Pascal compiler and kept changing it until it was easy to describe.

The compiler project is divided into phases that correspond to the chapters. After reading a chapter, you will be ready to program the corresponding part of the project. By writing your own compiler in Pascal, you will become familiar with the programming techniques described. In the project description, I have indicated how many Pascal lines I had to write in each phase of the compiler project.

The book does not attempt to cover different compilation methods. Such an attempt is often confusing for the beginner, who may have difficulty seeing how all the parts of a compiler fit together. Instead, I explain a single compiler in detail. Like most other Pascal compilers, this one is written in Pascal itself using the recursive-descent method. The great advantage of this method is that the compiler can be derived directly from the syntax of the programming language. Semantic analysis and code generation are easily added to this type of compiler.

Now, why should you be interested in compilers? After all, most programmers in industry never write one. Well, there are several reasons why compilers are worth studying: In most computer courses, you write small programs only. The compiler course is probably the only chance you will get as a student to write a realistic program of 1000 lines (or more) and make it work. If you can manage the details of a compiler, if you know how to test it systematically so that it never fails, and if you can write an understandable description of it, you know how to program!

The programming methods used in a compiler are also useful in other kinds of programs. For example, hashing is used in operating systems to look up file names in disk directories. Syntax checking of text is an important method for discovering invalid records in commercial data processing. Syntax-directed programming based on BNF rules is also an elegant method of organizing word processing programs.

Finally, it must be said that, like a good driver, a good programmer should know what is "under the hood." An understanding of how programs are compiled and executed will help you understand the basic limitations of present computers. Without that understanding, it is not easy to write efficient programs that push computers to their limits.

The programming language used in this book is a Pascal variant called Pascal* ("Pascal Star"). Pascal* omits some of the less important concepts of Pascal and includes a few new features that are useful for writing compilers and operating systems.

PER BRINCH HANSEN

1

WHAT A COMPILER DOES

A program written in a programming language is a piece of text; for example,

```
program P;
var x: integer;
begin x := 1 end.
```

This Pascal program describes the following sequence of actions:

(1) Allocate storage for a variable x.

(2) Assign the value 1 to x.

(3) Release the storage space of x.

Before a computer can execute this program, it must be *translated* from Pascal into *machine code*. The machine code is a sequence of numbers that instruct the computer to perform the actions. In this example, the machine code might be the following numbers:

```
24 1 2 5 1
37 3
3 1
38
7
```

Each line defines a computer instruction consisting of an operation code possibly followed by some arguments. The code becomes a bit more readable if we replace the operation codes by readable names and enclose the arguments in parentheses:

```
Program(1, 2, 5, 1)
LocalVar(3)
Constant(1)
SimpleAssign
EndProgram
```

A system program, known as a *compiler*, performs the translation from Pascal to machine code. Compilers play a crucial role in software development: They enable you to ignore the complicated instruction sets of computers and write programs in a readable notation. Compilers also detect numerous programming errors even before you begin testing your programs.

However, you can ignore the code generated by a compiler only if you know that the compiler never makes a mistake! If a compiler does not always work, programming becomes extremely complicated. In that case, you will discover that the Pascal report no longer defines exactly what your program does. This is obviously unacceptable.

So the following design rule is essential:

Rule 1.1:
A compiler must be error-free.

This requirement is quite a challenge to the compiler designer when you consider that a compiler is a program of several thousand lines. Compiler writing forces you to apply very systematic methods of program design, testing, and documentation. It is one of the best educational experiences for a software engineer.

The input to a compiler is a program text. The first task of the compiler is to read the program text character by character and recognize the symbols of the language. The compiler will, for example, read the characters

p r o g r a m

and recognize them as the single word **program**. At this point, the compiler views the previous program example as the following sequence of symbols:

program name P **semicolon**
var name x **colon name** integer **semicolon**
begin name x **becomes numeral** 1 **end period**

This phase of compilation is called *lexical analysis.* (The word *lexical* means "pertaining to the words or vocabulary of a language.")

The next task of the compiler is to check that the symbols occur in the right order. For example, the compiler recognizes the sentence

x := 1

as an assignment statement. But if you write

x = 1

instead, the compiler will indicate that this is not a valid statement. This phase of compilation is called *syntax analysis.* (The word *syntax* means "the structure of the word order in a sentence.")

The syntax analysis is concerned only with the sequence of symbols in sentences. As long as a sentence consists of a name followed by the := symbol and an expression, it will be recognized as an assignment statement. But even though the syntax of the statement is correct, it may still be meaningless, as in the following example:

y := 1

which refers to an undefined variable y. The assignment statement

x := true

is also meaningless because the variable x and the value *true* are of different types (integer and Boolean). The phase of compilation that detects meaningless sentences such as these is called *semantic analysis.* (The word *semantics* means "the study of meaning.")

As these examples show, the compiler must perform two kinds of semantic checks: First, the compiler must make sure that the names used in a program refer to known objects: either predefined standard objects, such as the type *integer*, or objects that are defined in the program, such as the variable *x*. The problem is to recognize a definition such as

var x: integer;

and determine in which part of the program the object x can be used. This task is called *scope analysis.* (The word *scope* means "the extent of application.") During this part of the compilation, the compiler will indicate if the program uses undefined names, such as y, or introduces ambiguous names in definitions, such as

var x: integer; x: integer;

Second, the compiler must check that the operands are of compatible types. This task is called *type analysis.*

When you compile a new program for the first time, the compiler nearly always finds some errors in it. It will often require several cycles of editing and recompilation before the compiler accepts the program as formally correct. So, *in designing a compiler, you must keep in mind that most of the time it will be used to compile incorrect programs!*

If there are many errors in a program, it is convenient to output the error messages in a file which can be inspected or printed after the compilation. However, the compiler will be able to complete this file and close it properly only if the compilation itself terminates properly. If the compilation of an incorrect program causes a run-time failure, such as an arithmetic overflow, the error messages will be lost and you will have to guess what happened.

To avoid this situation, we must impose the following design requirement:

Rule 1.2:

A compilation must always terminate, no matter what the input looks like.

The easiest way to satisfy this requirement is to terminate the compilation when the first error has been detected. The user must then remove this error and recompile the program to find the next error, and so on.

Since a compilation may take several minutes, this method is just too slow. To speed up the program development process, we must add another design requirement:

Rule 1.3:

A compiler should attempt to find as many errors as possible during a single compilation.

As you will see later, this goal is not easy to achieve.

There is one exception to the rule that a compilation must always terminate: If a program is so big that the compiler exceeds the limits of its tables, the only reasonable thing to do is to report this and stop the compilation. This is called a compilation *failure.*

If the compiler finds no formal errors in a program, it proceeds to the last phase of compilation, *code generation.* In this phase, the compiler determines the amount of storage needed for the code and variables of the program and emits final instructions. The main difficulty is that most computers have very unsystematic instruction sets that are ill suited for automatic code generation.

These, then, are the major tasks of a compiler:

Lexical analysis
Syntax analysis
Scope analysis
Type analysis
Code generation

Each of these tasks will be discussed in a separate chapter.

2

A PASCAL SUBSET

The compiler described in this book accepts a subset of the programming language Pascal known as Pascal— ("Pascal Minus"). This chapter describes Pascal— and defines the syntax of the language. I assume that you already know Pascal.

2.1 PASCAL MINUS

The Boolean and integer types are the only simple types in Pascal—. These types are standard types. The language does not have characters, reals, subrange types, or enumerated types.

The structured types are array types and record types. Packed types and variant records are not supported, nor are sets, pointers, and file types.

Every type has a name: either a standard name (*integer* or *Boolean*) or a name introduced by a type definition: for example,

```
type
  table = array [1 . . 100] of integer;
  stack = record contents: table; size: integer end;
```

A variable definition, such as

var A: table;

is correct, but the following is not:

var A: **array** [1 . . 100] **of** integer;

since it introduces an array type that has no name.

A type definition cannot rename an already existing type, as in the example:

type number = integer;

Most operations on a pair of operands are valid only if the operands are of the same type. Since every type has a name (and one name only!), it is tempting to suggest that two types are the same if, and only if, they have the same name. A name can, however, be defined as a type name in one block and as a variable name in another block. When this is taken into account, we end up with the following rule: Two types are the same only if they have the same name and the same scope. In Pascal, the rules for type compatibility are more complicated [IEEE, 1983].

Constant definitions, such as

const max = 100; on = true;

introduce names for constants.

In Pascal—, all constants have simple types. There are no string constants.

Variable definitions have the same form as in Pascal; for example,

var x, y: integer; yes: Boolean; lifo: stack;

The relational operators

< = > <= <> >=

can be applied only to operands of simple types.

Pascal— includes assignment statements, procedure statements, if statements, while statements, and compound statements. Following are some examples of these statements.

```
x := x - 1

search(x, yes, i)

if x > 0 then x := x - 1

while index < limit do
  if A[index] = value then limit := index
  else index := index + 1

begin
  lifo.size := lifo.size + 1;
  lifo.contents[lifo.size] := x
end
```

There are no goto statements (or labels), no case or repeat statements, and no for or with statements.

Pascal— supports nested procedures with value parameters and variable parameters. A procedure cannot be used as a parameter of another procedure, and functions cannot be defined.

The only standard procedures are

read(x)

which inputs an integer value and assigns it to a variable x, and

write(e)

which outputs an integer value given by an expression e.

Algorithm 2.1 illustrates most of the features of Pascal—.

To summarize, Pascal— includes the following features of Pascal:

Standard types (Boolean, integer)
Standard procedures (read, write)
Constant definitions
Type definitions (arrays, records)
Variable definitions
Expressions
Assignment statements
Procedure statements
If statements
While statements
Compound statements
Procedure definitions

```
program ProgramExample;
const n = 100;
type table = array [1 . . n] of integer;
var A: table; i, x: integer; yes: Boolean;

procedure search(value: integer;
  var found: Boolean; var index: integer);
var limit: integer;
begin index := 1; limit := n;
  while index < limit do
    if A[index] = value then limit := index
    else index := index + 1;
  found := A[index] = value
end;

begin {input table} i := 1;
  while i <= n do
    begin read(A[i]); i := i + 1 end;
  {test search} read(x);
  while x <> 0 do
    begin search(x, yes, i);
      write(x);
      if yes then write(i);
      read(x)
    end
end.
```

Algorithm 2.1

and excludes the following concepts:

- Char and real
- Subrange types
- Enumerated types
- Variant records
- Set types
- Pointer types
- File types
- Packed types
- Nameless types
- Renamed types
- Function definitions
- Procedural parameters

Goto statements (and labels)
Case statements
Repeat statements
For statements
With statements

Pascal— has enough features to illustrate all the problems of compilation. The omitted features add more detail to a compiler, but the added logic is basically "more of the same."

2.2 VOCABULARY

The vocabulary of a natural language like English is *words*. The vocabulary of a programming language like Pascal— is symbols such as

begin sort 13 :=

Pascal— has four kinds of symbols, called word symbols, names, numerals, and special symbols.

The *word symbols* are

and **array** **begin** **const** **div** **do** **else**
end **if** **mod** **not** **of** **or** **procedure**
program **record** **then** **type** **var** **while**

In this book, the word symbols are shown in boldface.

The *special symbols* are

+ − * < = > <= <> >= :=
( ) [ ] , . : ; ..

A *numeral* is a decimal notation for a nonnegative integer; for example,

0 1351

A *name* consists of a letter which may be followed by more letters and digits; for example,

x Edison RC4000

In word symbols and names, capital letters are considered equivalent to the corresponding small letters. So the following names are equivalent to one another:

PASCAL   pascal   Pascal

Although a word symbol, such as **then,** is printed in boldface here, it will normally be displayed in roman type on a computer terminal, as in the following example:

```
if x > 0 then x := x - 1
```

You may omit some of the spaces between the symbols; for example,

```
if x>0 then x:=x-1
```

But if you remove the space between the word *then* and the name x, you get an incorrect sentence:

```
if x>0 thenx:=x-1
```

in which the Boolean expression x>0 is followed by an undefined name *thenx* instead of a **then** symbol. The purpose of the *space* is to separate the two symbols **then** and x.

Every line of program text ends with a *newline* character. Two symbols can also be separated by a newline character; for example,

```
if x>0 then
x:=x-1
```

or by a *comment* enclosed in braces:

```
if x>0 then{reserve resource}x:=x-1
```

A comment may extend over several lines and may contain other (nested) comments:

```
{This is a {nested} comment
that extends over two lines}
```

The character { cannot occur within a comment (except as part of a nested comment).

Spaces, newline characters, and comments are called *separators.* Any symbol may be preceded by one or more separators. Two adjacent word symbols, names, and numerals must be separated by at least one separator.

2.3 SYNTACTIC RULES

A sequence of symbols that is formed according according to the rules of a programming language is called a *sentence* in the language. In Pascal—, a variable definition, such as

var x: integer;

and an assignment statement, such as

x := x − 1

are sentences. However, as the following example shows, not every sequence of symbols is a sentence:

x − x := 1

The rules that define all possible sentences of a programming language are called the *grammar* of the language. We will define the grammar of Pascal— in a notation known as the extended *Backus-Naur form* (or BNF).

We will introduce BNF rules by means of examples that define the syntax of very simple arithmetic expressions. In these expressions, the only operands are numerals and the operators are either + or −. Some examples of these expressions are

−5   3 + 1066 − 4   118 − (7 + 12)

The following grammar defines all possible expressions of this form:

(1) Expression = [Operator] Term { Operator Term } .

(2) Operator = "+" | "−" .

(3) Term = Numeral | "(" Expression ")" .

(4) Numeral = Digit { Digit } .

(5) Digit = "0" | "1" | "2" | "3" | "4" |
"5" | "6" | "7" | "8" | "9" .

The grammar consists of five BNF rules:

Rule 1 says that an expression consists of three parts. The first part is either an operator or nothing. This is expressed by the notation

[Operator]

The second part is a term. The third part is zero or more occurrences of an operator followed by another term. This is expressed by the notation

{ Operator Term }

Rule 2 says that an operator is either a "+" or a "—".

Rule 3 says that a term is either a numeral or another expression enclosed in parentheses "(" and ")". The choice between the two possibilities is expressed by a vertical bar | that can be pronounced as "or". This rule illustrates the use of BNF to define sentences recursively.

Rule 4 says that a numeral consists of at least one digit possibly followed by more digits.

Rule 5 defines a digit as one of the characters "0", "1", . . . , "9".

To show that the sentence

118 — (7 + 12)

is an expression, we first use rules 4 and 5 to recognize all numerals in the sentence:

Numeral — (Numeral + Numeral)   Rules, 4, 5

By applying the other rules as well, we can gradually recognize the structure of the sentence and see that it is indeed an expression.

Numeral Operator (Numeral Operator Numeral)	Rule 2
Term Operator (Term Operator Term)	Rule 3
Term Operator (Expression)	Rule 1
Term Operator Term	Rule 3
Expression	Rule 1

After seeing this example, it is not hard to follow a more formal definition of BNF rules. The sentences of a programming language are divided into classes called *syntactic units*. Each syntactic unit has a name; for example,

Expression   Operator   Term   Numeral

The name of a syntactic unit consists of one or more letters.

A *BNF rule* has the form

N = E .

N is the name of a syntactic unit and E is a syntax expression that defines the corresponding class of sentences.

A *syntax expression* E has the form

T1 | T2 | . . . | Tn

T1, T2, . . . , Tn are called the syntax terms of E. The expression defines sentences of the form T1, or T2, . . . , or Tn.

A *syntax term* T has the form

F1 F2 . . . Fn

F1, F2, . . . , Fn are called the syntax factors of T. The term defines sentences that consist of a sentence of the form F1 followed by a sentence of the form F2 . . . followed by a sentence of the form Fn.

A *syntax factor* F of the form

[E]

describes sentences that are either empty or of the form E (where E is a syntax expression).

A syntax factor of the form

{ E }

describes sentences that consist of zero or more sentences of the form E (where E is a syntax expression).

A syntax factor of the form

N

refers to the sentences that are defined by the syntactic rule named N.

A syntax factor of the form

"ab . . . z"

defines the symbol ab . . . z.

The structure of a *BNF grammar* can be described in the BNF notation itself:

```
Grammar = { SyntacticRule } .
SyntacticRule = Name "=" SyntaxExpression "." .
SyntaxExpression = SyntaxTerm { "|" SyntaxTerm } .
SyntaxTerm = SyntaxFactor { SyntaxFactor } .
SyntaxFactor =
  "[" SyntaxExpression "]" | "{" SyntaxExpression "}" |
  Name | " " " Symbol " " " .
Name = Letter { Letter } .
Symbol = GraphicCharacter { Graphic Character } .
```

In the literature, syntactic rules are also called *productions* since they are rules for producing all the possible sentences of a language. The symbols of the language are called *terminal symbols.* The names of the productions are called *nonterminal symbols.* The nonterminal symbol that is the starting point of the grammar is called the *start symbol.* In the preceding example, the start symbol is the name Expression.

A BNF rule

N = E .

specifies that a nonterminal symbol N can be replaced by the syntax expression E regardless of the context in which N occurs. BNF grammars are therefore said to be *context-free.*

2.4 GRAMMAR

The following BNF grammar defines the syntax of Pascal– . The empty sentence is denoted Empty.

Program = "**program**" ProgramName ";" BlockBody "." .
BlockBody =
  [ConstantDefinitionPart] [TypeDefinitionPart]
  [VariableDefinitionPart] { ProcedureDefinition }
  CompoundStatement .
ConstantDefinitionPart =
  "**const**" ConstantDefinition { ConstantDefinition } .
ConstantDefinition = ConstantName "=" Constant ";" .
TypeDefinitionPart =
  "**type**" TypeDefinition { TypeDefinition } .
TypeDefinition = TypeName "=" New Type ";" .
NewType = NewArrayType | NewRecordType .
NewArrayType =
  "**array**" "[" IndexRange "]" "**of**" TypeName .
IndexRange = Constant ". ." Constant .
NewRecordType = "**record**" FieldList "**end**" .
FieldList = RecordSection { ";" RecordSection } .
RecordSection =
  FieldName { "," FieldName } ":" TypeName .
VariableDefinitionPart =
  "**var**" VariableDefinition { VariableDefinition } .
VariableDefinition = VariableGroup ";" .
VariableGroup =
  VariableName { "," VariableName } ":" TypeName .

ProcedureDefinition =
  "**procedure**" ProcedureName ProcedureBlock ";" .
ProcedureBlock =
  ["(" FormalParameterList ")"] ";" BlockBody .
FormalParameterList =
  ParameterDefinition { ";" ParameterDefinition } .
ParameterDefinition = ["**var**"] VariableGroup .
Statement =
  AssignmentStatement | ProcedureStatement |
  IfStatement | WhileStatement |
  CompoundStatement | Empty .
AssignmentStatement =
  VariableAccess ":=" Expression .
ProcedureStatement =
  ProcedureName ["(" ActualParameterList ")"] .
ActualParameterList =
  ActualParameter { "," ActualParameter } .
ActualParameter = Expression | VariableAccess .
IfStatement =
  "**if**" Expression "**then**" Statement
    ["**else**" Statement] .
WhileStatement =
  "**while**" Expression "**do**" Statement .
CompoundStatement =
  "**begin**" Statement { ";" Statement } "**end**" .
Expression = SimpleExpression
  [RelationalOperator SimpleExpression] .
RelationalOperator =
  "<" | "=" | ">" | "<=" | "<>" | ">=" .
SimpleExpression =
  [SignOperator] Term { AddingOperator Term } .
SignOperator = "+" | "—" .
AddingOperator = "+" | "—" | "**or**" .
Term = Factor { MultiplyingOperator Factor } .
MultiplyingOperator = "*" | "**div**" | "**mod**" | "**and**" .
Factor = Constant | VariableAccess |
  "(" Expression ")" | "**not**" Factor .
VariableAccess = VariableName { Selector } .
Selector = IndexedSelector | FieldSelector .
IndexedSelector = "[" Expression "]" .
FieldSelector = "." FieldName .
Constant = Numeral | ConstantName .
Numeral = Digit { Digit } .
Name = Letter { Letter | Digit } .

3

COMPILER ORGANIZATION

We are now ready to discuss the design of the Pascal— compiler. To make it understandable, the compiler is written in Pascal*. This chapter describes how the compiler was designed to work on a small computer.

3.1 A PERSONAL COMPUTER

In writing compilers for all kinds of computers, I have found it most rewarding to work on small computers because they force you to think hard and adopt the simplest possible solutions. Furthermore, solutions that work well on small computers can nearly always be scaled up and used on large computers as well. So I have decided to use a personal computer as an example.

The computer is an IBM Personal Computer with the following configuration:

Intel 8088 Processor (16 bits)
Memory (64 K bytes)
Display terminal
Single diskette drive (320 K bytes)
Printer

The computer has a single drive for 5¼-inch diskettes. For the compiler writer, the most interesting performance figures of the disk drive are

Program loading	1 msec/word
Data input	2.5 msec/word
Data output	2 msec/word

These figures include both processor time and disk access time.

It is the word length that makes this computer small. With a 16-bit address the processor can access only 32 K words directly, since 2 ** 16 = 64 K bytes (= 32 K words). Although you can add more memory to the computer, it can still address only 32 K words at a time. The ability to work on 32 K words at a time in a larger memory can (with some difficulty) be used by a programmer who writes in assembly language, but it is very difficult to utilize this ad hoc feature systematically in a compiler. To keep the compiler simple, I decided to limit the memory to 32 K words.

3.2 SINGLE-PASS COMPILATION

The software system I will use as an example is written in a variant of Pascal known as Pascal*. [Brinch Hansen, 1985]. Let us assume, for the moment, that the Pascal* compiler is a single Pascal program (of about 3500 lines) which operates as follows. First, the compiler is loaded from the disk and is placed in memory. Then the compiler inputs the source text of a Pascal program from a disk file and outputs the corresponding code in another disk file. This form of compilation is called single-pass compilation, because the compiler scans the source text once only (Fig. 3.1).

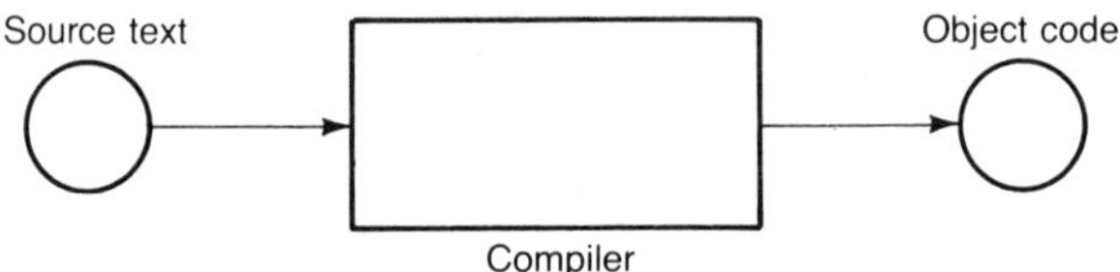

Fig. 3.1 Single-pass compiler (data flow).

Is this method practical for the personal computer? To answer that question, we must look at how the memory is used.

The Pascal* System always keeps a kernel and an operating system in memory. The kernel is an assembly language program that performs basic input/output operations and executes compiled Pascal code. The operating system is a single-user system written in Pascal*. The code and variables of these two programs occupy the following amounts of memory:

Kernel	2,000 words
Operating system	10,000 words
System space	12,000 words

This leaves 20,000 words for the compiler.

One of the goals of the Pascal* System was that the compiler should be able to compile any one of the system programs on the available machine configuration. In particular, the compiler should be able to compile itself.

If a single-pass Pascal* compiler compiles itself, the system will need approximately the following memory space for the compilation:

Compiler code	15,000 words
Compiler variables	46,000 words
Compiler space	61,000 words

Unfortunately, this exceeds the available memory space by 41,000 words.

So single-pass compilation of large programs requires much more memory. In this case, 128 K words would be adequate. Addressing this amount of memory is not a problem on a 32-bit processor, but, since 32 K words is a practical limit for a 16-bit processor, we must conclude that a single-pass compiler that can compile itself is not practical on a small personal computer.

However, if you intend to compile very small programs only, the tables used by the compiler can be made small enough to fit in the available memory. Single-pass compilation is therefore the method used in the compiler project described in Appendix B.

3.3 MULTIPASS COMPILATION

Figure 3.2 shows a different compilation method known as multipass compilation. The compiler now consists of a main program which calls several subprograms. The main program is known as the *compiler administra-*

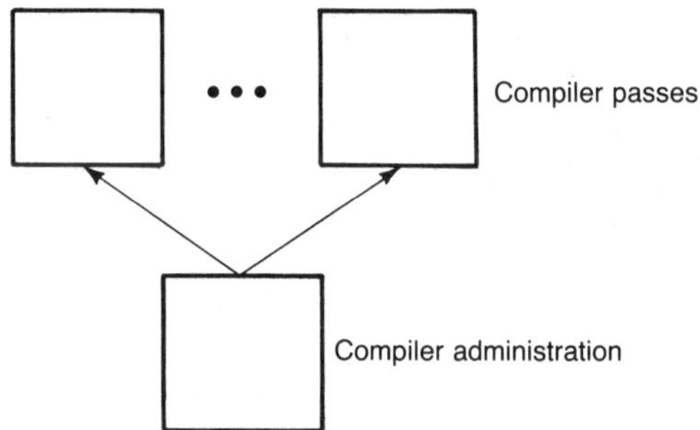

Fig. 3.2 Multipass compiler (control flow).

tion. The subprograms are called the *compiler passes*. At any moment, the memory holds the compiler administration and one of the passes only.

The trick is to divide the compilation task among the passes in such a way that the following is achieved:

(1) Each pass is loaded once only during a compilation. Otherwise, the disk becomes a bottleneck.

(2) The tables used by the compiler are distributed among the passes so that only a subset of them is needed in memory at any given moment. The administration, which remains in memory throughout a compilation, has few (if any) tables.

The first idea we will consider is to let each pass handle a fixed subset of the language features. One pass may, for example, handle all definitions and build a table describing the named objects used in a Pascal program. Another pass may compile expressions, and a third one may handle statements.

Although this scheme is very logical, it is disastrous in practice. Since every procedure in a program normally includes definitions, expressions, and statements, every pass of the compiler will be reloaded once for every procedure compiled. If we assume that the total size of the subprograms is about 14,000 words, it will take 14 sec to load all of them once. If the average procedure is about 15 lines long, the loading time alone is about 1 sec per line! (If you correctly regard this as an impractical method, keep in mind that a single-pass compiler running on a computer with "virtual memory" will behave exactly like this in situations where the system frequently transfers code from the disk to "real memory.")

Another major disadvantage is that the table of named objects built by one of the passes is needed by the other passes to check that the objects are used correctly. This large table must therefore remain in memory throughout the compilation.

Figure 3.3 shows an efficient multipass compiler. The compiler is divided into a series of smaller compilers known as Pass 1, Pass 2, and Pass 3. Each pass is loaded once only and performs a partial compilation of a whole program. The passes are loaded in their natural order beginning with Pass 1.

Pass 1 reads the source text once, performs lexical analysis, and outputs intermediate code in a temporary file.

Pass 2 inputs the intermediate code once, checks the syntax and semantics of the program, and outputs new intermediate code in another temporary file.

Pass 3 scans the output from pass 2 twice and outputs final code in a disk file.

The temporary files are deleted at the end of the compilation.

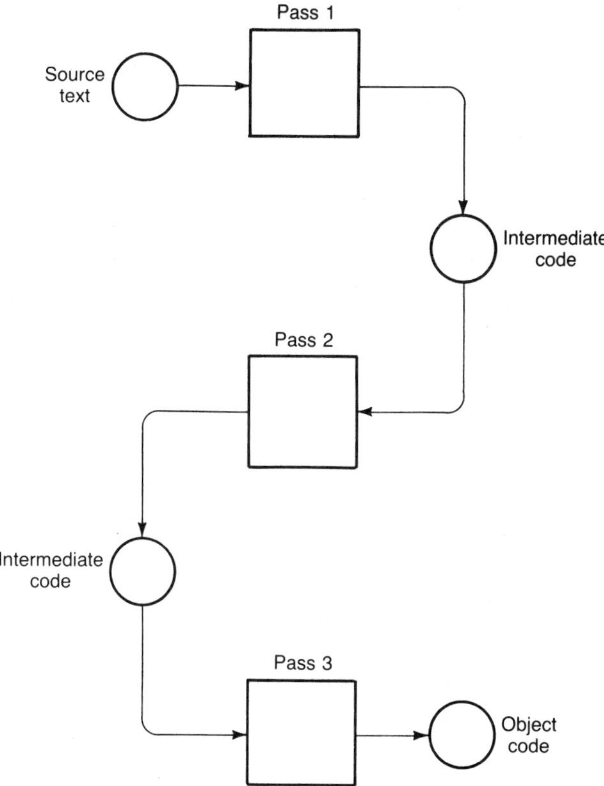

Fig. 3.3 Multipass compiler (data flow).

If the passes detect errors in a program, the compiler outputs error messages in a text file and generates no code.

This type of compiler uses the disk very efficiently. Since each part of the compiler is loaded once only, the loading of a multipass compiler is almost as fast as the loading of a single-pass compiler (if the two compilers are of the same total size). Furthermore, every pass (except the last one) reads the program text (or the intermediate code) once only. So the additional disk transfers are roughly proportional to the number of passes only.

A multipass compiler also makes efficient use of the memory. Less space is needed to hold a single pass at a time, and each pass needs storage for simple tables only to perform its own compilation tasks. These tables disappear from the memory as soon as the pass has finished its part of the compilation.

When the compiler compiles itself, the tables become even smaller since the compiler can now compile the passes separately as smaller programs. When the largest pass of the Pascal* compiler compiles itself, the memory is used as follows:

System space	12,000 words
Compiler administration	1,000 words
Pass 2	15,000 words
Memory used	28,000 words

A multipass compiler is ideal not just for a single processor with a small memory but also for a *multiprocessor system*. Look again at Fig. 3.3 and imagine that the passes are executed simultaneously by three different processors. Each pass will then be able to accept the input from the previous pass as fast as it is produced. So it is no longer necessary to store the intermediate code on a disk; it can be sent directly from one processor to another.

3.4 THE PASCAL MINUS COMPILER

The rest of this chapter describes the administration of the Pascal— compiler. This program is stored on the disk as a file named Pascal.

The operating system accepts one command at a time from the keyboard and interprets it; for example,

Command = *pascal*
  Source name = *sorttext*
  Code name = *sort*

This command starts the compilation of a program text named sorttext. If no errors are found, the code will be output in a new file named sort. The text shown in roman type is displayed by the system and the text you type is shown in *italics*.

It is the operating system that asks you to type the name of the compiler administration (*pascal*). The operating system then locates the compiler administration on the disk and activates it.

The compiler administration keeps the file names in two variables of type string (a standard type in Pascal*):

```
var Source, Code:  String;
```

The administration asks you to name the source and code files by executing the following statements:

```
WriteStr(' Source name = ');
ReadStr(Source);
WriteStr(' Code name = ');
ReadStr(Code)
```

There are no standard procedures for input/output in Pascal*. Instead, the compiler calls a set of external procedures implemented by the operating system. WriteStr and ReadStr are two of these procedures.

The compiler operates on two files at a time only: an input file and an output file. A *file* is a sequence of characters, integers, or enumeration values stored on the disk. The operating system defines the following operations on files:

Reset(f)	Opens an existing file named f for input.
EOF	Has the value true if the end of the input file has been reached; otherwise, the value is false.
Read(x)	Assigns the next value in the input file to a variable x.
Rewrite(f)	Creates a new file named f and opens it for output.
Write(x)	Appends a value x to the output file.
Close	Completes the output file and makes it inaccessible.

Before calling pass 1, the compiler administration opens the source file for input and creates a temporary file named temp1 for output of intermediate code:

```
Reset(Source); Rewrite ('temp1')
```

The administration then calls pass 1 by executing a *program statement*:

```
call Descriptor ('pass1'), Read, EOF, Emit,
  NewLine, Error, TestLimit
```

The effect of this statement is to load pass 1 from the disk and execute it. During its execution, pass 1 may call a set of external procedures and functions named Read, EOF, Emit, NewLine, Error, and TestLimit. The first two of these procedures are implemented by the operating system; the rest are part of the compiler administration.

The program statement is an extension to Pascal that makes it possible to write operating systems and multipass compilers in Pascal*. For our purpose it is unnecessary to discuss this new statement in detail. It is defined concisely in the handbook on Pascal* [Brinch Hansen, 1985].

After the execution of pass 1, the compiler administration closes the output file and opens it for input to pass 2. The intermediate code output by pass 2 is stored in another temporary file named temp2:

```
Reset ('temp1'); Rewrite('temp2');
call Descriptor('pass2'), Read, Emit,
  NewLine, Error, TestLimit;
Close; Delete('temp1')
```

After pass 2, the output file is closed and the input file (temp1) is deleted since it is no longer needed. (Delete is an operating system procedure.)

Finally, pass 3 is activated:

```
Reset('temp2'); Rewrite(Code);
call Descriptor('pass3'), Read, Emit,
  Rerun;
Close; Delete('temp2')
```

For reasons that will be described in Chapter 9, pass 3 scans its input twice. During both scans the pass attempts to output almost the same code by calling a procedure named Emit in the compiler administration. The latter uses a Boolean named Emitting to suppress output during the first scan (Algorithm 3.1).

```
procedure Emit(Value: integer);
begin if Emitting then Write(chr(Value))
end;
```

Algorithm 3.1

After the first scan, pass 3 calls a procedure named Rerun to reopen the input file from the beginning and activate disk output (Algorithm 3.2).

```
procedure Rerun;
begin Reset('temp2'); Emitting := true end;
```

Algorithm 3.2

3.5 ERRORS AND FAILURES

When the compiler finds an error in a program, it outputs an error message, such as

Line 328 Invalid Syntax

The error messages have the following meaning:

Ambiguous Name:
A block defines two or more objects with the same name.

Invalid Comment:
The closing delimiter } of a comment is missing.

Invalid Name Kind:
A name of the wrong kind is used in some context.

Invalid Numeral:
A numeral is outside the range 0 . . 32767.

Invalid Index Range:
The index range of an array type has a lower bound that exceeds the upper bound.

Invalid Syntax:
The program syntax is incorrect.

Invalid Type:
A name of the wrong type is used in some context.

Undefined Name:
A name is used without being defined.

Since these error messages are rather short they may be hard to understand for beginners who are still learning Pascal. You may therefore wish to change some of them later. This is difficult to do if the text of the messages is scattered throughout the passes.

It is much better to put all of them in one place: the compiler administration. The passes will then need some other means of reporting errors to the administration. For this purpose we introduce the following data type:

```
type ErrorKind = (Ambiguous3, Comment3, Kind3,
  Numeral3, Range3, Syntax3, Type3, Undefined3);
```

When a pass discovers an error it calls a procedure named Error in the administration; for example,

```
Error(Syntax3)
```

The compiler administration outputs readable error messages in a file named notes and displays the message

Compilation Errors

at the end of the compilation.

The error handling just described needs some refinements. Since the operating system supports one output file only, the compiler can output either code or error messages but not both at the same time. This constraint is satisfied by using two Boolean variables:

```
var Emitting, Errors: Boolean;
```

The first variable has already been introduced to suppress superfluous code output by pass 3.

When a compilation begins, no errors have yet been found and the compiler is ready to emit code. When the compiler finds the first error in a program, it closes the output of code and opens a message file:

```
procedure Error(Kind: ErrorKind);
begin
  if not Errors then
    begin Close; Rewrite('notes');
      Emitting := false; Errors := true
    end;
  . . .
end;
```

From now on, the procedure Emit prevents further output of intermediate (or final) code. Consequently, the output of the current pass will be incomplete, and very little is gained by executing the next pass. So each pass will be executed only if the previous passes found no errors in the program.

A single error may sometimes cause the compiler to produce a burst of redundant error messages. The superfluous messages are suppressed by a simple, effective method. At the beginning of each line of program text, the passes call a procedure in the compiler administration to record a line number and indicate that no errors have yet been found on the new line (Algorithm 3.3).

```
var LineNo: integer; CorrectLine: Boolean;

procedure NewLine(Number: integer);
begin LineNo := Number; CorrectLine := true
end;
```

Algorithm 3.3

When an error is reported, a message is output and the line is marked as incorrect to suppress further messages relating to that line (Algorithm 3.4).

```
procedure Error(Kind: ErrorKind);
var Text: String;
begin
  if not Errors then
    . . . same as before . . .

  if Kind = Ambiguous3 then
    Text := 'Ambiguous Name'
  else if Kind = Comment3 then
    Text := 'Invalid Comment'
  . . . ;
  if CorrectLine then
    begin
      WriteStr('Line');
      WriteInt(LineNo, 4);
      WriteStr(' '); WriteStr(Text);
      Write(NL); CorrectLine := false
    end
end;
```

Algorithm 3.4

The external procedures WriteStr and WriteInt write strings and integers in the output file. Every output line ends with a newline character named NL.

The passes use several arrays of fixed length in which space is allocated one element at a time from the beginning. When a pass needs room for another element in a table, it calls a procedure in the compiler administration:

TestLimit(Length, Maximum)

If the current length of the table is less than its maximum length, the procedure has no effect; otherwise, it displays the message

Program Too Big

and stops the compilation. This is a compilation failure.

Appendix A.1 contains the complete text of the compiler administration.

4

LEXICAL ANALYSIS

The part of a compiler that performs lexical analysis is called the *scanner*. This chapter describes the Pascal— scanner (pass 1) and explains how it recognizes symbols in a program text and replaces them by a more convenient representation. Much of the discussion concerns the problem of searching for word symbols and names in a symbol table.

4.1 SOURCE TEXT

The scanner reads a program text character by character. It uses a control character to indicate that it has reached the end of the source text

const ETX = 3C;

This is the Pascal* notation for ASCII character number three, known as ETX (End of Text).

When the scanner finds a character that cannot occur in any symbol, it reports the problem. A line number in the error message helps you locate the error in the program text and correct it. However, if an *invisible character* causes an error message, it is very confusing since you cannot see where the problem is by looking at the printed program text. To avoid this situation we must make sure that "what you see is what the compiler gets." In other words, the compiler must ignore all control characters (except NL and ETX).

The set of invisible characters is stored in a variable of type CharSet:

```
type CharSet = set of char;
var Invisible: CharSet;
```

The scanner uses Algorithm 4.1 to input the next character and store it in a global variable named ch. This procedure illustrates the use of set types in a compiler. Later, we will see many other examples of this.

```
procedure NextChar;
begin
  if EOF then ch := ETX
  else
    begin Read(ch);
      if ch in Invisible then NextChar
    end
end;
```

Algorithm 4.1

4.2 INTERMEDIATE CODE

In the source text, a word symbol such as **const** consists of a sequence of letters, in this case **c o n s t**. This representation of symbols is very bulky and awkward to work with in Pascal. If you store a symbol as a string of characters

```
var Symbol: String;
```

you can easily test, for example, if the symbol is the word **const**:

```
if Symbol = 'const' then . . .
```

But you cannot easily form sets of strings and ask whether the current symbol is either **const**, **type**, **var**, or **procedure**.

The use of symbol sets plays an important role in syntax analysis (Chapter 5). To be able to define symbol sets, we must represent the symbols by simple values. These values should, however, have readable names to make the compiler understandable. What we need, then, is an enumerated type that introduces a name for each symbol in the language:

```
type SymbolType =
  (And1, Array1, Asterisk1, Becomes1, Begin1, Colon1,
  Comma1, Const1, Div1, Do1, DoubleDot1, Else1, End1,
  EndText1, Equal1, Greater1, If1, LeftBracket1,
  LeftParenthesis1, Less1, Minus1, Mod1, Name1,
  NewLine1, Not1, NotEqual1, NotGreater1, NotLess1,
  Numeral1, Of1, Or1, Period1, Plus1, Procedure1,
  Program1, Record1, RightBracket1, RightParenthesis1,
  Semicolon1, Then1, Type1, Var1, While1, Unknown1);
```

When the scanner recognizes a word symbol such as **div** in the input, it outputs the corresponding symbol value Div1:

```
Emit1(Div1)
```

Pass 2 can now store a symbol in a simple variable

```
var Symbol: SymbolType
```

and use symbol sets

```
type Symbols = set of SymbolType;
var AddSymbols: Symbols
```

in statements, such as

```
while Symbol in AddSymbols do . . .
```

The scanner outputs a *numeral* as a symbol named Numeral1 followed by the value of the numeral:

```
Emit2(Numeral1, Value)
```

A *name* is output as the symbol Name1 followed by an integer. The integer is called a name index. The standard names have fixed indices:

```
const Integer0 = 1; Boolean0 = 2; False0 = 3;
  True0 = 4; Read0 = 5; Write0 = 6;
```

All other names are assigned consecutive indices in their order of appearance in the program text.

At the beginning of each line, the scanner outputs the symbol NewLine1 followed by a *line number*.

When the scanner detects an *unknown* sequence of characters, it outputs the symbol Unknown1. Pass 2 reports a syntax error when it inputs this symbol.

When the scanner reaches the end of the source text, it outputs the symbol EndText1 and terminates.

Notice that the scanner merely produces a more convenient encoding of the program text without changing its structure.

Throughout this chapter I will use a program text of about 2000 lines to study the performance of the Pascal— scanner. A compilation of this *sample program* shows that the intermediate code output by pass 1 occupies significantly less space than the source text:

Source text	54,600 characters
Intermediate code	17,200 words

Each character and symbol value occupies one machine word on the disk.

The reduction of the program to less than a third of its original size reduces the amount of disk input that pass 2 must perform during a compilation.

4.3 SCANNING

Now we will look at the scanning algorithm.

The following symbols are trivial to recognize:

+ − * = ( ) [ ] , ;

Each of these symbols consists of a single character only which does not occur at the beginning of any other symbol.

However, in some cases, two or more symbols begin with the same character; for example,

< <= <>

When the scanner has input the first character of a symbol and recognized it as the character "<", it must input another character to determine whether the first character is part of one of the symbols "<=" or "<>". If the second character is neither "=" nor ">", the scanner knows that the first character simply denotes the symbol "<". However, when the scanner discovers this, it has already input the first character of the next symbol.

It turns out that this happens in several cases. When the scanner inputs the first digit of a numeral, it can find out where the numeral ends only by reading more characters until it finds one that is not a digit. So the scanner will again input a symbol (a numeral) plus an extra character. The same thing happens when the scanner reads a word symbol or a name.

When a new symbol is scanned, the scanner must know whether it needs to input the first character of the symbol or whether it has done that already during the input of the preceding symbol. Instead of remembering this distinction, it is simpler to make a rule of the exception so that there is one possibility only:

Rule 4.1:

The scanner is always one character ahead.

This rule is implemented as follows:

(1) When the scanner is activated, it immediately inputs the first character of the program text.

(2) Whenever the scanner has recognized a character as being part of a particular symbol, it immediately inputs the next character.

The same principle will be used in the rest of the compiler and is called *single-symbol look-ahead*.

Algorithm 4.2 defines the procedure that scans a single symbol. Notice again the use of set variables

```
var Letters, Digits: CharSet;
```

to classify characters.

```
procedure NextSymbol;
begin
  SkipSeparators;
  if ch in Letters then
    ScanWord
  else if ch in Digits then
    ScanNumeral
  else if ch = '+' then
    ScanPlus
    . . .
  else if ch = '<' then
    ScanLess
    . . .
  else if ch <> ETX then
    ScanUnknown
end;
```

Algorithm 4.2

The scanning algorithm is now straightforward:

```
NextChar;
while ch <> ETX do NextSymbol;
Emit1(EndText1)
```

Separators

The scanner skips any spaces, newline characters, and comments before each symbol (Algorithm 4.3). The separators begin with the following characters:

```
Separators := CharSet[SP, NL, '{']
```

Notice that a set constructor written in Pascal* must include the name of the set type (CharSet). At the end of each line, the scanner calls a procedure EndLine, which increments the *line number* by one and outputs it together with a NewLine symbol.

```
{SkipSeparators}
  while ch in Separators do
     if ch = SP then NextChar
     else if ch = NL then
       begin EndLine; NextChar end
     else Comment
```

Algorithm 4.3

A *comment* may extend over several lines and contain nested comments. The scanning of a comment is therefore recursive (Algorithm 4.4).

```
procedure Comment;
begin { ch = '{' } NextChar;
  while not (ch in EndComment) do
    if ch = '{' then Comment
    else
      begin
        if ch = NL then EndLine;
        NextChar
      end;
  if ch = '}' then NextChar
  else Error(Comment3)
end;
```

Algorithm 4.4

If a comment is not properly terminated by the character "}", the scanner skips the rest of the program text looking for the missing terminator. If the scanner attempts to read past the end of the source text, the operating system will stop the compilation. In that case, the user gets no error message from the compiler and is left with the (correct) impression that there is something wrong with the compiler.

The scanner has indeed violated the basic principle that a compilation must always terminate properly no matter what the input text is (Rule 1.2). We can prevent this from happening by assuming that the last character in a comment is either "}" or ETX:

```
EndComment := CharSet['}', ETX]
```

Special Symbols

After skipping separators, the scanner inputs a single symbol. If it is a special symbol like "+", the scanner immediately outputs the symbol and reads one character ahead (Algorithm 4.5).

```
{ScanPlus: ch = '+'}
  Emit1(Plus1); NextChar
```

Algorithm 4.5

The look-ahead principle also makes it easy to distinguish symbols that begin with the same character, such as "<", "<=", and "<>" (Algorithm 4.6).

```
{ScanLess: ch = '<'}
  NextChar;
  if ch = '=' then
    begin Emit1(NotGreater1); NextChar end
  else if ch = '>' then
    begin Emit1(NotEqual1); NextChar end
  else Emit1(Less1)
```

Algorithm 4.6

Numerals

The following algorithm describes the input of a numeral:

```
Value := 0;
while ch in Digits do
  begin
    Value := 10 * Value + (ord(ch) - ord('0'));
    NextChar
  end;
Emit2(Numeral1, Value)
```

Unfortunately, it suffers from the same problem as the first algorithm for skipping comments: If the program text contains a numeral that exceeds the largest possible integer

```
const MaxInt = 32767
```

the algorithm above will cause overflow and abortion of the compilation with the message

```
pass 1  line 278  range error
```

Again the user cannot tell whether this message is caused by a programming error in the compiler or in the program being compiled.

So we must be a bit more careful with the preceding algorithm (see Algorithm 4.7).

```
var Value, Digit: integer; Digits: CharSet;

{Scan Numeral: ch in Digits}
  Value := 0;
  while ch in Digits do
    begin
      Digit := ord(ch) - ord('0');
      if Value <= (MaxInt - Digit) div 10 then
        begin
          Value := 10 * Value + Digit;
          NextChar
        end
      else
        begin Error(Numeral3);
          while ch in Digits do NextChar
        end
    end;
  Emit2(Numeral1, Value)
```

Algorithm 4.7

Words

So far we have not discussed the real problem of lexical analysis, which is the recognition of *words*, that is, word symbols and names. The input of a word is simple enough (Algorithm 4.8a).

```
var Text: String; Length: integer;
  AlphaNumeric, CapitalLetters: CharSet;

{Scan Word: ch in Letters}
  Length := 0;
  while ch in AlphaNumeric do
     begin
       if ch in CapitalLetters then
         ch := chr(ord(ch) + ord('a') - ord('A'));
       Length := Length + 1;
       Text[Length] := ch; NextChar
     end;
  {continued below}
```

Algorithm 4.8a

When the scanner has input a word it calls a search procedure that recognizes the word as either a word symbol or a name. If it is a word symbol, the scanner outputs its ordinal value. A name is output as a symbol followed by a name index (Algorithm 4.8b).

```
var IsName: Boolean; Index: integer;

{Scan Word, continued}
  Search(Text, Length, IsName, Index);
  if IsName then Emit2(Name1, Index)
  else Emit(Index)
```

Algorithm 4.8b

In the following we will discuss efficient methods of storing words in tables and searching for them.

4.4 SEARCHING

The search problem is easy to state but nontrivial to solve. The scanner builds a table of all the words used in a program text. Each entry in this *symbol table* describes a single word with the following attributes:

(1) The sequence of characters in the word

(2) A Boolean that indicates whether it is a name or word symbol

(3) A name index or the ordinal value of a word symbol

Initially, the scanner puts all the word symbols and standard names in the symbol table. When a word has been input, the scanner first tries to find it in the table. If it is not there, it is inserted and described as a name with a new name index. The word is then output as a symbol value possibly followed by a name index.

It is important to realize that the scanner is not aware of the syntax and block structure of a program. It views the source text as an arbitrary sequence of symbols. The scanner cannot tell whether a name was introduced by a definition before it is referenced. The scanner just inserts a name in the symbol table the first time it occurs in the program text. If the same name is used for different purposes in different blocks, the scanner still assigns the same index to all occurrences of the name. Two words are distinguished only if they are *spelled* differently. The use of the same name to denote different objects in different blocks is recognized later during scope analysis (Chapter 6).

The only operations on the symbol table are insertions of new words and searches for previous words. The sample program mentioned earlier uses 431 distinct words which occur a total of 4830 times. *Searches are therefore more than 10 times as frequent as insertions in the symbol table.*

Linear Searching

To illustrate how important efficient searching is in lexical analysis, we will look first at a very inefficient method called *linear searching*. The idea behind it is the simplest possible: The symbol table is organized as a *linked list* of records each describing one word. The list is unordered and is always searched from the beginning. New words can be inserted anywhere in the list.

Figure 4.1 shows a linked list after the compilation of the sample program. The list begins with the word symbols **and** and **array** and ends with the name *programx*. Since the list can be extended dynamically, it adjusts itself

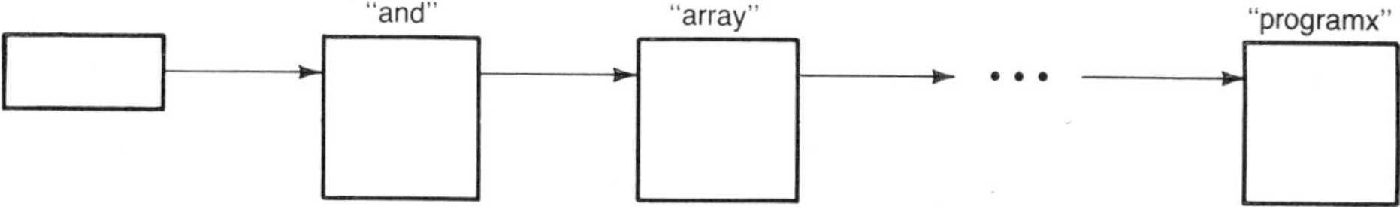

Fig. 4.1 Symbol table for linear searching.

nicely to the compilation of programs of different sizes. The inefficiency of linear searching matters very little if a compiler is used for small programs only.

The Pascal– compiler is, however, built to compile program texts of the order of 2000 lines with up to 500 names. The sample program is roughly of that size. When the scanner uses linear searching, a linked list with up to 431 words is searched 4830 times. The relevant performance measure is the average number of times each word must be compared to another word during a search. Toward the end of the compilation, you would expect an average of 431/2 = 216 comparisons for each occurrence of a word if all the words occur with the same frequency (which they do not). Since the list holds a smaller number of words to begin with, the actual number of comparisons per word is somewhat less (184). But the scanning still requires a total of 886,444 comparisons and takes an unreasonable amount of time (later we will see how much).

Letter Indexing

Well then, let's improve things a bit by using a "thumb index" of the words as in a dictionary. Instead of a single linked list we will use a separate list for each letter of the alphabet (Fig. 4.2). The first list will hold all words beginning with the letter "A". The second list is for the letter "B", and so on. The first letter of each word is used as an index in an array to locate the start of the corresponding list. Each list is unordered.

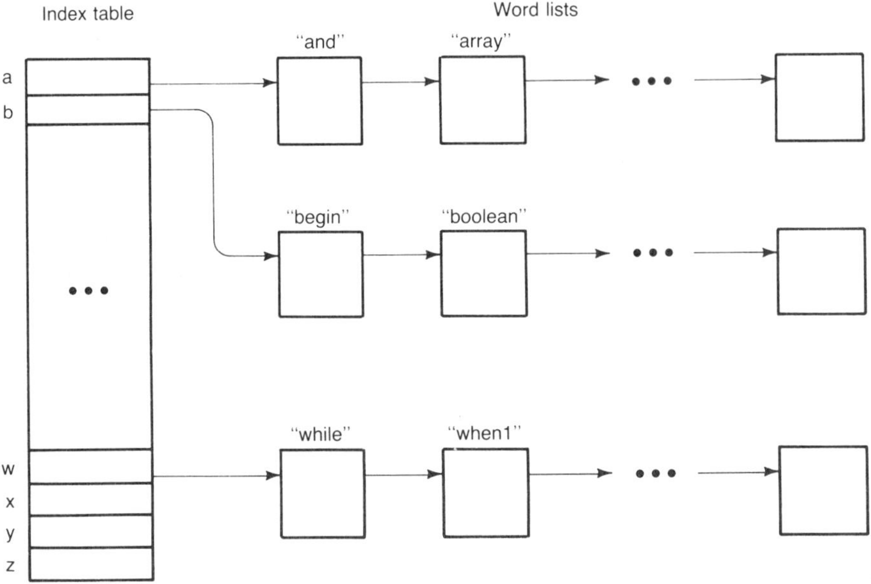

Fig. 4.2 Symbol table for letter indexing.

This method, which I will call *letter indexing*, is obviously a generalization of linear searching. It is also a special case of a superior method called *hashing*. Although letter indexing is not the best search method, it is surprisingly good compared to linear searching.

If we assume that the words of the sample program are divided evenly among the 26 lists and occur with the same frequency, the search for a single word will require an average of 431/52 = 8 comparisons. In reality, the scanner makes 12 comparisons per word.

The actual performance is less than expected because the assumptions behind the prediction are unrealistic. The words of English (or Pascal) are not divided evenly among the letters of the alphabet. My English dictionary has 147 pages of words beginning with C but only 18 pages of words beginning with K. Figure 4.3 shows the alphabetic distribution of the 431 words of the sample program. It should also be kept in mind that some words are used much more often than others in English (or Pascal).

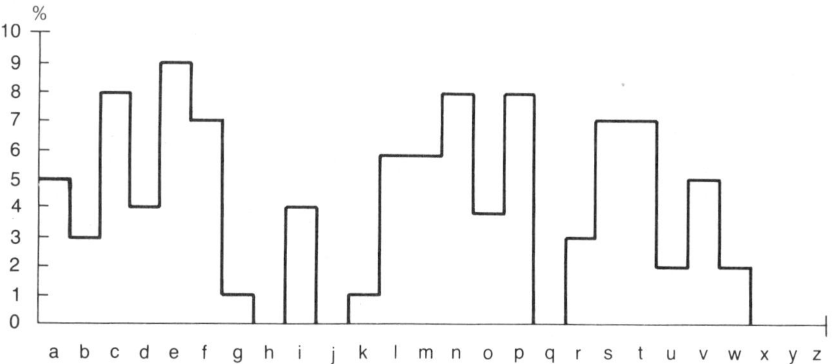

Fig. 4.3 Alphabetic distribution of words.

However, the most serious limitation of letter indexing is not that it distributes words unevenly among the lists, but that it divides them into 26 groups only (one for each letter of the alphabet).

Letter indexing would be ideal in a hypothetical language that uses an alphabet with hundreds of letters and a dictionary with roughly the same number of words for each letter of the alphabet. Although such a language does not exist, hashing is a pretty good approximation of this ideal situation.

Hashing

To use hashing you must decide how many word lists you are going to need. Let us call this number N. You must then define a function H that transforms any word into a number between 1 and N. The number H(w) is used as an index to select the list in which a word w belongs.

The function H is called a *hash function* because it chops a word into small pieces (individual characters) and performs somewhat arbitrary (arithmetic) operations on the pieces to compute a number. The number H(w) is called the *hash key* of the word w.

The aim is to find a hash function that distributes the words evenly among the lists. If it was possible to place every word on a different list, the number of comparisons would drop to one per word. This obviously requires that the number of words M does not exceed the number of lists N.

However, even if we assume that all hash keys are equally likely and that the hash function H distributes them uniformly over the range from 1 to N, there is still some probability that certain words will have the same hash key and therefore end up on the same list. Such coincidences are known as word *collisions*.

The famous "birthday paradox" is a well-known example of this phenomenon: If there are 23 people in a room, there is a better than even chance that at least two of them have the same birthday. With 50 persons, the probability is 0.97 [Weaver, 1963]. In the context of hashing this result can be restated as follows: If a symbol table with 365 lists contains 50 words only, there is a 97 percent chance that some of the lists will contain more than one word.

The hash function must be selected with care to reduce the chance of collision in the symbol table. Experiments have shown that the following algorithm works well: Add the individual characters of a word, divide the sum by the table length and use the remainder as the hash key. The table length should preferably be a prime number. Algorithm 4.9 defines the hash function just described.

```
function Key(Text: String; Length: integer)
  : integer;
const W = 32641; N = MaxKey;
var Sum, i: integer;
begin Sum := 0; i := 1;
  while i <= Length do
     begin
       Sum := (Sum + ord(Text[i])) mod W;
       i := i + 1
     end;
  Key := Sum mod N + 1
end;
```

Algorithm 4.9

To prevent arithmetic overflow during the addition of characters, we must make sure that when the largest of the 128 ASCII characters is added to the sum, the result does not exceed the largest integer. So the algorithm must satisfy the constraint

$$\text{Sum} + 127 < 32768$$

This is achieved by taking the remainder of the sum modulo $32768 - 127 = 32641$ after each addition.

The table length N (also known as MaxKey) is the prime number 631. (Later, I will explain how this number was chosen.) The hash key of a word is a number in the range

$$1 \leqslant \text{Key} \leqslant \text{MaxKey}$$

The following are some examples of the keys computed by the hash function. The last two words illustrate the collision phenomenon.

Word	*Hash Key*
object	1
baseno	2
charno	5
record	9
factor	9

To find out how good this hash function is I compiled the sample program and obtained these results:

Length of List	*Number of Lists*
1	181
2	90
3	15
4	5
5	1

As you can see, 181 lists contained one word only, and 90 lists had 2 words each. No list contained more than 5 words.

Direct Chaining

Figure 4.4 shows the symbol table after the compilation of the sample program. The hash key of each word is used as an index in a table to locate a list of all words that have the same hash key. In this example, the names

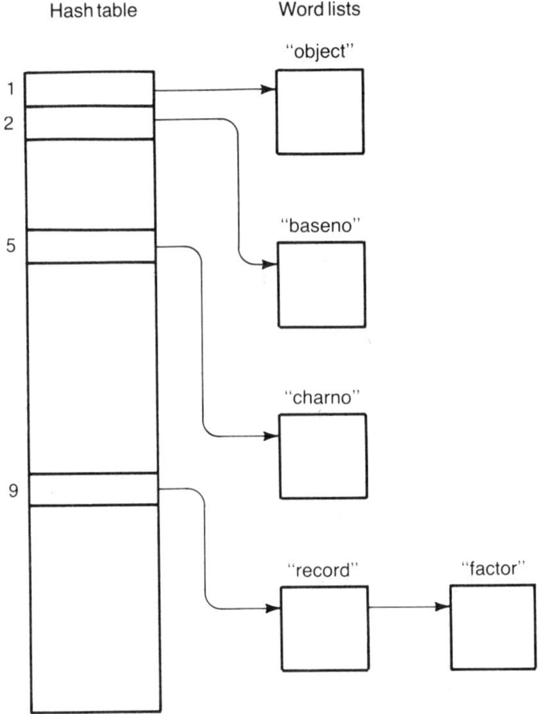

Fig. 4.4 Hash table with direct chaining.

object, baseno, and charno are the only words with hash keys 1, 2, and 5, respectively. There are no words with hash keys 3, 4, 6, 7, and 8. The words record and factor both have the hash key 9.

This method is called hashing with *direct chaining*. It is very simple to implement in a programming language like Pascal that supports pointers.

A detailed analysis shows that the average number C of comparisons for a successful search is approximately

$$C = \frac{1}{f} \ln \frac{1}{1 - f}$$

where f = M/N is the *loading factor* of the symbol table [Knuth, 1973]. The following table lists C as a function of f:

f	*C*
0.2	1.1
0.4	1.3
0.6	1.5

f	C
0.7	1.7
0.8	2.0
0.9	2.6

As a design guideline we will attempt to keep the number of comparisons per word less than 2 during the compilation of a large program with 500 names. This means that the load factor should be at most 0.8 at the end of the compilation. To ensure this we need a table with at least 500/0.8 = 625 lists. To make the size of the table a prime number, we will use N = 631 lists in the Pascal— compiler.

When the sample program is scanned, the actual load factor is less than 431/631 = 0.7. The expected number of comparisons at the end of the scan is therefore 1.7 per word. The number measured is only 1.3 comparisons per word! This is because the loading factor is smaller at the beginning of a compilation.

Linear Probing

Another variant of hashing is known as *linear probing*. In this method the symbol table is just an array of size N. There are no linked lists because the words are stored in the array itself. The search for a word w begins at table element number H(w) and continues with elements number H(w)+1, H(w)+2, and so on. If element number N is reached, the search continues cyclically from element number 1. The search ends when a word is found or an empty element is reached. In the latter case, the word is inserted at the empty spot.

Figure 4.5 shows a symbol table with linear probing. The name *object*, which has the hash key 1, is described by entry number 1 and can therefore

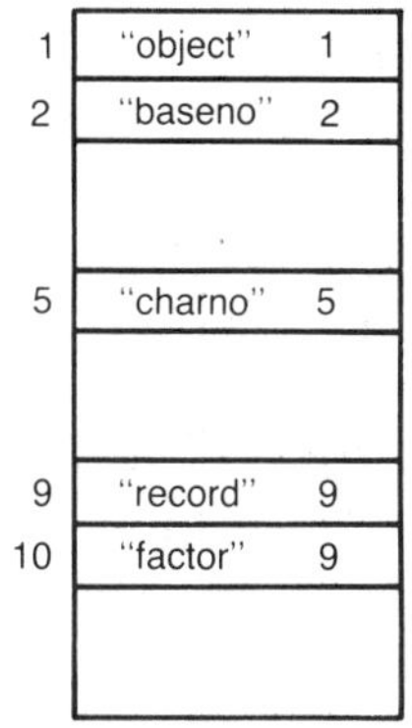

1	"object"	1
2	"baseno"	2
5	"charno"	5
9	"record"	9
10	"factor"	9

Fig. 4.5 Hash table for linear probing.

be found after one comparison only. The words *record* and *factor* both have the hash key 9. The first of them is placed in entry number 9 and the second one ends up in entry number 10. Consequently, a search for the name *factor* requires two comparisons.

Further down in the table we find the following cluster of words:

Entry Number	*Word*	*Hash Key*
19	expect	19
20	recordlength	20
21	number	19
22	funcno	19

When the last two names were inserted, the first two names were already in the table, so they were placed in the nearest empty locations (entries 21 and 22). This example illustrates the main problem of linear probing: Names with different hash keys have a tendency to form clusters when the load factor increases. This makes linear probing somewhat slower than direct chaining.

For linear probing the expected number of comparisons for a successful search is approximately [Knuth, 1973]

$$C = 1 + \frac{f}{2(1 - f)}$$

Some numerical values are

f	*C*
0.2	1.1
0.4	1.3
0.6	1.8
0.7	2.2
0.8	3.0
0.9	5.5

During a compilation of the sample program with linear probing, the number of comparisons was 1.7 per word.

Linear probing is the natural method to use in a programming language like Edison that does not support pointers [Brinch Hansen, 1983]. Since Pascal does not allow pointer values to be copied to and from a disk, linear probing is also useful for searching a directory of files maintained by an operating system.

Comparison of Methods

The experiments with the sample program gave the following results:

Linear search	184 comparisons/word
Letter indexing	12 comparisons/word
Hashing (linear probing)	1.7 comparisons/word
Hashing (direct chaining)	1.3 comparisons/word

Hashing is obviously superior to the other methods. There is not much difference between the two kinds of hashing. Since the algorithms of the two methods are of almost the same length, there is no reason not to prefer the best one. Consequently, direct chaining is used in the Pascal— compiler.

It is somewhat startling to discover that hashing can be faster than searching a binary tree of words. A binary search among 431 words requires up to 9 comparisons, where less than 2 is sufficient with hashing. However, if you feed the scanner with words that all have the same hash key, hashing will be just as slow as linear searching and require 184 comparisons per word. In the same situation, a binary search will still require no more than 9 comparisons. Binary searching always *guarantees* you an upper bound on the search time. Hashing, on the other hand, gives superior performance with high *probability* because extreme clustering of words rarely occurs.

Since the length of a hash table is fixed, you must be able to make a reasonable estimate of how many words a large Pascal program may contain. It is not very difficult to make such an estimate. Just write your compiler in its own language and use it to compile itself. On a small computer you will often find that the compiler is about the largest program your system is able to edit, compile, and run. The number of words in the largest pass of the compiler is the number you are looking for. (The sample program is indeed the largest pass of the Pascal* compiler.)

4.5 SYMBOL TABLE

Before we can implement the symbol table in Pascal, we have one final decision to make: How do we store the characters of each word in the symbol table?

The most obvious solution is to store the characters of a word as an array in the record that describes the word (Fig. 4.4). Since arrays are of fixed length in Pascal, we must then decide how long a word can be. In the original Pascal report, Wirth recommends that compilers should recognize the first eight characters of a word only [Jensen and Wirth, 1974]. With this restriction, a compiler cannot distinguish long readable names, such as

ConstantDefinition
ConstantDefinitionPart

These are the names of two procedures in the Pascal— compiler. You are therefore forced to use cryptic abbreviations, such as

ConDef
ConDefPart

By contrast, the IEEE Pascal Standard [1983] says that "all characters of an identifier shall be significant in distinguishing between identifiers." Since this rule encourages the use of long names, we will comply with it in the Pascal— compiler.

How long can names be then? Well, we know that separators can occur before and after a symbol but not within it. Since every line ends with a separator (a newline character) it follows that a name cannot be longer than a single line. It would therefore be acceptable to store each word as a string of, say, 80 characters. However, if we wish to compile programs with up to 500 names, the strings alone will occupy 40,000 words in a memory of 64 K words only. So this idea is impractical for a small computer.

Now, in practice, few names are 80 characters long, so there is no reason to waste memory like that. The longest word in the sample program is the name

ConstantDefinitionPart

which consists of 22 characters. The shortest word consists of the single letter n. The 431 distinct words occupy a total of 3624 characters, or an average of 8 characters per word.

Figure 4.6 shows an efficient way of storing the characters of all words in a separate table known as the *spelling table*. Each word record defines the length of a word and the index of its last character in the spelling table.

We can now put the pieces of the symbol table together.

The hash table is an array of pointers:

```
const MaxKey = 631;
type WordPointer = @ WordRecord;
  HashTable = array [1 . . MaxKey] of WordPointer;
var Hash: HashTable;
```

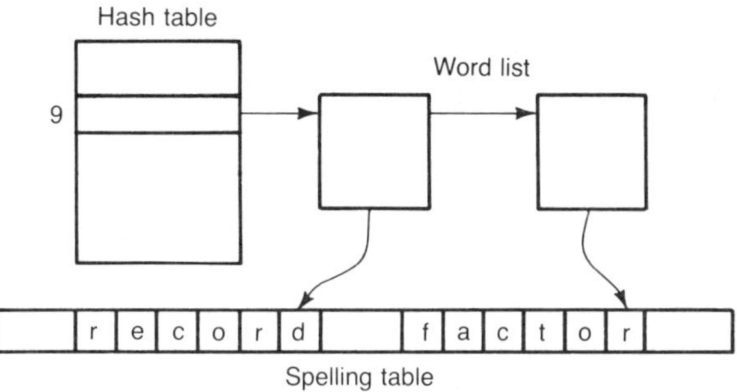

Fig. 4.6 Symbol table.

If a word list is empty, the corresponding pointer in the hash table has the value nil; otherwise, it points to the first word record in the list.

Each word in a list is described by a record that defines whether the word is a name or a word symbol:

```
type
  WordRecord =
    record
      NextWord: WordPointer;
      IsName: Boolean;
      Index, Length, LastChar: integer
    end;
```

The index of a word is either a name index or the ordinal value of a word symbol. The spelling of the word is given by its length (in characters) and by the index of its last character in the spelling table.

The spelling table is an array of characters:

```
const MaxChar = 5000;
type SpellingTable = array [1 . . MaxChar] of char;
var Spelling: SpellingTable; Characters: integer;
```

A variable defines the total number of characters stored in the table.

Algorithm 4.10 defines the insertion of a new word in the symbol table. The procedure TestLimit checks whether there is room in the spelling table for a new word (Section 3.5). The standard operation **New** creates a new word record and assigns its pointer value to a variable. Since a word record may be inserted anywhere in the list, we will insert it at the beginning.

```
procedure Insert(IsName: Boolean; Text: String;
  Length, Index, KeyNo: integer);
var Pointer: WordPointer; M, N: integer;
begin
  {Insert the word in the spelling table}
  Characters := Characters + Length;
  TestLimit(Characters, MaxChar);
  M := Length; N := Characters - M;
  while M > 0 do
     begin Spelling[M + N] := Text[M];
       M := M - 1
     end;
  {Insert the word in a word list}
  New(Pointer);
  Pointer@.NextWord := Hash[KeyNo];
  Pointer@.IsName := IsName;
  Pointer@.Index := Index;
  Pointer@.Length := Length;
  Pointer@.LastChar := Characters;
  Hash[KeyNo] := Pointer
end;
```

Algorithm 4.10

Initially, the scanner makes the symbol table empty:

```
var KeyNo: integer;

KeyNo := 1;
while KeyNo <= MaxKey do
   begin
     Hash[KeyNo] := nil WordPointer;
     KeyNo := KeyNo + 1
   end;
Characters := 0;
```

In Pascal*, the pointer value **nil** must include the name of a pointer type, in this case

nil WordPointer

The word symbols and standard names are inserted in the table by means of Algorithm 4.11.

```
procedure Define(IsName: Boolean; Text: String;
  Length, Index: integer);
begin
  Insert(IsName, Text, Length, Index,
    Key(Text, Length))
end;
```

Algorithm 4.11

This procedure is called as follows:

```
{Insert the word symbols}
Define(false, 'and', 3, ord(And1));
  . . .
Define(false, 'while', 5, ord(While1));
{Insert the standard names}
Define(true, 'integer', 7, Integer0);
  . . .
Define(true, 'write', 5, Write0)
```

The scanner uses Algorithm 4.12 to search the symbol table for a particular word. The hash key of the word is used to select a list that is then

```
procedure Search(Text: String; Length: integer;
  var IsName: Boolean; var Index: integer);
var KeyNo: integer; Pointer: WordPointer;
  Done: Boolean;
begin
  KeyNo := Key(Text, Length);
  Pointer := Hash[KeyNo]; Done := false;
  while not Done do
    if Pointer = nil WordPointer then
      begin IsName := true;
        Names := Names + 1; Index := Names;
        Insert(true, Text, Length, Index, KeyNo);
        Done := true
      end
    else if Found(Text, Length, Pointer) then
      begin IsName := Pointer@.IsName;
        Index := Pointer@.Index; Done := true
      end
    else Pointer := Pointer@.NextWord
end;
```

Algorithm 4.12

searched linearly. If the word is found, its symbol value (or name index) is retrieved from the table; otherwise, the word is inserted in the list and described as a name. (Since all the word symbols are already in the table, a new word can only be a name.)

The scanner uses a variable

```
var Names: integer;
```

to count the total number of names used in the program text. The initial value of this counter is equal to the number of standard names in the symbol table.

Algorithm 4.13 determines whether or not a given word is the same as a word in the symbol table. To speed up the algorithm, two words are compared only if they are of the same length.

```
function Found(Text: String; Length: integer;
  Pointer: WordPointer): Boolean;
var Same: Boolean; M, N: integer;
begin
  if Pointer@.Length <> Length then
    Same := false
  else
    begin Same := true; M := Length;
      N := Pointer@.LastChar - M;
      while Same and (M > 0) do
        begin
          Same := Text[M] = Spelling[M + N];
          M := M - 1
        end
    end;
  Found := Same
end;
```

Algorithm 4.13

This completes the discussion of the scanning algorithm. Appendix A.2 contains the complete program text of the scanner. It is a sobering thought that this whole chapter describes a subtle program of less than 400 lines. But this is true of most nontrivial programs: *A good description of a program is often longer than the program itself.* To be a good programmer you must also be a good writer!

4.6 TESTING

Now that we have written a scanner, it must be tested systematically. The testing is a series of experiments designed to reveal programming errors in the scanner. In each experiment, the scanner is executed with some input and the computed results are compared with the expected results.

To be sure that we are testing the scanner in its normal mode of operation, it must be executed with its usual input (a program text). Since a compiler must be able to translate an infinite number of possible Pascal programs, it is very unlikely that a few "typical" programs chosen at random will test the scanner systematically. We must therefore carefully construct small programs for test purposes only. These programs are called *test programs.*

Rule 4.2:
A compiler is tested by letting it compile small programs constructed specifically for testing.

The choice of the *test output* is crucial. It will generally be the printed values of certain variables of the scanner. The trick is to obtain enough output to determine what happened during a test compilation without being drowned in data.

You might, for example, extend the scanner with an algorithm for printing the symbol table at the end of the scan. But this method has several flaws:

(1) Perhaps the scanner will not terminate and print the table.

(2) The scanner may contain several errors that are hard to distinguish when you look at the final state of the symbol table only.

(3) The symbol table may be unprintable because it is constructed incorrectly.

(4) Even if the symbol table is correct, the scanner may still output the wrong intermediate code.

The first problem is a serious one. If the scanner produces no test output, you have no idea of what is wrong with it. To solve this problem we introduce

Rule 4.3:
The compiler displays the test program as it inputs it character by character.

The display requires a trivial change only of the compiler administration. If the scanner goes into an endless loop or crashes during the input of a symbol S, the screen will show exactly where S is in the test program. (Even if the scanner does not succeed in inputting the symbol S completely, the screen will still show all the previous symbols, so that you can find S on a printout of the test program.) When you know which symbol the scanner cannot handle, you can find the programming error by studying the corresponding part of the scanner carefully. When the scanner finally works, the display mechanism may be removed.

The second problem is merely a matter of printing the symbol table more often. The most radical approach is to print the table after each insertion of a new word. If you do that, it is not a good idea to use the sample program as a test program. If each word in the table can be described on one printed line, the test output will consist of $1 + 2 + \cdots + 431 = 93{,}096$ lines! It is clearly essential to construct a much smaller test program for the scanner.

Considering that printing the symbol table repeatedly does not solve problems three and four, you probably suspect by now that we are not doing this right. So let us try something else:

Rule 4.4:

The test output of the compiler consists of the intermediate code printed as a sequence of integers.

If the scanner terminates after outputting a symbol incorrectly, the corresponding symbol in the test program will show you exactly where the scanner failed. Since the scanner uses a different algorithm for each kind of symbol, you can immediately locate the incorrect algorithm. By simulating the execution of the algorithm manually, you can determine exactly where the error is. After correcting the scanner, you can then run the same test again.

What we have done is to print the sequence of values assigned to a single variable of the scanner (the variable that holds the current output symbol). If there is anything wrong with the symbol table, the test output will reveal it indirectly.

In constructing the test program we will follow a general guideline:

Rule 4.5:

The test program must be written in such a way that it forces the compiler to execute every statement at least once.

This means that every conditional statement must be executed both when the condition is true and false.

In practice, it is easy to invent a systematic set of test cases that satisfies this rule. Take, for example, the following part of the scanner:

```
(T) if ch = '<' then
(S)   begin NextChar;
(F)     if ch = '=' then
          begin Emit1(NotGreater1); NextChar end
(T)     else if ch = '>' then
(S)       begin Emit1(NotEqual1); NextChar end
        else Emit1(Less1)
      end
```

Every line that is executed when the symbol "<>" is scanned is marked with one of three letters:

(T) True condition tested

(F) False condition tested

(S) Simple statement tested

It is obvious that the three symbols

< <= <>

comprise a complete test of this program piece.

The construction of test cases continues until all conditions are marked T and F and all simple statements are marked S.

The test program does not have to be a complete Pascal program. It need only be a sequence of symbols that is acceptable to the scanner.

The algorithm for scanning a word has the form

```
while ch in AlphaNumeric do
  begin
    if ch in CapitalLetters then . . .
  end;
Search( . . . );
if IsName then . . .
else . . .
```

Any word will make the condition

ch **in** AlphaNumeric

true initially and false at the end. To test the if statement within the loop, the sample word must include both small and capital letters. The if statement after the loop requires both a name and a word symbol. So the following test cases will apparently do the job:

And   DNA

However, at this point, Rule 4.5 should be supplemented by a few other rules:

Rule 4.6:

When the compiler uses a variable restricted to a subrange of values, the test should preferably cover the whole range of values (or at least the extreme values of the range).

During the scanning of a single word, the variable ch holds alphanumeric characters only. The test should therefore preferably include a name consisting of all the letters and digits; for example,

abcdefghijklmnopqrstuvwxyz0123456789

To test the equivalence of small and capital letters, the same name should also occur in the following form in the test program:

ABCDEFGHIJKLMNOPQRSTUVWXYZ0123456789

These test cases will verify that the compiler initializes the set variables

AlphaNumeric   CapitalLetters

correctly.

If you find it a bit too much to test all the letters and digits, you may prefer to construct a name that includes the first and last character of each kind only:

az09

and then check the initialization of the set constants by proofreading the scanner carefully.

When you are constructing the test cases for the algorithm above, the call of the search procedure is regarded as a simple statement that needs to be executed once only.

When you are reading the search procedure in detail, you must construct other test cases to execute all the statements of this procedure. The body of the search loop has the form

```
if Pointer = nil WordPointer then
  {1: The list does not contain a given word}
else if Found ( . . . ) then
  {2: The list contains the word}
else Pointer := Pointer@.NextWord
  {3: The list contains another word}
```

The following sequence of words covers all three test cases:

And DNA DNA

Since the addition of characters modulo W is a commutative operation, the words above have the same hash key because they are permutations of the same letters. When the scanner initializes the symbol table, the first thing it does is to insert the word **and.** When the scanner finds the same word in the test program, the word is already in the table (case 2). When the name DNA is input the first time, the list already contains another word (the word **and**—see case 3), but it does not yet contain the name DNA (case 1).

During the testing of the search procedure, the call of the function named Found is regarded as a condition that needs to be tested twice only (when it has the values true and false). To construct a more complete test of this function we must study it in detail to discover the following test cases:

(1) The scanner must be able to compare two words of different lengths with the same hash key.

You can easily construct two names of this kind by looking at a table of the ASCII characters [Brinch Hansen, 1983]. You may, for example, find that the name "a12" has the hash key 97 + 49 + 50 = 196. Since this sum can be rewritten as 97 + 99, the name "ac" has the same hash key.

(2) The scanner must also be able to compare two words of the same length with the same hash key. In one case the two words must be identical; in another, they must be different.

These cases are already covered by the words **and** and DNA.

With these test cases we can determine whether the search algorithm works in general. But we must do a bit more for the word symbols and standard names. These fixed words may be regarded as a constant part of the symbol table. The testing of constant tables is governed by the following rule:

Rule 4.7:

Use every element of a constant table at least once.

The test program should therefore include each of the fixed words at least once.

The remaining test cases for the scanner are constructed by following the same rules. Test 1 is a complete test program for correct symbols.

```
{ Pascal— Test 1: Correct Symbols }

{abcdefghijklmnopqrstuvwxyz
{ABCDEFGHIJKLMNOPQRSTUVWXYZ
 1234567890} !"#$%&'()*+,-.
 /:;<=>?@[\]_~`}

+ - * < = > <= <> >= :=
( ) [ ] , . : ; ..

0 32767

And array begin const div do else
end if mod not of or procedure
program record then type var while

Integer Boolean false true read write
abcdefghijklmnopqrstuvwxyz0123456789
ABCDEFGHIJKLMNOPQRSTUVWXYZ0123456789
DNA a12 ac DNA a12 ac
```

Test 1

The printed test output is a sequence of numbers:

23	1	23	2	23	3	23	4
23	5	23	6	23	7	23	8
32	20	2	19	14	15	26	25
27	3	23	9	18	37	17	36
6	31	5	38	10	23	10	23
11	28	0	28	32767	23	12	23
13	0	1	4	7	8	9	11
23	14	12	16	21	24	29	30
33	23	15	34	35	39	40	41
42	23	16	23	17	22	1	22
2	22	3	22	4	22	5	22
6	23	18	22	7	23	19	22
7	23	20	22	8	22	9	22
10	22	8	22	9	22	10	23
21	13						

If you replace the ordinal values of the symbols by their names, the test output looks like this:

> NewLine 1 NewLine 2 NewLine 3 NewLine 4 NewLine 5
> NewLine 6 NewLine 7 NewLine 8 Plus Minus Asterisk
> Less Equal Greater NotGreater NotEqual NotLess
> Becomes NewLine 9 LeftParenthesis RightParenthesis
> LeftBracket RightBracket Comma Period Colon
> Semicolon DoubleDot NewLine 10 NewLine 11 Numeral 0
> Numeral 32767 NewLine 12 NewLine 13 And Array Begin
> Const Div Do Else NewLine 14 End If Mod Not Of Or
> Procedure NewLine 15 Program Record Then Type Var
> While NewLine 16 NewLine 17 Name 1 Name 2 Name 3
> Name 4 Name 5 Name 6 NewLine 18 Name 7 NewLine 19
> Name 7 NewLine 20 Name 8 Name 9 Name 10 Name 8
> Name 9 Name 10 NewLine 21 EndText

When the scanner works it would seem that we no longer need the test programs. However, there are several reasons why it would be a mistake to throw them away:

(1) If we ever decide to add a new standard procedure to Pascal— or extend the language in any other way, the compiler must also be extended. When this has been done, it is wise to run all the previous tests of the compiler to verify that the changes have no influence on the existing logic.

(2) If you decide to move the compiler with minimal changes to a new operating system or a new computer, the compiler must be tested systematically from scratch.

This brings us to yet another rule of testing:

Rule 4.8:
The test cases and their expected output must be well documented and reproducible.

If you keep the test programs and their correct output, the compiler can be retested completely simply by running the same tests and comparing the new test output with the old output.

Since the proofreading of test output can be a bit tedious, I offer the following final advice for testing a compiler:

Rule 4.9:
Use check sums of the test output to reduce the proofreading when a test is repeated.

In testing the Pascal— compiler, I used the following algorithm to compute check sums:

```
{Initial sum}
 Sum := 0;
   ...
{After the output of an integer value}
 Sum := (Sum + Value mod 8191) mod 8191;
```

When a test is repeated you need only look at a single number (the check sum).

5

SYNTAX ANALYSIS

A program that performs syntax analysis is called a *parser*. (The word *parse* means "to describe a series of words grammatically.") This chapter describes the Pascal— parser (pass 2) and explains how it recognizes correct sentences and detects syntax errors. The difficult problem of error recovery is discussed in detail. The method of compilation, which is known as recursive-descent, imposes certain restrictions on the grammar of the language.

5.1 SYMBOL INPUT

When the scanner has converted a program text into a sequence of symbols, the parser performs a single scan of the symbols and checks whether they form Pascal sentences. In this chapter we assume that the only task of pass 2 is to input symbols and output error messages if the program syntax is wrong. Semantic analysis and code generation will be discussed later.

The compiler passes use two procedures named Read and Emit to input and output intermediate (and final) code. The compiler administration makes these procedures available to the passes (Section 3.4).

The intermediate code consists of symbols represented by enumeration values of type SymbolType (Section 4.2). Some symbols are followed by an integer argument n:

Name n   NewLine n   Numeral n

These symbols are called *long symbols.*

The intermediate code is therefore a sequence of symbol values and integers. This mixture of types causes a minor problem in a language like Pascal in which each variable must be of a single type only.

As an arbitrary convention, the parameters of the procedures Read and Emit are defined to be of type integer. This convention forces the scanner to output the ordinal value of a symbol (rather than the symbol itself):

```
Emit(ord(Symbol))
```

When the parser inputs the ordinal value of a symbol it replaces it by the corresponding symbol value. In Pascal* this type conversion is expressed as follows

```
Read(Symbol:integer)
```

The parser uses two variables to hold a symbol and its argument (if any):

```
var Symbol: SymbolType; Argument: integer;
```

Algorithm 5.1 defines the input of the next symbol.

```
var LineNo: integer;
procedure NextSymbol;
begin Read(Symbol:integer);
  while Symbol = NewLine1 do
    begin
      Read(LineNo); NewLine(LineNo);
      Read(Symbol:integer)
    end;
  if Symbol in LongSymbols then
    Read(Argument)
end;
```

Algorithm 5.1

The only purpose of *line numbers* is to help you locate errors in the program text. They are not part of the Pascal sentences as such. It is therefore convenient to let the input procedure act as a filter that skips line numbers after transmitting them to the compiler administration (Section 3.5).

The procedure NextSymbol illustrates the use of sets to classify symbols during syntax analysis:

```
type Symbols = set of SymbolType;
var LongSymbols: Symbols;
LongSymbols := Symbols[Name1, Numeral1]
```

Whereas the source text of a program may be an arbitrary sequence of characters, the intermediate code output by the scanner is always a sequence of correct symbols terminated by an EndText symbol. Consequently, the parser does not have to call the function EOF to find out if it has reached the end of the input. It just terminates when it reaches the EndText symbol. Perhaps, I should be a bit more careful and say instead that *the parser must never try to scan past the EndText symbol*!

5.2 PARSER CONSTRUCTION

The parser uses the single-symbol look-ahead method (Section 4.3). After initializing its variables, the parser reads the first symbol of the intermediate code and calls a procedure named Programx to check the syntax of a program:

```
begin Initialize; NextSymbol; Programx end.
```

The parser is constructed directly from the BNF grammar of Pascal— (Section 2.4) by following a set of programming rules. The first of these rules is:

Rule 5.1:

For every BNF rule

N = E .

the parser defines a procedure of the same name:

```
procedure N; begin a(E) end;
```

The procedure defines a parsing algorithm a(E). When the algorithm is executed it examines one or more symbols and determines whether they form a sentence described by the syntax expression E. If they do, the algorithm inputs the whole sentence plus the first symbol that follows after it; otherwise, the algorithm reports a syntax error after inputting an unknown number of symbols. Later we will see how the parser deals with this uncertainty after a syntax error. Informally, we will say that the parsing algorithm *recognizes* sentences of the form E.

The starting point of the grammar is the BNF rule that defines the syntax of a whole program:

Program = "**program**" ProgramName ";" BlockBody "." .

To recognize a program we need a procedure:

```
procedure Programx;
begin
  a("program" ProgramName ";" BlockBody ".")
end;
```

that defines an algorithm:

a("**program**" ProgramName ";" BlockBody ".")

The algorithm scans a sentence consisting of the word **program** followed by a name, a semicolon, a block body, and a period.

We will construct this complicated algorithm out of five simpler algorithms:

a("**program**")	Recognizes the word **program**
a(ProgramName)	Recognizes a name
a(";")	Recognizes a semicolon
a(BlockBody)	Recognizes a block body
a(".")	Recognizes a period

When we know how to program these algorithms, we can construct the original algorithm as a sequence of the simpler algorithms:

```
a("program" ProgramName ";" BlockBody ".") =
  a("program"); a(ProgramName);
  a(";"); a(BlockBody); a(".")
```

This is an example of the use of the following construction rule:

Rule 5.2:

A sequence of sentences of the forms F1, F2, . . . , Fn is recognized by scanning the individual sentences one at a time in the order written:

a(F1 F2 . . . Fn) = a(F1); a(F2); . . . ; a(Fn)

Another frequently used rule is:

Rule 5.3:

When the parser expects a single symbol s, it uses the following algorithm:

```
a(s) = if Symbol = s then NextSymbol
       else SyntaxError
```

This algorithm is implemented as a procedure:

```
procedure Expect(s:  Symbol)
```

It is now trivial to construct all but one of the algorithms above:

```
a("program") = Expect(Program1)
a(ProgramName) = Expect(Name1)
a(";") = Expect(Semicolon1)
a(".") = Expect(Period1)
```

Since a block body is defined by another BNF rule, it must be recognized by a separate procedure that we have not yet written (Rule 5.1). In the procedure named Programx, all we need to do to recognize a block body is to call a procedure named BlockBody. In other words,

```
a(BlockBody) = BlockBody
```

However trivial this may seem, we have just found yet another construction rule for parsing:

Rule 5.4:

To recognize a sentence described by a BNF rule named N the parser calls the corresponding procedure named N:

```
a(N) = N
```

By combining the smaller algorithms according to Rule 5.2, we obtain the procedure Programx (Algorithm 5.2).

```
procedure Programx;
begin
  Expect(Program1); Expect(Name1);
  Expect(Semicolon1); BlockBody;
  Expect(Period1)
end;
```

Algorithm 5.2

You may, of course, feel that there is no need to be so formal about it—it is all quite obvious. But be patient! Although an experienced programmer does not need a set of construction rules to write a complete parser of 1000 lines or more, the task becomes so much easier when all you have to do is to follow a set of mechanical rules. You will also discover that a careful analysis of the parsing method reveals some subtle restrictions that must be imposed on the BNF grammar.

A block body is described by the BNF rule:

```
BlockBody =
  [ ConstantDefinitionPart ] [ TypeDefinitionPart ]
  [ VariableDefinitionPart ] { ProcedureDefinition }
  CompoundStatement .
```

and is recognized by the Algorithm 5.3.

```
procedure BlockBody;
begin
  if Symbol = Const1 then
    ConstantDefinitionPart;
  if Symbol = Type1 then
    TypeDefinitionPart;
  if Symbol = Var1 then
    VariableDefinitionPart;
  while Symbol = Procedure1 do
    ProcedureDefinition;
  CompoundStatement
end;
```

Algorithm 5.3

The syntax factor

```
[ ConstantDefinitionPart ]
```

shows that a block body may or may not begin with a constant definition part. The BNF rule

```
ConstantDefinitionPart =
  "const" ConstantDefinition { ConstantDefinition } .
```

shows that the first symbol of a constant definition part is the word **const**. Consequently, the parser can find out if there is a constant definition part by looking at the next symbol only:

```
if Symbol = Const1 then
  ConstantDefinitionPart
```

In general, a sentence of some form E may begin with any one of several symbols. A statement may, for example, begin with a name or one of the words **if, while,** or **begin.** The set of possible symbols that may appear at the beginning of a sentence of the form E is denoted First(E).

It is also useful to have a notation for the set of symbols that can follow immediately after a nonterminal symbol N. This set is denoted Follow(N).

It is fairly easy to determine the set First(E) by looking at the syntax expression E and the BNF rules that are mentioned in E. It is more difficult to find the set Follow(N) since you have to look at all BNF rules that refer to N. Here are some examples from Pascal—:

```
First(ConstantDefinitionPart) =
  Symbols[Const1]
Follow(ConstantDefinitionPart) =
  Symbols[Type1, Var1, Procedure1, Begin1]

First(Statement) =
  Symbols[Name1, If1, While1, Begin1]
Follow(Statement) =
  Symbols[Semicolon1, Else1, End1, Period1]
```

We are now ready to describe a programming rule that was used intuitively to parse a block body:

Rule 5.5:

The parser uses the following algorithm to recognize a possibly empty sentence of the form [E]:

```
a([ E ]) = if Symbol in First(E) then a(E)
```

A block body may include zero or more procedure definitions:

```
{ ProcedureDefinition }
```

Since a procedure definition begins with the word **procedure,** a (possibly empty) sequence of procedure definitions is recognized by a while statement:

```
while Symbol = Procedure1 do
  ProcedureDefinition
```

This example illustrates the use of

Rule 5.6:

To recognize a sentence of the form { E } use the following algorithm:

a({ E }) = **while** Symbol **in** First(E) **do** a(E)

It is now obvious how to parse a constant definition part (see Algorithm 5.4).

```
procedure ConstantDefinitionPart;
begin
  Expect(Const1);
  ConstantDefinition;
  while Symbol = Name1 do
    ConstantDefinition
end;
```

Algorithm 5.4

To make the parser more readable, it is a good idea to write each BNF rule as a comment before the corresponding procedure (see Algorithm 5.5).

```
{ ConstantDefinition =
    ConstantName "=" Constant ";" . }

procedure ConstantDefinition;
begin
  Expect(Name1); Expect(Equal1);
  Constant; Expect(Semicolon1)
end;
```

Algorithm 5.5

Algorithm 5.6 defines the parsing of a constant (which is either a numeral or a name).

```
{ Constant = Numeral | ConstantName . }

procedure Constant;
begin
  if Symbol = Numeral1 then NextSymbol
  else if Symbol = Name1 then NextSymbol
  else SyntaxError
end;
```

Algorithm 5.6

Here we have used yet another rule of parsing:

Rule 5.7

If all sentences of the forms T1, T2, . . . , Tn are nonempty, the following algorithm will recognize a sentence of the form T1 | T2 | . . . | Tn:

```
a(T1 | T2 | . . . | Tn) =
  if Symbol in First(T1) then a(T1)
  else if Symbol in First(T2) then a(T2)
    . . .
  else if Symbol in First(Tn) then a(Tn)
  else SyntaxError
```

If any of the Ti sentences may be empty, the error reporting at the end of the algorithm is omitted.

When the parser scans a program that begins like this:

```
program P;
const N = 100;
  . . .
```

it will initially call the following sequence of procedures:

Procedure	*Initial Symbol*
Programx	**program**
BlockBody	**const**
ConstantDefinitionPart	**const**
ConstantDefinition	N
Constant	100

This list also shows what the next symbol is at the beginning of each procedure ("the initial symbol").

The parser recognizes a sentence by looking at it as a whole before it looks at smaller parts of the sentence. As the parser gradually recognizes a sentence, it never ends up in a situation where it has to look at the same symbols again to make another guess of what kind of sentence (if any) they form. A compilation method with these characteristics is known as *top-down parsing without backtracking.*

5.3 FIRST SYMBOLS

The construction of the parsing algorithm for a sentence involves finding the set of symbols that may occur at the beginning of the sentence. This is done by using the following rules:

(1) The empty sentence has no first symbol:

First(Empty) = Symbols[]

In Pascal, the empty statement is an example of a sentence expressed by writing nothing.

(2) The first symbol of a single symbol s is s itself:

First(s) = Symbols[s]

For example:

First("**record**") = Symbols[Record1]

(3) If all sentences of the form E are nonempty, all sentences of the form E F must begin with one of the first symbols of E, so

First(E F) = First(E)

For example:

First(VariableName { Selector })
= First(VariableName)
= Symbols[Name1]

(4) If some sentences of the form E are empty, all sentences of the form E F must begin with one of the first symbols of either E or F, that is,

First(E F) = First(E) + First(F)

For example:

First(["**var**"] VariableGroup)
= First(["**var**"]) + First(VariableGroup)
= Symbols[Var1, Name1]

(5) All sentences of the form E | F must begin with one of the first symbols of either E or F:

First(E | F) = First(E) + First(F)

For example:

First (NewArrayType | NewRecordType)
  = First (NewArrayType) + First (NewRecordType)
  = Symbols[Array1, Record1]

(6) By rewriting N = [E] and N = { E } as

N = Empty | E   N = Empty | E N

and using the preceding rules, you can easily derive the following rules:

First ([E]) = First (E)
First ({ E }) = First (E)

First ([E] F) = First (E) + First (F)
First ({ E } F) = First (E) + First (F)

A tedious, but necessary step in the compiler construction is to use rules 1 to 6 to find the first symbols of all the sentence forms of Pascal— (Section 2.4). It is most convenient to do this *bottom-up* starting with the simplest sentences working toward the composite sentences. The following list shows the result of such an analysis:

BNF Rule	*First Symbols*
Name	name
Numeral	numeral
Constant	name numeral
IndexedSelector	[
FieldSelector	.
Selector	[.
VariableAccess	name
Factor	name numeral (**not**
MultiplyingOperator	* **div mod and**
Term	name numeral (**not**
AddingOperator	+ − **or**
SignOperator	+ −
SimpleExpression	+ − name numeral (**not**
RelationalOperator	< = > <= <> >=
Expression	+ − name numeral (**not**
ActualParameter	+ − name numeral (**not**
ActualParameterList	+ − name numeral (**not**

BNF Rule	*First Symbols*
AssignmentStatement	name
ProcedureStatement	name
IfStatement	**if**
WhileStatement	**while**
CompoundStatement	**begin**
Statement	name **if while begin**
ParameterDefinition	**var** name
FormalParameterList	**var** name
ProcedureBlock	(;
ProcedureDefinition	**procedure**
VariableGroup	name
VariableDefinition	name
VariableDefinitionPart	**var**
RecordSection	name
FieldList	name
NewRecordType	**record**
IndexRange	name numeral
NewArrayType	**array**
NewType	**array record**
TypeDefinition	name
TypeDefinitionPart	**type**
ConstantDefinition	name
ConstantDefinitionPart	**const**
BlockBody	**const type var procedure begin**
Program	**program**

5.4 FOLLOW SYMBOLS

To find the set of symbols that may follow after a nonterminal symbol T, you must look at all productions of the forms

N = S T U .   N = S [T] U .   N = S { T } U .

If all sentences of the form U are nonempty, Follow(T) includes First(U). If some sentences of the form U are empty, Follow(T) also includes Follow(N).

Productions of the forms

N = S T .   N = S [T] .   N = S { T } .

show that Follow(T) includes Follow(N).

If T occurs in the form { T }, Follow(T) also includes First(T).

By using these rules you can find the follow symbols of all BNF rules of Pascal—. This time it is more convenient to do it in *top-down order* starting with the BNF rule

Program = "**program**" ProgramName ";" BlockBody "." .

This rule shows that Follow(BlockBody) includes First(".") = Symbols[Period1]. Since a BlockBody also is a part of a ProcedureBlock, we can only conclude at this point that

Follow(BlockBody)
  = Symbols[Period1] + Follow(ProcedureBlock)

The next BNF rule is

BlockBody =
  [ConstantDefinitionPart] [TypeDefinitionPart]
  [VariableDefinitionPart] { ProcedureDefinition }
  CompoundStatement

Since a ConstantDefinitionPart does not occur anywhere else in the grammar, it follows immediately that

Follow(ConstantDefinitionPart)
  = First(the rest of the rule)
  = Symbols[Type1, Var1, Procedure1, Begin1]

Similarly, we have

Follow(TypeDefinitionPart)
  = Symbols[Var1, Procedure1, Begin1]

Follow(VariableDefinitionPart)
  = Symbols[Procedure1, Begin1)

The production

{ ProcedureDefinition } CompoundStatement

shows that Follow(ProcedureDefinition) includes both First(ProcedureDefinition) and First(CompoundStatement). Since a ProcedureDefinition is not mentioned anywhere else, we have

Follow(ProcedureDefinition)
= Symbols[Procedure1, Begin1]

The last part of a block body is a compound statement. Consequently, Follow(CompoundStatement) includes Follow(BlockBody). Since a CompoundStatement also occurs as a Statement in the grammar, we conclude that

Follow(CompoundStatement)
= Follow(BlockBody) + Follow(Statement)

Here is a complete list of the follow symbols of Pascal—:

BNF Rule	*Follow Symbols*
BlockBody	; .
ConstantDefinitionPart	**type var procedure begin**
TypeDefinitionPart	**var procedure begin**
VariableDefinitionPart	**procedure begin**
ProcedureDefinition	**procedure begin**
ConstantDefinition	name **type var procedure begin**
TypeDefinition	name **var procedure begin**
NewType	;
NewArrayType	;
NewRecordType	;
IndexRange	]
FieldList	**end**
RecordSection	; **end**
VariableDefinition	name **procedure begin**
VariableGroup	;)
ProcedureBlock	;
FormalParameterList	)
ParameterDefinition	;)
AssignmentStatement	; **else end**
ProcedureStatement	; **else end**

BNF Rule	*Follow Symbols*
IfStatement	; **else end**
WhileStatement	; **else end**
CompoundStatement	; **else end** .
Statement	; **else end** .
VariableAccess	* **div mod and** + − **or** < = > <= <> >= ,)] ; := **then else do end**
Expression	,)] ; **then else do end**
ActualParameterList	)
ActualParameter	,)
SimpleExpression	< = > <= <> >= ,)] ; **then else do end**
RelationalOperator	< = > <= <> >= ,)] ; **then else do end**
SignOperator	name numeral (**not**
AddingOperator	name numeral (**not**
Term	+ − **or** < = > <= <> >= ,)] ; **then else do end**
Factor	* **div mod and** + − **or** < = > <= <> >= ,)] ; **then else do end**
MultiplyingOperator	name numeral (**not**
Constant	* **div mod and** + − **or** < = > <= <> >= ,)] ; . . **then else do end**
Selector	* **div mod and** + − **or** < = > <= <> >= ,) [ ] ; := . **then else do end**

5.5 GRAMMAR RESTRICTIONS

When the parser has reached a point in the program text where several different kinds of sentences may occur, it must decide which of these possibilities to pursue. To avoid backtracking one must design the programming language in such a way that a choice among alternative sentences can always be made by looking at the next symbol only.

The decision is, of course, trivial when a sentence form begins with a unique symbol:

Sentence Form	*First Symbols*
Program	**program**
ConstantDefinitionPart	**const**
TypeDefinitionPart	**type**
VariableDefinitionPart	**var**
ProcedureDefinition	**procedure**
CompoundStatement	**begin**
NewArrayType	**array**
NewRecordType	**record**
IfStatement	**if**
WhileStatement	**while**
IndexedSelector	[
FieldSelector	.

It is possible to change Pascal so that each kind of sentence begins with a unique symbol. But this makes the language notation somewhat clumsy, as shown below:

assign x := x + 1   **call** P(. .)

To abbreviate the notation, Pascal allows a name to occur at the beginning of many kinds of sentences:

ConstantDefinition
TypeDefinition
IndexRange
FieldList
RecordSection
VariableDefinition
VariableGroup
FormalParameterList
ParameterDefinition
Statement
AssignmentStatement
ProcedureStatement

ActualParameterList
ActualParameter
Expression
SimpleExpression
Term
Factor
VariableAccess
Constant

To deal with this ambiguity we must be a bit more clever. We know that each kind of sentence can occur at certain points in a program only. So at each point in the program text, the parser must choose between a small number of alternatives only. If these alternatives all begin with different symbols, the parser can immediately make the right choice. To make this possible, the BNF grammar of the programming language must be restricted as follows:

Restriction 1:

Consider all sentences of the form

N = E | F .

To decide whether the next symbol is the beginning of an E or F sentence, the parser must assume that the two kinds of sentences always begin with different symbols. So the BNF grammar must satisfy the following condition:

First(E) * First(F) = Symbols[ ] .

By using the first symbols listed in Section 5.3, you can, for example, verify that the BNF rule

NewType = NewArrayType | NewRecordType .

satisfies this condition since

```
First(NewArrayType) * First(NewRecordType)
  = Symbols[Array1] * Symbols[Record1]
  = Symbols[ ]
```

However, if you look at the BNF rule for a statement, it is obvious that the parser cannot distinguish an assignment statement from a procedure statement, since both kinds of statements begin with a name. This is a violation of the restriction above.

The ambiguity can be resolved (somewhat artificially) by describing the two kinds of statements by a single BNF rule:

```
NameStatement = Name Operands .
Operands =
  { Selector } ":=" Expression |
  [ "(" ActualParameterList ")" ] .
```

The use of names to denote both constants and variables also makes the following BNF rules ambiguous:

```
ActualParameter = Expression | VariableAccess .

Factor = Constant | VariableAccess | . . . .
```

Since the syntax of an expression includes a variable access as a special case, the first BNF rule can simply be rewritten as

```
ActualParameter = Expression .
```

As the parser cannot tell the difference between a constant name and a variable name, the second rule can be rewritten as follows for the purpose of parsing only:

```
Factor = Numeral | VariableAccess | . . . .
```

In this chapter we accept these ad hoc solutions. Later, we will see how the parser can use semantic information stored in a name table to distinguish between the names of constants, types, variables, and procedures (Chapter 7).

Restriction 1 is not sufficient for single-symbol look-ahead parsing. If a sentence of some form N may be empty, the parser must be able to decide whether the next symbol is the beginning of a nonempty or an empty sentence of that form. In the former case, the next symbol will be one of the first symbols of N. In the latter case, it will be one of the follow symbols of N. To make this choice unambiguous, we need another restriction:

Restriction 2:

If some of the sentences described by a BNF rule N may be empty, the grammar must be constrained as follows:

```
First(N) * Follow(N) = Symbols[ ] .
```

A statement is an example of a sentence that may be empty. In this case, we have

```
First(Statement) * Follow(Statement)
  = Symbols[Name1, If1, While1, Begin1]
    * Symbols[Semicolon1, Else1, End1, Period1]
  = Symbols[ ]
```

as required by the second restriction.

In the context of this restriction, any syntax factors of the forms [E] and { E } must be considered abbreviations for BNF rules of the forms

```
N = Empty | E .     N = Empty | E N .
```

In the case of the BNF rule

```
ParameterDefinition = [ "var" ] VariableGroup .
```

we find

```
First([ "var" ]) * Follow([ "var" ])
  = First("var") * First(VariableGroup)
  = Symbols[Var1] * Symbols[Name1]
  = Symbols[ ]
```

as required.

For the BNF rule

```
ConstantDefinitionPart =
  "const" ConstantDefinition { ConstantDefinition } .
```

we have

```
First({ ConstantDefinition })
  * Follow({ ConstantDefinition })
  = First(ConstantDefinition)
    * Follow(ConstantDefinitionPart)
  = Symbols[Name1]
    * Symbols[Type1, Var1, Procedure1, Begin1]
  = Symbols[ ]
```

Before writing a parser, you must verify that all the sentence forms of the programming language are restricted as defined here.

5.6 RECURSION

If the grammar of a programming language includes recursive BNF rules, the corresponding parsing algorithms will be recursive procedures. Let us, for example, look at some very simple expressions of the form

```
Expression = Term { Operator Term } .
Operator = "+" | "—" .
Term = Numeral | "(" Expression ")" .
```

A parser for these expressions consists of two recursive procedures named Term and Expression. Since these procedures must refer to each other, we need a forward declaration of one of them (see Algorithm 5.7).

```
procedure Expression; forward;

procedure Term;
begin
  if Symbol = Numeral1 then NextSymbol
  else if Symbol = LeftParenthesis1 then
    begin NextSymbol; Expression;
      Expect(RightParenthesis1)
    end
  else SyntaxError
end;

procedure Expression;
begin Term;
  while Symbol in Operators do
    begin NextSymbol; Term end
end;
```

Algorithm 5.7

This algorithm uses the following set of symbols:

Operators = Symbols[Plus1, Minus1]

When the algorithm recognizes the expression

$$118 - (7 + 12)$$

it executes the following sequence of procedure calls:

Procedure Called	*Part Recognized*
1. Expression	118 − (7 + 12)
2. Term	118
3. Term	(7 + 12)
4. Expression	7 + 12
5. Term	7
6. Term	12

Figure 5.1 shows the same sequence of actions as a tree structure. Each node of the tree corresponds to the recognition of a nonterminal or terminal symbol of the expression. The terminal symbols are at the leaves of the tree. This tree, which shows the grammatical composition of the expression, is called a *parse tree.* Conceptually, the parser builds this tree one branch at a time and removes each branch again as soon as it has recognized the sentence or symbol that corresponds to the branch.

Since all programming languages include expressions, a parser is normally a collection of recursive procedures. These procedures analyze a sentence from the top down in more and more detail until they have recognized the individual symbols of the sentence. The method is therefore known as *recursive-descent parsing.*

It should be obvious at this point that a compiler should be written in a programming language that supports recursion. This requirement makes Pascal a good choice and Fortran a poor one.

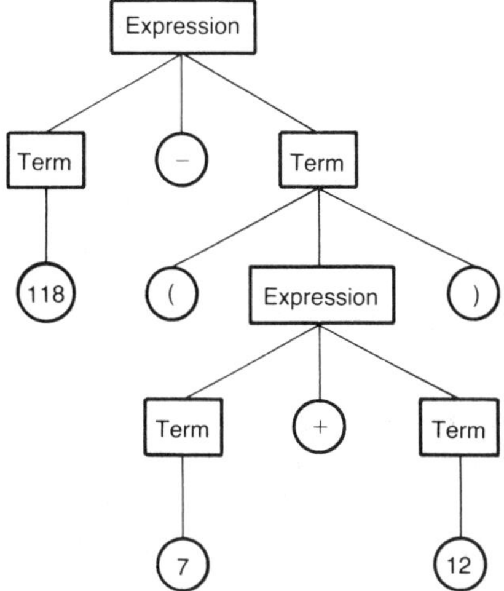

Fig. 5.1 Parse tree.

The BNF rule for an expression of the previous type can be rewritten like this:

Expression = Term [Operator Expression] .

The parsing algorithm for this recursive rule is as follows:

```
procedure Expression;
begin Term;
  if Symbol in Operators then
    begin NextSymbol; Expression end
end;
```

Since the procedure Term is called once only, we can replace the call of this procedure by its statement part and write the expression parser as a single procedure (Algorithm 5.8).

```
procedure Expression;
begin
  if Symbol = Numeral1 then NextSymbol
  else if Symbol = LeftParenthesis1 then
    begin NextSymbol; Expression;
      Expect(RightParenthesis1)
    end
  else SyntaxError;
  if Symbol in Operators then
    begin NextSymbol; Expression end
end;
```

Algorithm 5.8

In later chapters I will show how the semantic analysis of a program text can be simplified by using recursive procedures of this type.

To satisfy the second restriction imposed on grammars (Section 5.5) we must assume the following about the context in which an expression can occur:

```
First([ Operator Expression ])
  * Follow([ Operator Expression ])
  = First(Operator) * Follow(Expression)
  = Symbols[Plus1, Minus1] * Follow(Expression)
  = Symbols[ ]
```

In other words, an expression cannot be followed by a "+" or "—" symbol.

The form of recursion used in the rule

Expression = Term [Operator Expression] .

is called *right recursion.*

The use of *left recursion* as in the rule

Expression = [Expression Operator] Term .

can cause problems in a recursive-descent parser. A naive parsing algorithm for this rule looks like this:

```
procedure Expression;
begin
  if Symbol in ExpressionSymbols then
    begin Expression;
      if Symbol in Operators then NextSymbol
      else SyntaxError
    end;
  Term
end;
```

The first symbol of an expression will immediately cause this procedure to call itself and look at the same symbol again and again until the computer runs out of memory for procedure calls. So the compiler now crashes while parsing a correct expression!

If we had checked the second restriction on the grammar, we would have found that the BNF rule above is unacceptable since

```
First([ Expression Operator ])
  * Follow([ Expression Operator ])
  = First(Expression) * First(Term)
  = First(Term) * First(Term)
  = Symbols[Numeral1, LeftParenthesis1]
```

which is a nonempty set.

5.7 TESTING

When the parser has been programmed it must be tested by means of a small program that forces the parser to execute all statements at least once (Section 4.6). It is convenient to write two different test programs for this purpose: one that tests the parsing of correct sentences and another one that tests the detection of syntax errors.

We will begin by looking at the test program for correct sentences (see Test 2, Appendix A.6). Let's look at the procedure that parses a constant definition part:

```
procedure ConstantDefinitionPart;
begin
  Expect(Const1);
  ConstantDefinition;
  while Symbol = Name1 do
    ConstantDefinition
end;
```

This procedure contains four statements. Any constant definition part will make the parser execute the first two statements. The while statement should be tested both when it is executed zero times and when it is executed one or more times. (The latter case automatically tests the statement within the loop.) So the following test cases are sufficient for this procedure:

(1) **const** a = 1;

(2) **const** a = 1; b = a;

The complete test program was constructed like that by studying each parsing procedure (see Appendix A.6).

Since the parser does not output intermediate code in its present form, the test program will not produce any output either, and the only evidence you have that the parser works is that it terminates. If the parser cannot recognize a correct sentence, it will either (1) cause a run-time failure with a line number that refers to the program text of the parser; (2) report a (non-existing) syntax error with a line number that refers to the test program; or (3) go into an endless loop.

In the first two cases, you can immediately locate the parser procedure that is wrong and the test case that revealed the problem. In the third case, it is very helpful to let the compiler administration display a line number at the beginning of each line in the test program. When a test case makes the parser go into an endless loop, you can see the corresponding line number on the screen.

When you have located the incorrect procedure and the test case it could not handle, you must find the programming error by studying the procedure and simulating the parsing of the test case manually.

The testing of the error detection reveals some unexpected problems that are discussed in the following.

5.8 ERROR RECOVERY

To test the ability of the parser to report syntax errors you must find all the parsing procedures that call the procedure named SyntaxError. There are remarkably few of these procedures:

Procedure	*Test Case*
Expect	**const** a :={?} 1;
Constant	**const** c = {?};
TypeDefinition	**type** S = recrod{?} f, g: integer **end**;
Factor	**if** {?}= 2 **then** x := 1

The test cases shown will make the parser execute every one of these calls. The syntax errors are marked {?}.

The steps performed by the compiler immediately after the discovery of a syntax error are known as *error recovery*. The purpose of the error recovery is to enable the compiler to continue the parsing of a program text to find as many errors as possible in a single compilation and make sure that every error is reported once only.

Initially, we will assume that the parser only reports a syntax error, *leaving the current symbol unchanged*:

```
procedure SyntaxError;
begin Error(Syntax3) end;
```

To see if the parser is able to continue after a syntax error, we will write a correct sentence after each incorrect one. Test 3 is the complete test program.

A test of the parser with this program gives a very disappointing result: After reporting the first syntax error in line 5, the parser immediately terminates and ignores the rest of the program. What happened?

When the parser has recognized the name "a" in line 5, it reaches the following statements in the procedure ConstantDefinition:

```
Expect(Equal1);
Constant;
Expect(Semicolon1)
```

Since the next symbol is not "=" as expected, but ":=" instead, the parser reports a syntax error and leaves the current symbol unchanged.

```
 1 { Pascal— Test 3: Syntax Errors }
 2
 3 program Test3;
 4 const
 5   a :={?} 1;
 6   b = 2;
 7   c = {?};
 8   d = 4;
 9 type
10   S = recrod{?} f, g: integer end;
11   T = array [1 . . 2] of integer;
12 var
13   x: integer;
14 begin
15   if {?} = 2 then
16     x := 1
17 end.
```

Test 3

During the subsequent calls of Constant and Expect, the parser reports the same symbol twice again as a syntax error. But these redundant error messages are suppressed by the compiler administration, which refuses to output more than one error message per line (Section 3.5).

When the execution of ConstantDefinition terminates, the parser reaches the following loop within the procedure ConstantDefinitionPart:

```
while Symbol = Name1 do
  ConstantDefinition
```

Since the current symbol is still ":=", the loop immediately terminates, and so does the procedure.

Afterward, the ":=" symbol also makes the procedures BlockBody and Programx terminate. At this point, the whole parser terminates.

A look at the parser construction rules makes it clear that this will happen in general (Section 5.2). When the parser finds an unknown symbol it performs some combination of the following actions: (1) call a procedure, (2) report a syntax error, (3) skip a conditional statement that is unable to recognize the symbol, or (4) execute a statement that recognizes the symbol as valid in its own context.

The last situation occurs when a symbol has been omitted, as in line 7 of the test program

```
c = {?} ;
```

Here the semicolon will first cause an error message in the procedure Constant but will then be accepted by the procedure ConstantDefinition as the expected symbol after the (missing) constant.

However, in most cases the compiler cannot depend on this kind of luck in its error recovery. An invalid symbol will normally not be recognized by any of the parsing procedures and will therefore terminate the parsing.

To prevent this from happening we might let the parser skip the offending symbol after a syntax error by rewriting the procedure SyntaxError as follows:

```
procedure SyntaxError;
begin Error(Syntax3); NextSymbol end;
```

But, alas, the problem of error recovery is more subtle than that. The parser now reports syntax errors in lines 5, 7, and 8 and terminates in line 9. Although the parser now detects two errors correctly, it also reports one that is not there (line 8).

The semicolon in line 7 causes an error message as described earlier and is then skipped. When the parser expects the semicolon it finds instead the name "d" in line 8 and reports it as another syntax error. From then on, the parser continues to report errors, skip symbols, and look at new symbols that are not recognized by any of the parsing procedures. If a sequence of unrecognized symbols is long enough, it will eventually make the parser return from all procedures and terminate.

Our next approach to error recovery will be to skip zero or more symbols until we reach a major symbol which the parser is certain to recognize at some level. We will call these major symbols the *stop symbols* and choose them as follows:

```
StopSymbols := Symbols[Const1, Type1, Var1,
  Procedure1, Begin1, If1, While1]
```

After a syntax error, the parser must now perform the following error recovery:

```
procedure SyntaxError;
begin Error(Syntax3);
  while not (Symbol in StopSymbols) do
    NextSymbol
end;
```

Although this idea looks promising, we must obviously try it in practice. The result is a complete failure! The test program crashes the parser with the message temp1 file limit

and all error messages from the compiler are lost.

The problem is revealed by the syntax error in line 15, which makes the parser search for a stop symbol. Since there are no stop symbols after that line, the parser eventually tries to read past the end of the input file ("temp1") and is then stopped by the operating system.

As I said earlier, "the parser must never try to scan past the EndText symbol!" So, after including EndText in the set of stop symbols, we run the same test again.

This time, the parser correctly reports errors in lines 5, 10, and 15. It ignores the error in line 7 and reports nonexisting errors in lines 9, 12, and 18.

The idea of skipping symbols until the parser reaches a stop symbol it recognizes is fine, but the algorithm is just too crude. The use of a small, fixed number of stop symbols makes the parser skip too many symbols after a syntax error. As a result, many sentences are not checked at all.

For example, after detecting the syntax error in line 5 of the test program, the parser skips all other constant definitions until it reaches the word **type**, which is a stop symbol:

```
4 const
5   a := 1;
6   b = 2;
7   c =  ;
8   d = 4;
9 type
```

If the set of stop symbols could be extended temporarily with the semicolon symbol during the parsing of a constant definition part, the parser would not skip the remaining constant definitions.

Once you get the idea of using different sets of stop symbols to parse different kinds of sentences, the next step is obviously to revise the *parser construction rules* (Section 5.2) to include this idea:

Rule 5.1 (revised):
For every BNF rule

N = E .

the parser defines a procedure of the same name:

```
procedure N(Stop: Symbols);
begin a(E, Stop) end;
```

The procedure defines a parsing algorithm a(E, Stop) that can recognize any sentence of the form E and check that the sentence is followed by a well-defined stop symbol. The stop symbols are precisely those symbols which the parser is prepared to recognize after an E sentence. The set of stop symbols is a parameter of the parsing algorithm.

When the algorithm recognizes an E sentence followed by one of the stop symbols, it inputs the whole sentence plus the stop symbol. However, if either the sentence or the first symbol after it is incorrect, the parser reports a syntax error and skips further input until it reaches one of the stop symbols. In other words, the parser recovers from a syntax error by searching for the first symbol that makes sense in the given context. To prevent the parser from reading past the end of the input during error recovery, the stop symbols must always include the EndText symbol.

From the above we conclude that the last symbol input by a parsing algorithm is always one of the stop symbols of the algorithm—even if the algorithm finds a syntax error! A parsing algorithm with this property is said to be *sound*. More formally, a parsing algorithm a(E, Stop) is sound if the assertion

Symbol **in** Stop

is true after the execution of the algorithm.

Rule 5.2 (revised):

A sequence of sentences of the forms F1, F2, . . . , Fn followed by a stop symbol is recognized by scanning the individual sentences one at a time in the order written.

```
a(F1 F2 . . . Fn, Stop) =
  a(F1, First(F2, . . . , Fn) + Stop);
  a(F2, First(F3, . . . , Fn) + Stop);
   . . .
  a(Fn, Stop)
```

If there is a syntax error in the F1 sentence, the parser immediately attempts to find the beginning of the F2 sentence. If the parser cannot find the first symbol of the F2 sentence, it tries to find the first symbol of the F3 sentence, and so on. If the parser does not recognize anything after the error, it skips input until it reaches one of the stop symbols of the whole sequence of sentences. The set of stop symbols used during the parsing of the F1 sentence is therefore the union of the first symbols of all the following sentences plus the stop symbols of the whole sequence. The stop symbols of the remaining sentences are similar.

If the n component algorithms are sound, the assertion

Symbol **in** Stop

is true after the execution of the last component algorithm. The whole algorithm is therefore also sound.

Rule 5.3 (revised):
When the parser expects a single symbol s followed by a stop symbol, it calls a procedure named Expect (Algorithm 5.9).

a(s, Stop) = Expect(s, Stop)

```
procedure Expect(s: Symbol; Stop: Symbols);
begin
  if Symbol = s then NextSymbol
  else SyntaxError(Stop);
  SyntaxCheck(Stop)
end;
```

Algorithm 5.9

After examining the current symbol, the parser always makes sure that the next symbol is one of the expected stop symbols. This check is performed by Algorithm 5.10.

```
procedure SyntaxCheck(Stop: Symbols);
begin
  if not (Symbol in Stop) then
    SyntaxError(Stop)
end;
```

Algorithm 5.10

After a syntax error, the parser skips input until it reaches one of the stop symbols (Algorithm 5.11).

```
procedure SyntaxError(Stop: Symbols);
begin Error(Syntax3);
  while not (Symbol in Stop) do
    NextSymbol
end;
```

Algorithm 5.11

These procedures obviously define sound parsing algorithms since all of them make the assertion

Symbol **in** Stop

true.

Rule 5.4 (revised):

To recognize a sentence described by a BNF rule named N the parser calls the corresponding procedure named N using the stop symbols of the sentence as a parameter:

a(N, Stop) = N(Stop)

If the procedure N defines a sound parsing algorithm, the call of the procedure is obviously also a sound parsing algorithm.

Algorithm 5.12 illustrates the use of the revised Rules 5.1 to 5.4.

```
{ Program =
    "program" ProgramName ";" BlockBody "." . }

procedure Programx(Stop: Symbols);
begin
  Expect(Program1, Symbols[Name1, Semicolon1,
    Period1] + BlockSymbols + Stop);
  Expect(Name1, Symbols[Semicolon1, Period1]
    + BlockSymbols + Stop);
  Expect(Semicolon1, Symbols[Period1]
    + BlockSymbols + Stop);
  BlockBody(Symbols[Period1] + Stop);
  Expect(Period1, Stop)
end;
```

Algorithm 5.12

The algorithm uses the following symbol set:

```
BlockSymbols = Symbols[Begin1, Const1,
  Procedure1, Type1, Var1]
```

After initializing its variables, the parser inputs the first symbol and calls the foregoing procedure to analyze the syntax of a whole program:

```
begin Initialize; NextSymbol;
  Programx(Symbols[EndText1])
end;
```

The only symbol that may follow after a whole program is EndText. So initially this is the only stop symbol. When the parser calls other procedures, such as Expect and BlockBody, it adds further symbols temporarily to the stop symbols without removing the previous ones.

Rule 5.5 (revised):

The parser uses the following algorithm to recognize a sentence of the form [E] followed by a stop symbol:

```
a([ E ], Stop) =
  SyntaxCheck(First(E) + Stop);
  if Symbol in First(E) then a(E, Stop)
```

After the execution of the syntax check, the assertion

Symbol **in** (First(E) + Stop)

is true. There are now two possibilities:

(1) If the current symbol is one of the first symbols of an E sentence, the component algorithm a(E, Stop) will be executed. If the component algorithm is sound, it will make the assertion "Symbol **in** Stop" true.

(2) If the current symbol is not one of the first symbols of an E sentence, it must be one of the stop symbols. In that case, the component algorithm is not executed, but the assertion "Symbol **in** Stop" is still true.

In either case, the current symbol will be one of the stop symbols after the execution of the whole algorithm. So if the component algorithm is sound, the whole algorithm is also sound.

If the parsing algorithm above is preceded by another algorithm that makes the assertion

Symbol **in** (First(E) + Stop)

true, the initial syntax check may, of course, be omitted.

Rule 5.6 (revised):

The parser uses the following algorithm to recognize a sentence of the form { E } followed by a stop symbol:

```
a({ E }, Stop) =
  SyntaxCheck(First(E) + Stop);
  while Symbol in First(E) do
    a(E, First(E) + Stop)
```

The syntax check makes the assertion "Symbol **in** (First(E) + Stop)" true to begin with. If the component algorithm a(E, . . .) is sound, it will make the same assertion true every time it is executed. When the while statement terminates, we know two things: (1) the current symbol is either the first symbol of an E sentence or a stop symbol (this is the loop invariant we have just discussed), and (2) the current symbol is not the first symbol of an E sentence (this is the termination condition of the loop). Consequently, the current symbol must be a stop symbol. So we may conclude that if the component algorithm is sound, the whole algorithm is also sound.

If we know that the assertion

Symbol **in** (First(E) + Stop)

already holds at the beginning of the algorithm, the initial syntax check may be omitted.

Algorithm 5.13 illustrates the use of the revised Rules 5.5 and 5.6.

```
{ BlockBody =
    [ ConstantDefinitionPart ] [ TypeDefinitionPart ]
    [ VariableDefinitionPart ] { ProcedureDefinition }
    CompoundStatement . }

procedure BlockBody(Stop: Symbols);
begin
  SyntaxCheck(BlockSymbols + Stop);
  if Symbol = Const1 then
    ConstantDefinitionPart(Symbols[Type1, Var1,
      Procedure1, Begin1] + Stop);
  if Symbol = Type1 then
    TypeDefinitionPart(Symbols[Var1, Procedure1,
      Begin1] + Stop);
  if Symbol = Var1 then
    VariableDefinitionPart(Symbols[Procedure1,
      Begin1] + Stop);
  while Symbol = Procedure1 do
    ProcedureDefinition(Symbols[Procedure1,
      Begin1] + Stop);
  CompoundStatement(Stop)
end;
```

Algorithm 5.13

Rule 5.7 (revised):

If all sentences of the forms T1, T2, . . . , Tn are nonempty, the following algorithm will recognize a sentence of the form T1 | T2 | . . . | Tn followed by a stop symbol:

```
a(T1 | T2 | . . . | Tn, Stop) =
  if Symbol in First(T1) then a(T1, Stop)
  else if Symbol in First(T2) then a(T2, Stop)
    . . .
  else if Symbol in First(Tn) then a(Tn, Stop)
  else SyntaxError(Stop)
```

If any of the Ti sentences may be empty, the error reporting at the end of the algorithm is replaced by a SyntaxCheck(Stop).

Algorithm 5.14 illustrates the use of this rule.

```
{ Constant = Numeral | ConstantName . }

procedure Constant(Stop: Symbols);
begin
  if Symbol = Numeral1 then
    Expect(Numeral1, Stop)
  else if Symbol = Name1 then
    Expect(Name1, Stop)
  else SyntaxError(Stop)
end;
```

Algorithm 5.14

By means of the previous rules you can derive two more rules for special cases that occur frequently in many programming languages:

Rule 5.8:

The following algorithm recognizes one or more sentences of the form F followed by a stop symbol:

```
a(F { F }, Stop) =
  a(F, First(F) + Stop);
  while Symbol in First(F) do
    a(F, First(F) + Stop)
```

Algorithm 5.15 illustrates the use of this rule.

```
{ ConstantDefinitionPart =
    "const" ConstantDefinition
      { ConstantDefinition } . }

procedure ConstantDefinitionPart(Stop: Symbols);
var Stop2: Symbols;
begin
  Stop2 := Symbols[Name1] + Stop;
  Expect(Const1, Stop2);
  ConstantDefinition(Stop2);
  while Symbol = Name1 do
    ConstantDefinition(Stop2)
end;
```

Algorithm 5.15

Rule 5.9:

The following algorithm recognizes one or more sentences of the form F separated by the symbol s and followed by a stop symbol:

```
a(F { s F }, Stop) =
  a(F, Symbols[s] + Stop);
  while Symbol = s do
    begin
      Expect(s, First(F) + Symbols[s] + Stop);
      a(F, Symbols[s] + Stop)
    end
```

Algorithm 5.16 illustrates the use of this rule.

```
{ FieldList =
    RecordSection { ";" RecordSection } . }

procedure FieldList(Stop: Symbols);
var Stop2: Symbols;
begin
  Stop2 := Symbols[Semicolon1] + Stop;
  RecordSection(Stop2);
  while Symbol = Semicolon1 do
    begin
      Expect(Semicolon1, Symbols[Name1] + Stop2);
      RecordSection(Stop2)
    end
end;
```

Algorithm 5.16

We have defined nine rules for constructing a parser. The composite parsing algorithms are sound as a whole if their component algorithms are sound. The elementary algorithm that recognizes a single symbol is always sound. Any parser constructed according to these rules only will therefore be sound.

The parser of Pascal— was derived directly from the grammar in Section 2.4 using the construction rules above. Appendix A.3 contains the parser extended with algorithms for semantic analysis and code generation. (The additional algorithms will be described in later chapters.)

6

SCOPE ANALYSIS

This chapter defines the scope rules of Pascal— and explains how they are enforced by the compiler. The scope analysis is an extension of the parser.

6.1 BLOCKS

A Pascal— program uses names to refer to constants, data types, record fields, variables, and procedures. These named entities are called the *objects* of the program.

The types integer and Boolean, the constants false and true, and the procedures read and write are predefined objects that may be used in any Pascal— program. They are called the *standard objects* of the language.

Any other object used in a program must be defined by a *definition* that introduces the name of the object and describes some of its properties.

A constant definition introduces a constant; for example,

const c = 10;

A type definition introduces a data type; for example,

type T = **array** [1 . . c] **of** integer;

A record type introduces one or more fields; for example,

type U = **record** f: T; g: Boolean **end;**

A variable definition introduces one or more variables; for example,

var x, y: T;

A procedure definition defines a procedure; for example,

```
procedure P(x, y: T);
begin . . . end;
```

This example includes definitions of two local variables x and y which are parameters of the procedure.

A program combines related definitions and statements into syntactic units called *blocks*. There are three kinds of blocks:

(1) The standard block

(2) Programs

(3) Procedures

The standard block is an imaginary block in which the standard objects are defined.

Blocks may contain other blocks. The following program example shows how blocks are *nested*:

```
{Standard Block:
  const false = . . . ; true = . . . ;
  type integer = . . . ; Boolean = . . . ;
  procedure read(var x: integer);
  begin . . . end;
  procedure write(x: integer);
  begin . . . end;}

  program P;
    . . .
    procedure Q( . . . );
      . . .
      procedure R( . . . );
      begin . . . end {R};
      . . .
    begin . . . end {Q};
    . . .
  end {P}.

{End Standard Block}
```

The standard block contains the whole program. The program itself contains procedures. Each procedure may in turn contain other procedures.

6.2 SCOPE RULES

The purpose of the block concept is to confine the use of an object to the block in which it is defined. To make this idea precise we need a set of rules that enable a programmer (and a compiler!) to associate every occurrence of a name with a definition of the corresponding object.

The following rule is necessary to distinguish between different objects defined in the same block:

Rule 6.1:

All constants, types, variables, and procedures defined in the same block must have different names.

(The rules of record fields are exceptions to the general rules and will be considered in Chapter 7.)

According to Rule 6.1, a block may contain the following definitions, which introduce objects of different names:

```
type T = array [1 . . 10] of integer;
var x, y:  T;
```

But the definitions shown below are meaningless since they introduce objects of the same name:

```
const x =10;
var x:  integer;
```

We must also specify in which part of a block an object can be referenced. This part of the block is called the *scope* of the object. An object is said to be *known* in its scope.

Roughly speaking, an object defined in a block is known from its definition to the end of the block. In the example below, a procedure Q defines a variable x. The lines in which the variable is known are marked (var x):

```
              procedure Q;
              var x:  T;
(var x)         . . .
(var x)         procedure R;
(var x)         begin
(var x)           . . . x . . .
(var x)         end;
(var x)         . . .
(var x)       begin
(var x)         . . . x . . .
              end;
```

Notice that the procedure Q contains another procedure R in which the variable x is also known. The variable is said to be *local* to Q and *global* to R.

If we say only that an object x is known "from its definition to the end of the block," it is not clear whether the scope of x extends from the *beginning* or the *end* of its definition.

It may seem obvious that we mean "from the end of its definition to the end of the block." But if that were the case, the name of a procedure would be known only after the end of the procedure, and it would be impossible to write a procedure that calls itself.

So if we wish to permit recursive procedures, the scope of a procedure must extend from the beginning of its definition. More precisely, a procedure Q must be known from the beginning of the procedure block, that is, right after the introduction of the procedure name Q (Section 2.4):

```
          program P;
            . . .
            procedure Q;
    (Q)     begin
    (Q)       . . . Q . . .
    (Q)     end;
    (Q)     . . .
    (Q)   begin
    (Q)     . . . Q . . .
          end.
```

However, if we allow the scope of any object to begin right after the introduction of its name, the language will permit meaningless recursive definitions, such as

```
const c = c;
type T = array [1 . . 10] of T;
  U = record f, g: U end;
```

These examples make it clear that the scope rules of a programming language must be formulated with great care. The insight we have gained so far is expressed in the following rule:

Rule 6.2:

A constant, type, or variable defined in a block is normally known from the end of its definition to the end of the block. A procedure defined in

a block B is normally known from the beginning of the procedure block to the end of the block B.

(The only exception to this rule will be defined later by Rule 6.3.)

Although objects defined in the same block must have different names, two or more objects may have the same name if they are defined in different blocks. As an example, consider the following program:

```
                program P;

                  procedure Q;
                  var x:  T;
(var x)           begin
(var x)             . . . x . . .
                  end;

                  procedure R;
                  const x = 10;
(const x)         begin
(const x)           . . . x . . .
                  end;

                begin . . . end.
```

Here procedure Q defines a variable x, while procedure R defines a constant which is also named x. Since procedure Q does not contain procedure R (or vice versa), Rule 6.2 makes it clear that the name x refers to the variable when it is used within Q and to the constant when it is used within R.

In the next example, a procedure Q contains another procedure R:

```
                procedure Q;
                var x:  T;
(var x)           . . .
(var x)           procedure R;
(var x)           const x = 10;
  (const x)         . . .
  (const x)       begin . . . end;
(var x)           . . .
(var x)         begin . . . end;
```

When two blocks Q and R are nested like this, the name x denotes the constant x when it is used within R and the variable x when it is used anywhere else in Q (outside R). Strictly speaking, this is not quite correct: According to Rule 6.2, the constant x is unknown in that part of R which precedes the definition of the constant. So to be accurate we must say instead that the variable x is unknown in the scope of the constant x.

This example illustrates the use of the following scope rule:

Rule 6.3:

Consider a block Q that defines an object x. If Q contains a block R that defines another object named x, the first object is unknown in the scope of the second object.

Scope Rules 6.2 and 6.3 can be reformulated as an algorithm for finding the definition that corresponds to a name used in a block. This search process is called a *binding.*

When a name is used in a block, you must first try to find a preceding definition of the name in the same block. If that fails, you must look for a preceding definition in the surrounding block, and so on, until you either find a definition or reach the standard block.

More precisely, when a name occurs in a block, a binding is performed as follows, starting with the smallest block that includes the occurrence of the name:

Step A: If a name x is preceded in the same block by a definition of an object named x, the name x refers to that object.

Step B: Otherwise, step A is repeated for the smallest block that contains the previous block. (If there is no such block, the name is undefined.)

6.3 COMPILATION METHOD

I will use the following program example to explain how the compiler performs scope analysis:

```
(Standard Block
  program P;
  type T = array [1 . . 100] of integer;
  var x: T;

    procedure Q(x: integer);
    const c = 13;
    begin . . . x . . . end;

    procedure R;
    var b, c: Boolean;
    begin . . . x . . . end;

  begin . . . end.
End Standard Block)
```

During scope analysis, the compiler maintains a *stack* of definitions. When the compiler recognizes a definition of a new object, it pushes the name of the object on the stack. Initially, the compiler pushes all the standard names on the stack. At the end of a block, the compiler removes all names defined in that block from the stack.

Figure 6.1 shows the stack at various stages during the compilation of the program example. (The stack grows from the top of the figure toward the bottom.)

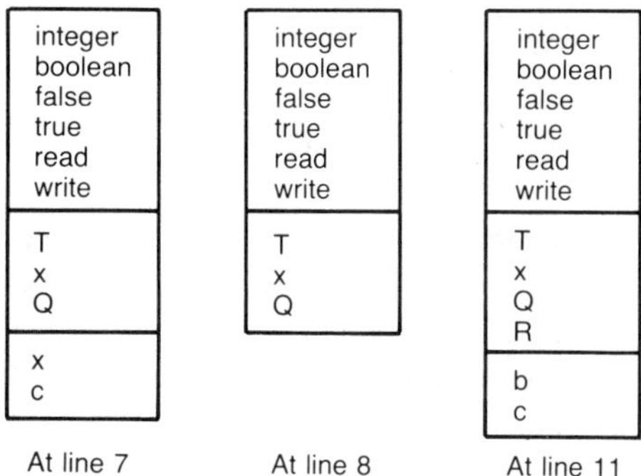

Fig. 6.1 Name stack.

When the compiler reaches line 7 of the program, the stack contains all the names introduced in the previous lines. Line 7 contains a reference to an object named x. To determine if such an object is known at that point, the compiler searches the stack from the top until it finds an object named x (in this case the parameter x) defined in procedure Q.

At line 8, the names defined within the procedure Q have been removed from the stack, and at line 11, the procedure R and its local variables b and c have been added to the stack. Line 11 also contains a reference to an object named x. In this case, a search of the stack shows that the name refers to an object (the variable x) that is defined in the program block.

In the following example, the name of a variable is misspelled in the definition of the variable but is spelled correctly in the rest of the program:

```
program P;
  . . .
var tabel:  T;
begin
  . . . table . . .
  . . . table . . .
  . . . table . . .
end.
```

A poor compiler will report every occurrence of the name "table" as an undefined name. To avoid this, we will use the following form of *error recov-*

ery: If a name is not found in the stack, it is reported as an *undefined* name. The name is then added to the stack so that other references to the same name will not cause further error messages.

When the compiler reaches a definition in a block, it compares the new name to all other names that have already been defined in the same block. If one of these names is the same as the new name, the name is reported as *ambiguous* and is not entered in the stack. However, since the stack already contains that name, any references to it will not cause further error messages.

6.4 DATA STRUCTURES

Before we can implement the stack in Pascal we need to define the concept of *block levels.* Every block in a program is assigned a level number as follows: The standard block is at level 0. The level number increases by one at the beginning of a new block and decreases by one at the end of the block. In the program example discussed in Section 6.3, the blocks have the following level numbers:

Block	*Level Number*
Standard block	0
Program P	1
Procedure Q	2
Procedure R	2

Figure 6.2 shows the stack at line 7 in the program example. At this point, the stack contains the names of objects defined in the following blocks:

Block	*Level Number*
Standard block	0
Program P	1
Procedure Q	2

All objects that are defined in the same block are represented by a linked list of records. Every record describes an object by its name index and a pointer:

```
type
  Pointer = @ ObjectRecord;
  ObjectRecord =
    record Name: integer; Previous: Pointer end;
```

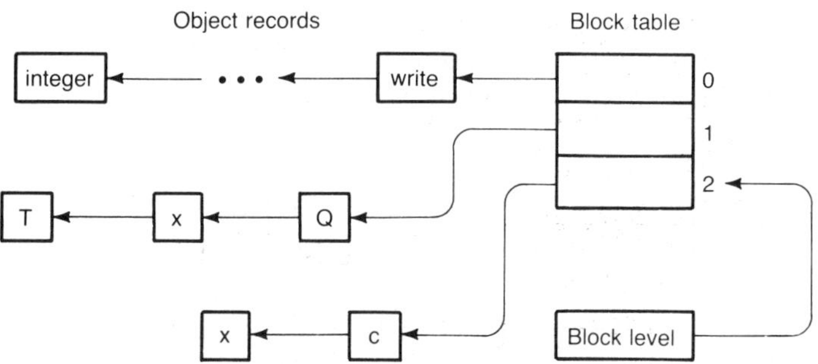

Fig. 6.2 The name stack represented by linked lists.

Since all objects defined in a block must have different names, it does not matter in which order they are linked together. In this case, the list begins with the *last object* defined in a block, and every object is linked to the *previous* object defined in the same block.

In the preceding example, the compiler is currently analyzing a procedure Q at level 2 which is contained in the program block at level 1 and the standard block at level 0. The objects defined in these nested blocks are described by three linked lists (Fig. 6.2). The compiler uses a *block table* to define where these lists begin:

```
const
  MaxLevel = 10;
type
  BlockRecord = record LastObject: Pointer end;
  BlockTable = array [0 . . MaxLevel] of BlockRecord;
var
  Block: BlockTable; BlockLevel: integer;
```

Each entry in the block table holds a pointer to the last object defined in a block. It seems likely, however, that we may need to add more attributes of blocks later to perform type analysis and code generation. By defining each block entry as a record (instead of just a pointer) we make it easier to add more fields later.

The compiler keeps the level number of the current block in a variable named BlockLevel.

6.5 ALGORITHMS

First, we need an algorithm to determine if a name has been defined in a given block. The block is identified by its level number (see Algorithm 6.1).

```
procedure Search(Name, LevelNo: integer;
  var Found: Boolean);
var More: Boolean; Object: Pointer;
begin
  More := true;
  Object := Block[LevelNo].LastObject;
  while More do
     if Object = nil Pointer then
       begin More := false; Found := false end
     else if Object@.Name = Name then
       begin More := false; Found := true end
     else
       Object := Object@.Previous
end;
```

Algorithm 6.1

The parser uses Algorithm 6.2 to define a new object. If the current block already defines another object of the same name, the name is reported as ambiguous. Otherwise, the new object is linked to the other objects defined in the same block.

```
procedure Define(Name: integer);
var Found: Boolean; Object: Pointer;
begin
  Search(Name, BlockLevel, Found);
  if Found then Error(Ambiguous3)
  else
    begin
      New(Object);
      Object@.Name := Name;
      Object@.Previous :=
         Block[BlockLevel].LastObject;
      Block[BlockLevel].LastObject := Object
    end
end;
```

Algorithm 6.2

When a name is used to refer to an object, the compiler first tries to find the object in the current block. If that fails, the compiler looks for the object in the surrounding block, and so forth. If the object is not described in the stack, the compiler reports it as undefined and creates a definition of the object in the stack (Algorithm 6.3).

```
procedure Find(Name: integer);
var More, Found: Boolean; LevelNo: integer;
begin
  More := true; LevelNo := BlockLevel;
  while More do
    begin Search(Name, LevelNo, Found);
      if Found or (LevelNo = 0) then More := false
      else LevelNo := LevelNo - 1
    end;
  if not Found then
    begin Error(Undefined3); Define(Name) end
end;
```

Algorithm 6.3

At the beginning of a new block, the compiler makes sure that the maximum number of block levels has not been reached (Section 3.5). It then increments the block level by one and creates an empty list of objects for the new block (Algorithm 6.4).

```
procedure NewBlock;
begin
  TestLimit(BlockLevel, MaxLevel);
  BlockLevel := Blocklevel + 1;
  Block[BlockLevel].LastObject := nil Pointer
end;
```

Algorithm 6.4

At the end of a block, the objects defined in the block are made inaccessible by decrementing the block level (Algorithm 6.5).

```
procedure EndBlock;
begin BlockLevel := BlockLevel - 1 end;
```

Algorithm 6.5

Initially, the compiler defines the standard objects at level 0 (see Section 4.1 and Algorithm 6.6).

This is all we need to add scope analysis to the parser. We will now look at some examples of how the parser uses these algorithms.

Let us first rewrite Algorithm 5.14, which parses a constant. The revised version (Algorithm 6.7) shows how the compiler uses the procedure Find to check whether a name refers to a known object.

```
procedure StandardBlock;
begin
  BlockLevel := -1;
  NewBlock;
  Define(Integer0);
  Define(Boolean0);
  Define(False0);
  Define(True0);
  Define(Read0);
  Define(Write0)
end;
```

Algorithm 6.6

```
{ Constant = Numeral | ConstantName . }

procedure Constant(Stop: Symbols);
begin
  if Symbol = Numeral1 then
    Expect(Numeral1, Stop)
  else if Symbol = Name1 then
    begin Find(Argument);
      Expect(Name1, Stop)
    end
  else SyntaxError(Stop)
end;
```

Algorithm 6.7

As an example of a definition, we will look at a constant definition. The parser must input a name at the beginning of the constant definition but must not enter it in the stack until it reaches the end of the constant definition. The delayed definition of the name prevents the use of recursive constant definitions, such as

```
const c = c;
```

The compiler will simply report the second occurrence of the name c as an undeclared name (unless c is already defined in a surrounding block).

If there is no name at the beginning of a constant definition, the parser must remember not to enter one at the end of the definition. This ugly exception is avoided by using Algorithm 6.8 wherever the parser expects a new name. If there is no name, the procedure reports a syntax error and returns an imaginary name index:

```
const NoName = 0;
```

The parser can then enter a description of that name just as it would have done if the name had been real. Since the scanner never outputs the imaginary name, the parser will never find a reference to it in the program text. So it does no harm to enter a description of it in the stack.

```
procedure ExpectName(var Name: integer;
  Stop: Symbols);
begin
  if Symbol = Name1 then
    begin Name := Argument; NextSymbol end
  else
    begin Name := NoName; SyntaxError(Stop) end;
  SyntaxCheck(Stop)
end;
```

Algorithm 6.8

Algorithm 6.8 is a variant of an earlier procedure named Expect (Algorithm 5.9). We can now use it to analyze a constant definition (see Algorithm 6.9).

```
{ ConstantDefinition =
    ConstantName "=" Constant ";" . }

procedure ConstantDefinition(Stop: Symbols);
var Name: integer;
begin
  ExpectName(Name, Symbols[Equal1, Semicolon1]
    + ConstantSymbols + Stop);
  Expect(Equal1, ConstantSymbols
    + Symbols[Semicolon1] + Stop);
  Constant(Symbols[Semicolon1] + Stop);
  Define(Name);
  Expect(Semicolon1, Stop)
end;
```

Algorithm 6.9

The parsing of a complete program illustrates the handling of blocks (see Algorithm 6.10).

Appendix A.3 contains the parser extended with scope analysis (plus type analysis and code generation).

The data structures used for the scope analysis make the algorithms very simple and do not put a fixed limit on the number of objects that can be used in a program.

```
{ Program =
    "program" ProgramName ";" BlockBody "." }

procedure Programx(Stop: Symbols);
begin
  Expect(Program1, Symbols[Name1, Semicolon1,
    Period1] + BlockSymbols + Stop);
  Expect(Name1, Symbols[Semicolon1, Period1]
    + BlockSymbols + Stop);
  Expect(Semicolon1, Symbols[Period1]
    + BlockSymbols + Stop);
  NewBlock;
  BlockBody(Symbols[Period1] + Stop);
  EndBlock;
  Expect(Period1, Stop)
end;
```

Algorithm 6.10

On the other hand, the method is somewhat careless in its use of storage: When the objects of a block are removed from the stack, this means only that the objects no longer can be reached from the block table. But since the object records are pointer elements allocated in the heap, they continue to occupy storage until the parser terminates. As we shall see later, the type analysis makes it necessary in any case to retain the descriptions of some objects (record fields and procedure parameters). So the disadvantage of the linked lists is not as great as you might think.

6.6 TESTING

The scope analysis is tested by writing a Pascal program that forces the parser to execute every statement of the new algorithms. A study of these algorithms shows that the test program must include sentences of the following kinds:

(1) A constant definition

(2) A type definition

(3) A variable definition

(4) A recursive procedure definition

(5) References to all standard objects

(6) References to all defined objects

Test 4 includes all these test cases (see Appendix A.6). Since the parser outputs no code yet, a compilation of this program will show only whether the parser is able to terminate without error messages when it analyzes the test cases. Later, we will write other programs to test the code generation. But that is not the purpose of the present test.

We must also show that the scope analysis can report the following kinds of errors:

(1) A definition of an ambiguous name

(2) A definition without a name

(3) Meaningless recursive definitions

(4) References to an undefined name

These test cases are covered by Test 5.

```
 1  { Pascal— Test 5:  Scope Errors }
 2
 3  program Test5;
 4  const
 5    {a} = 1;
 6    b = b;
 7  type
 8    T = array [1 . . 10] of T;
 9    U = record f, g:  U end;
10  var
11    x, y, x:  integer;
12  begin
13    x :=  a;
14    y := a
15  end.
```

Test 5

If the scope analysis works, the parser should report the following errors in this program:

Line 5: Invalid Syntax
Line 6: Undefined Name
Line 8: Undefined Name
Line 9: Undefined Name
Line 11: Ambiguous Name
Line 13: Undefined Name

Notice that the first reference to the undefined name "a" (in line 13) is reported but the other one (in line 14) is not.

7

TYPE ANALYSIS

This chapter explains how the compiler uses definitions of objects to perform type analysis of sentences. The type analysis is an extension of the parser, which already performs scope analysis.

7.1 KINDS OF OBJECTS

During scope analysis, an object is described by its name only and is linked to all previous objects defined in the same block (Section 6.4):

```
type
  Pointer = @ ObjectRecord;
  ObjectRecord =
     record Name:  integer; Previous:  Pointer end;
```

To perform type analysis, the compiler must, however, be able to distinguish between different *kinds* of objects: constants, types, variables, procedures, and so on. We will use the following data type to classify objects:

```
type
  Class = (Constantx, StandardType, ArrayType,
    RecordType, Field, Variable, ValueParameter,
    VarParameter, Procedur, StandardProc,
    Undefined);
```

The parser must now store all information contained in the definition of an object (including its kind). The parser collects different kinds of information about different kinds of objects. A constant is, for example, described by its type and value. On the other hand, a procedure is characterized by its list of parameters. Since the information varies from one kind of object to another, it is most convenient to describe the objects by *variant records* of the following type:

```
type
  ObjectRecord =
    record
      Name: integer; Previous: Pointer;
      case Kind: Class of
        Constantx: ( . . . );
        ArrayType: ( . . . );
          . . .
        Procedur: ( . . . )
    end;
```

After extending the object records with a variant part, we must modify the scope analysis procedures to enable the parser to classify objects and access their records through pointers. The following explains how these procedures work when they have been revised.

When the parser recognizes the definition of an object it calls the following procedure (Algorithm 6.2):

```
procedure Define(Name: integer; Kind: Class;
  var Object: Pointer);
```

This procedure creates a record with the name and kind of the object and returns a pointer to it. The parser uses the pointer to fill in the variant part of the record with additional information about the object.

When the parser encounters a reference to an object, it calls the following procedure (Algorithm 6.3):

```
procedure Find(Name: integer;
  var Object: Pointer);
```

This procedure tries to find the record of an object with a given name. If the object does not exist, the procedure creates a record of a fictitious kind (called Undefined). In either case, the procedure returns a pointer to the chosen record, which the parser then uses to access the available information about the object.

The following sections explain how objects of different kinds are handled.

7.2 STANDARD TYPES

Each standard type (integer or Boolean) is described by an object record:

```
type
  ObjectRecord =
    record
      Name: integer; Previous: Pointer;
      case Kind: Class of
        . . .
    end;
```

The fixed part of the record defines the name of the type and links it to the previous objects defined in the standard block. The link is used for scope analysis only and plays no role in the type analysis. The variant part of the record consists of a kind field only with the value StandardType.

This is how the parser defines the standard types:

```
var TypeInteger, TypeBoolean: Pointer;

Define(Integer0, StandardType, TypeInteger);
Define(Boolean0, StandardType, TypeBoolean)
```

The name indices of the standard types are called Integer0 and Boolean0 (Section 4.2). During type analysis, each type is represented by a pointer to the corresponding record. These pointers are stored in two variables named TypeInteger and TypeBoolean.

Figure 7.1 shows the record that describes the type Boolean and the variable that points to it. The link to a previous object is omitted because it is not used in the type analysis.

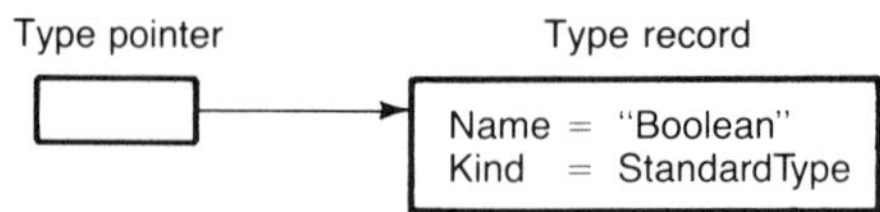

Fig. 7.1 Data representation of the type Boolean.

7.3 CONSTANTS

A constant is described by an object record that includes the name of the constant:

```
type
  ObjectRecord =
    record
      Name: integer; Previous: Pointer;
      case Kind: Class of
        Constantx:
          (ConstValue: integer;
            ConstType: Pointer);
        . . .
    end;
```

The variant part of the record consists of a kind field with the value Constantx and two fields that define the type and value of the constant.

Figure 7.2 shows the record that describes the standard constant *false*. The type field of the record points to the record that describes the type Boolean (Section 7.2). The parser creates this data representation in the following way:

```
var Constx: Pointer;

Define(False0, Constantx, Constx);
Constx@.ConstValue := ord(false);
Constx@.ConstType := TypeBoolean
```

The name index of the constant is called False0 (Section 4.2). The parser creates a similar description of the standard constant *true*.

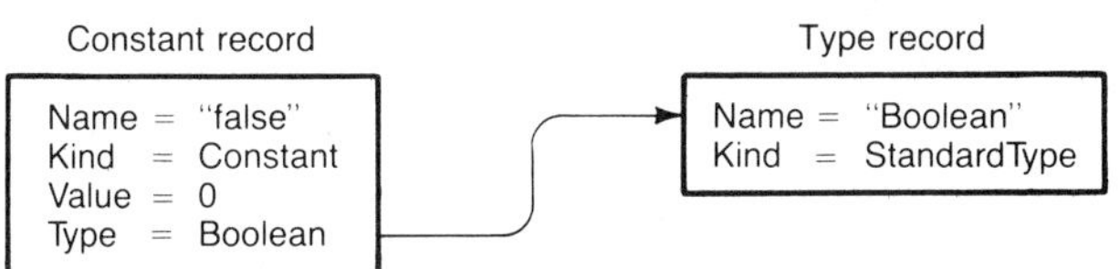

Fig. 7.2 Data representation of the constant false.

When the parser encounters a constant it must determine the type and value of the constant. This information is provided by a revised version of Algorithm 6.7 (see Algorithm 7.1). If parsing is based on syntax alone, the compiler cannot distinguish between the names of constants and other kinds of objects (Section 5.5). This ambiguity is resolved by the use of object classes.

```
{ Constant = Numeral | ConstantName . }

procedure Constant(var Value: integer;
  var Typex: Pointer; Stop: Symbols);
var Object: Pointer;
begin
  if Symbol = Numeral1 then
    begin
      Value := Argument;
      Typex := TypeInteger;
      Expect(Numeral1, Stop)
    end
  else if Symbol = Name1 then
    begin
      Find(Argument, Object);
      if Object@.Kind = Constantx then
        begin
          Value := Object@.ConstValue;
          Typex := Object@.ConstType
        end
      else
        begin KindError(Object);
          Value := 0;
          Typex := TypeUniversal
        end;
      Expect(Name1, Stop)
    end
  else
    begin SyntaxError(Stop):
      Value := 0;
      Typex := TypeUniversal
    end
end;
```

Algorithm 7.1

Algorithm 7.1 illustrates two forms of *error recovery* used during type analysis:

(1) When the parser encounters a name that does not refer to a constant, it reports it as a name of the wrong kind by executing Algorithm 7.2. If the name refers to an undefined object, it has already caused an error message during scope analysis. In that case, the algorithm will not output another error message.

```
procedure KindError(Object: Pointer);
begin
  if Object@.Kind <> Undefined then
    Error(Kind3)
end;
```

Algorithm 7.2

(2) If the parser does not recognize a constant, it returns a value (zero) of a fictitious type known as the *universal type*. The parser makes sure that an operand of this type never causes another error message during type checking.

The universal type is defined as a standard type with an imaginary name index (zero):

```
const NoName = 0;
var TypeUniversal: Pointer;

Define(NoName, StandardType, TypeUniversal)
```

We can now extend Algorithm 6.9, which parses a constant definition with statements that create an object record (see Algorithm 7.3).

```
{ ConstantDefinition =
    ConstantName "=" Constant ";" . }

procedure ConstantDefinition(Stop: Symbols);
var Name, Value: integer;
  Constx, Typex: Pointer;
begin
  ExpectName(Name, Symbols[Equal1, Semicolon1]
    + ConstantSymbols + Stop);
  Expect(Equal1, ConstantSymbols
    + Symbols[Semicolon1] + Stop);
  Constant(Value, Typex, Symbols[Semicolon1]
    + Stop);
  Define(Name, Constantx, Constx);
  Constx@.ConstValue := Value;
  Constx@.ConstType := Typex;
  Expect(Semicolon1, Stop)
end;
```

Algorithm 7.3

7.4 VARIABLES

The following procedure definition illustrates the different kinds of variables used in Pascal—:

```
procedure P(u: integer; var v: integer);
var x, y: Boolean;
begin . . . end;
```

It defines a *value parameter* u, a *variable parameter* v, and two local *variables* x and y.

During compilation, each variable is described by its name, kind, and type:

```
type
  ObjectRecord =
    record
      Name: integer; Previous: Pointer;
      case Kind: Class of
        . . .
        Variable, ValueParameter, VarParameter:
          (VarType: Pointer);
        . . .
    end;
```

The value of the kind field is either Variable, ValueParameter, or VarParameter.

Figure 7.3 shows two records that describe the local variables x and y. The type fields of these records point to the record that describes the type Boolean (Section 7.2).

The object records of parameters and local variables differ only in the value of the kind field. We can therefore use a single parsing procedure to

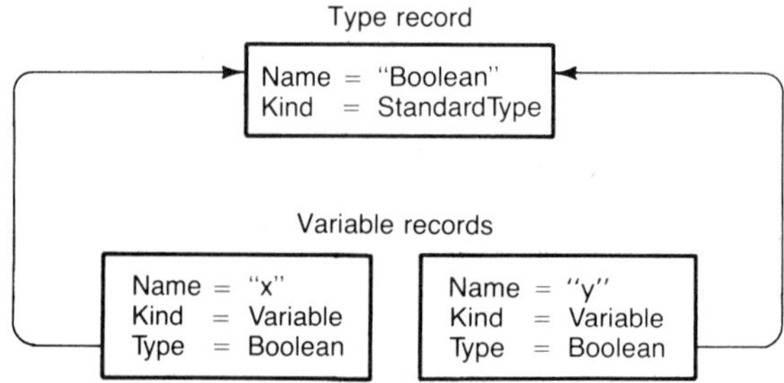

Fig. 7.3 Data representation of two variables.

construct any kind of variable record. If you ignore the symbols **var** and ";", you will see that parameter definitions and variable definitions have the same syntax (Section 2.4). Both are defined by sentences of the form

```
VariableGroup =
  VariableName { "," VariableName } ":" TypeName .
```

All we have to do then is to extend the parsing procedure for variable groups with a kind parameter

```
procedure VariableGroup(Kind: Class; Stop: Symbols);
```

and add statements to create variable records.

Unfortunately, this procedure is somewhat awkward to write. First, it must scan the list of variable names and create the corresponding records. Then, when it reaches the type name, it must go back through these records again and insert pointers to the type record. The variable records can be accessed the second time by following the chain of pointers that links every object to the previous objects defined in the same block. This is a case in which the links established for scope analysis can be used for type analysis also.

We will instead write a more elegant procedure in which iterative statements are replaced by recursive calls of the same procedure. To do this, we must rewrite the syntax rule for variable groups:

```
VariableGroup = VariableName GroupTail .
GroupTail = "," VariableGroup | ":" TypeName .
```

According to these rules, a variable group such as

```
x, y: integer
```

consists of a variable name x followed by a group tail

```
, y: integer
```

The latter consists of a comma followed by a variable group:

```
y: integer
```

This variable group, in turn, consists of a variable name y followed by a group tail:

```
: integer
```

Algorithm 7.4 defines the recursive parsing procedure. If this procedure encounters a variable name followed by a comma, it calls itself. Each variable name is therefore handled by a separate call of the procedure. The last of these calls occurs when the procedure reaches the type name and obtains a pointer to the corresponding type record. This pointer is assigned to a variable parameter named Typex, which is shared by all the procedure calls. At the end, each procedure call completes its own variable record with a copy of the type pointer and terminates.

```
procedure VariableGroup(Kind: Class;
  var LastVar, Typex: Pointer; Stop: Symbols);
var Name: integer; Varx: Pointer;
begin
  ExpectName(Name, Symbols[Comma1, Colon1]
    + Stop);
  Define(Name, Kind, Varx);
  if Symbol = Comma1 then
    begin
      Expect(Comma1, Symbols[Name1] + Stop);
      VariableGroup(Kind, LastVar, Typex, Stop)
    end
  else
    begin LastVar := Varx;
      if Symbol = Colon1 then
        begin
          Expect(Colon1, Symbols[Name1] + Stop);
          TypeName(Typex, Stop)
        end
      else
        begin
          SyntaxError(Stop);
          Typex := TypeUniversal
        end
    end;
  Varx@.VarType := Typex
end;
```

Algorithm 7.4

This recursive procedure implements a two-pass scan of a variable group. First, the variable names are scanned from left to right while the procedure calls itself and creates the corresponding records. Just before the calls terminate, the records are updated one more time in reverse order. We are simply using the chain of procedure calls to remember the chain of variable records.

The procedure above also returns a pointer to the last variable record in a group. I will explain the need for this pointer during the discussion of procedures.

When the parser expects to find a type name in a sentence, it executes Algorithm 7.5 to obtain a pointer to the corresponding type record. If there is no name (or if the name does not refer to a type), this procedure returns a pointer to the universal type, so that the rest of the parser is not affected by the error.

```
{ TypeName = Name . }

procedure TypeName(var Typex: Pointer;
  Stop: Symbols);
var Object: Pointer;
begin
  if Symbol = Name1 then
    begin
      Find(Argument, Object);
      if Object@.Kind in Types then
        Typex := Object
      else
        begin KindError(Object);
          Typex := TypeUniversal
        end
    end
  else Typex := TypeUniversal;
  Expect(Name1, Stop)
end;
```

Algorithm 7.5

The compiler uses a set value to determine whether a name refers to a type:

```
type Classes = set of Class;
var Types: Classes;

Types := Classes[StandardType, Array Type,
  RecordType]
```

It is now trivial to parse variable definitions by means of Algorithm 7.6.

```
{ VariableDefinition = VariableGroup ";" . }

procedure VariableDefinition(Stop: Symbols);
var LastVar, Typex: Pointer;
begin
  VariableGroup(Variable, LastVar, Typex,
    Symbols[Semicolon1] + Stop);
  Expect(Semicolon1, Stop)
end;
```

Algorithm 7.6

Parameter definitions are also straightforward (see Algorithm 7.7).

```
{ ParameterDefinition =
    [ "var" ] VariableGroup . }

procedure ParameterDefinition(
  var LastParam: Pointer; Stop: Symbols);
var Kind: Class; Typex: Pointer;
begin
  SyntaxCheck(Symbols[Var1, Name1] + Stop);
  if Symbol = Var1 then
    begin Kind := VarParameter;
      Expect(Var1, Symbols[Name1] + Stop)
    end
  else Kind := ValueParameter;
  VariableGroup(Kind, LastParam, Typex, Stop)
end;
```

Algorithm 7.7

A reference to a variable is called a *variable access.* When the parser encounters a variable name, it uses the corresponding record to determine the type of the variable. When a variable name x stands alone, it refers to a variable as a whole. If a variable is of an array type, the variable name x may be followed by an index expression e that selects an element of the array:

x[e]

The symbol "[e]" is called an *indexed selector.*

If a variable is of a record type, the variable name x may be followed by a name f, which selects a field of the record:

x.f

The symbol ".f" is called a *field selector.*

In Pascal—, the elements of an array may be records, and the fields of a record may be arrays. A variable access may therefore include a list of selectors that gradually select smaller and smaller parts of a whole variable; for example,

x.f[i] [j].g

In its most general form, a variable access has the following syntax:

VariableAccess = VariableName { Selector } .
Selector = IndexedSelector | FieldSelector .

and is parsed by Algorithm 7.8. This procedure uses the following set values:

Variables = Classes[Variable, ValueParameter,
  VarParameter]

SelectorSymbols = Symbols[LeftBracket1, Period1]

The procedure returns a pointer to the type of the variable to be used elsewhere for type checking.

```
procedure VariableAccess(var Typex: Pointer;
  Stop: Symbols);
var Stop2: Symbols; Object: Pointer;
begin
  if Symbol = Name1 then
    begin
      Stop2 := SelectorSymbols + Stop;
      Find(Argument, Object);
      Expect(Name1, Stop2);
      if Object@.Kind in Variables then
        Typex := Object@.VarType
      else
        begin KindError(Object);
          Typex := TypeUniversal
        end;
      while Symbol in SelectorSymbols do
        if Symbol = LeftBracket1 then
          IndexedSelector(Typex, Stop2)
        else {Symbol = Period1}
          FieldSelector(Typex, Stop2)
    end
  else
    begin SyntaxError(Stop);
      Typex := TypeUniversal
    end
end;
```

Algorithm 7.8

In the following sections we discuss selectors.

7.5 ARRAYS

An array type is described by an object record:

```
type
  ObjectRecord =
    record
      Name: integer; Previous: Pointer;
      case Kind: Class of
        . . .
        ArrayType:
          (LowerBound, UpperBound: integer;
            IndexType, ElementType: Pointer);
        . . .
    end;
```

The variant part consists of a kind field with the value ArrayType and four other fields. Three of these fields define the type and bounds of the array indices. The last field defines the type of the array elements.

Figure 7.4 shows a record that describes the array type

type T = **array** [1 . . 10] **of** Boolean;

The lower and upper bounds of the indices are 1 and 10. The type fields point to the records that describe the types integer and Boolean (Section 7.2).

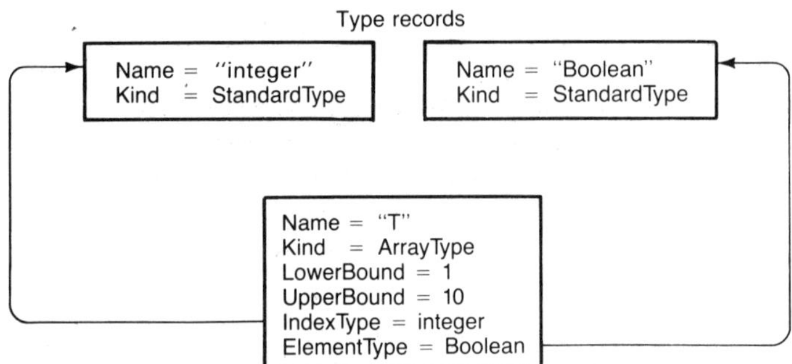

Fig. 7.4 Data representation of an array type.

A complete type definition has the following syntax:

TypeDefinition = TypeName "=" NewType ";" .
NewType = NewArrayType | NewRecordType .

The procedure that parses a type definition inputs the name of a new array type and passes it as a parameter to Algorithm 7.9. This procedure parses the definition of a new array type and constructs the corresponding record. To make the procedure easier to look at, the various stop symbols are replaced by dots (. . .):

```
{ NewArrayType =
    "array" "[" IndexRange "]" "of" TypeName .
  IndexRange = Constant ". ." Constant . }

procedure NewArrayType(Name: integer;
  Stop: Symbols);
var NewType, LowerType, UpperType,
  ElementType: Pointer;
  LowerBound, UpperBound: integer;
begin
  Expect(Array1, . . . );
  Expect(LeftBracket1, . . . );
  Constant(LowerBound, LowerType, . . . );
  Expect(DoubleDot1, . . . );
  Constant(UpperBound, UpperType, . . . );
  CheckTypes(LowerType, UpperType);
  if LowerBound > UpperBound then
    begin Error(Range3);
      LowerBound := UpperBound
    end;
  Expect(RightBracket1, . . . );
  Expect(Of1, . . . );
  TypeName(ElementType, Stop);
  Define(Name, ArrayType, NewType);
  NewType@.LowerBound := LowerBound;
  NewType@.UpperBound := UpperBound;
  NewType@.IndexType := LowerType;
  NewType@.ElementType := ElementType
end;
```

Algorithm 7.9

The parser uses Algorithm 7.10 to check that the bounds of the index range are of the same type. If the two types are different, the parser reports a *type error*—unless one of the types is the universal type, which is compatible with any other type (Section 7.3). After a type error, the first type is replaced by the universal type to suppress further error messages.

```
procedure CheckTypes(
  var Type1: Pointer; Type2: Pointer);
begin
  if Type1 <> Type2 then
    begin
      if (Type1 <> TypeUniversal) and
        (Type2 <> TypeUniversal) then
          Error(Type3);
      Type1 := TypeUniversal
    end
end;
```

Algorithm 7.10

Consider now a *variable access* of the form

x[i + 1]

where

```
type T = array [1 . . 10] of Boolean;
var x: T; i: integer;
```

The procedure named VariableAccess inputs the variable name x and obtains a pointer to the record that describes its type T. The procedure then calls another procedure to parse the indexed selector

[i + 1]

This procedure checks that the variable type T is an array type with indices of the same type as the expression

i + 1

The procedure then returns the type of the indexed variable x[i + 1] (which is of type Boolean).

This type transformation is performed by Algorithm 7.11. At the beginning of this procedure, the parameter named Typex points to the type of the array variable. At the end, it points to the type of the indexed variable—unless the parser finds a kind error. Later, we will see how the parser determines the type of an expression.

```
{ IndexedSelector = "[" Expression "]" . }

procedure Expression(var Typex: Pointer;
  Stop: Symbols); forward;

procedure IndexedSelector(var Typex: Pointer;
  Stop: Symbols);
var ExprType: Pointer;
begin
  Expect(LeftBracket1, . . . );
  Expression(ExprType, . . . );
  if Typex@.Kind = ArrayType then
    begin
      CheckTypes(ExprType, Typex@.IndexType);
      Typex := Typex@.ElementType
    end
  else
    begin KindError(Typex);
      Typex := TypeUniversal
    end;
  Expect(RightBracket1, . . . )
end;
```

Algorithm 7.11

7.6 RECORDS

We will now discuss the scope and type analysis of record types. The example

```
type R = record f: Boolean; g: T end;
var x: R;
```

defines a variable x of a record type R. The whole variable x consists of two field variables:

x.f x.g

The scope rules of fields, like f and g, are quite different from the scope rules of other objects. When a name x is used several times in a block, it usually refers to the same object (in this case, a variable). But a field name f may refer to different objects in the same block, and some of these objects may not even be fields!

In a block with the definitions

```
type
  R = record f:  Boolean; g:  T end;
  S = record a, b:  integer; f:  R end;
var f:  integer; x:  R; y:  S;
```

the name f may denote four different objects:

(1) The variable f of type integer

(2) The field variable x.f of type Boolean

(3) The field variable y.f of type R

(4) The field variable y.f.f of type Boolean

In the last case, the name f is used with two different meanings in a single variable access! The first f selects a field of type R within the variable y. The second f selects a subfield of type Boolean within the previous field.

To determine whether x.f refers to a field variable, the parser must look at the definition of x and check that it is a variable of a record type that includes a field f. Since this requires type analysis, it cannot be done during the regular scope analysis (Chapter 6).

After this introduction, we will define the scope rules of fields precisely:

Rule 7.1:
All fields defined by the same record type must have different names.

Rule 7.2:
A field f of a variable x is denoted

x.f

and is known only within the scope of x. The variable x must be of a record type that defines a field f. If the name f is used in any other way in the scope of x, it denotes another object.

Figure 7.5 shows the object records that describe the type

type R = **record** f: Boolean; g: T **end**;

The record that describes the type R is linked to another record that describes the last field g. The field record is linked to another record that describes the previous field f. The two field records are also linked to two records that describe their types T and Boolean (see also Fig. 7.4).

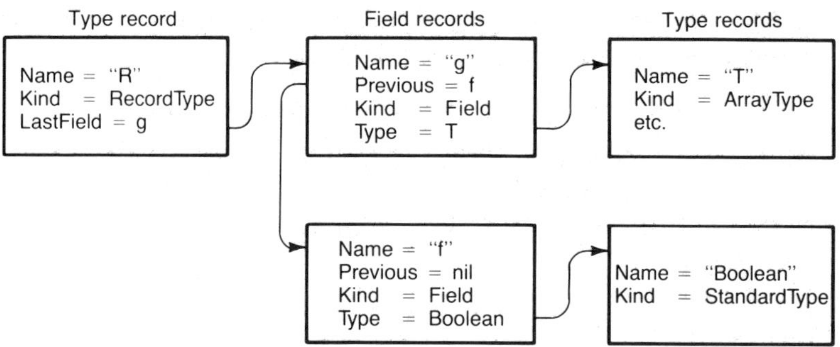

Fig. 7.5 Data representation of a record type and its fields.

More precisely, a record type is described by an object record of the following kind:

```
type
  ObjectRecord =
    record
      Name: integer; Previous: Pointer;
      case Kind: Class of
        . . .
        RecordType:
          (LastField: Pointer);
        . . .
    end;
```

The variant part points to another record that describes the last field of the record type.

The fields are described by another kind of object record:

```
type
  ObjectRecord =
    record
      Name: integer; Previous: Pointer;
      case Kind: Class of
        . . .
        Field:
          (FieldType: Pointer);
        . . .
    end;
```

The fixed part links a field to the previous fields of the same record type. The variant part points to the field type.

The parser must check that the fields of a record type have different names and must link them together as a separate chain (see Fig. 7.5). The scope analysis procedures will do this automatically if we treat a new record type as a block (see Algorithms 6.2 and 7.12).

```
{ NewRecordType = "record" FieldList "end" . }

procedure NewRecordType(Name: integer;
  Stop: Symbols);
var NewType, LastField: Pointer;
begin
  NewBlock;
  Expect(Record1, . . . );
  FieldList(LastField, . . . );
  Expect(End1, Stop);
  EndBlock;
  Define(Name, RecordType, NewType);
  NewType@.LastField := LastField
end;
```

Algorithm 7.12

The field list is parsed one section at a time by means of Algorithm 7.13.

```
{ FieldList =
    RecordSection { ";" RecordSection } . }

procedure FieldList(var LastField: Pointer;
  Stop: Symbols);
var Typex: Pointer;
begin
  RecordSection(LastField, Typex, . . . );
  while Symbol = Semicolon1 do
    begin
      Expect(Semicolon1, . . . );
      RecordSection(LastField, Typex, . . . )
    end
end;
```

Algorithm 7.13

A record section has the same syntax as a variable group (Section 7.4):

```
RecordSection = FieldName SectionTail .
SectionTail = "," RecordSection | ":" TypeName .
```

and is parsed by a procedure

```
procedure RecordSection(var LastField,
  Typex: Pointer; Stop: Symbols);
```

which is identical to the procedure VariableGroup except that it creates object records of the kind Field (see Algorithm 7.4).

Let us now turn from the definition of record types to field variables. Consider again a *variable access* x.f, where x is a variable of type R:

```
type R = record f: Boolean; g: T end;
var x: R;
```

The parser calls the procedure VariableAccess to input the variable name x and obtain a pointer to its type R (Algorithm 7.8). Afterward, it executes Algorithm 7.14 to check the field selector ".f". At the beginning of

```
{ FieldSelector = "." FieldName . }

procedure FieldSelector(var Typex: Pointer;
  Stop: Symbols);
var Found: Boolean; Fieldx: Pointer;
begin
  Expect(Period1, . . . );
  if Symbol = Name1 then
    begin
      if Typex@.Kind = RecordType then
        begin
          Found := false;
          Fieldx := Typex@.LastField;
          while not Found and
            (Fieldx <> nil Pointer) do
              if Fieldx@.Name <> Argument then
                Fieldx := Fieldx@.Previous
              else Found := true;
          if Found then Typex := Fieldx@.FieldType
          else
            begin Error(Undefined3);
              Typex := TypeUniversal
            end
        end
      else
        begin KindError(Typex);
          Typex := TypeUniversal)
        end;
      Expect(Name1, Stop)
    end
  else
    begin SyntaxError(Stop);
      Typex := TypeUniversal
    end
end;
```

Algorithm 7.14

this procedure, the parameter named Typex points to the type of the variable x. If it is a record type, the procedure examines the fields looking for the field name f. At the end of the procedure, Typex points to the type of the selected field—unless the parser finds an error, in which case the field type is set to "universal" to suppress further error messages.

7.7 EXPRESSIONS

The type of an expression is determined by four procedures, named Expression, SimpleExpression, Term, and Factor. The dependence diagram in Fig. 7.6 shows the order in which these procedures may call one another.

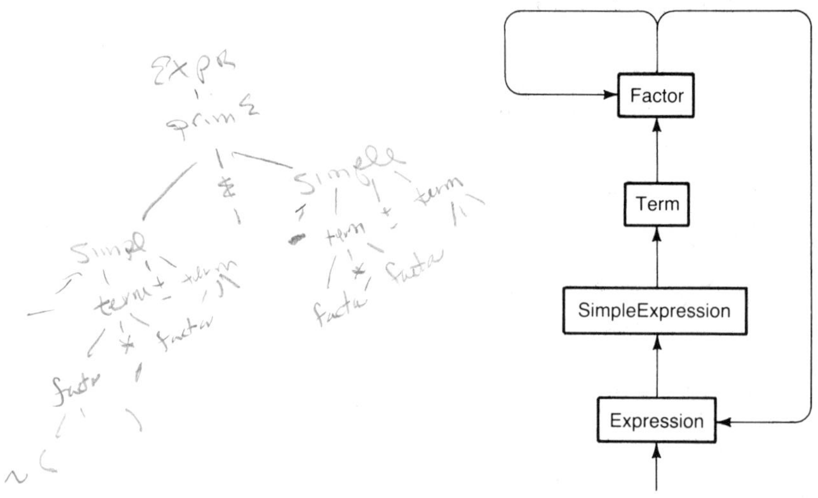

Fig. 7.6 Dependence diagram for expressions.

We will look at factors first (Algorithm 7.15). This procedure illustrates the recursive nature of compilation. If it encounters an expression enclosed in parentheses, it calls the procedure Expression recursively. If it finds a **not** operator in front of an operand, it calls itself. Notice how the procedure checks that the operand of the **not** operator is of type Boolean.

A term is parsed by means of Algorithm 7.16 using the following set of symbols:

```
MultiplySymbols =
  Symbols[And1, Asterisk1, Div1, Mod1]
```

The procedure checks that arithmetic operators are applied to integer operands only, and that the **and** operator has Boolean operands. Otherwise, a type error is reported by means of Algorithm 7.17.

```
{ Factor = Constant | VariableAccess |
    "(" Expression")" | "not" Factor . }

procedure Factor(var Typex: Pointer;
  Stop: Symbols);
var Object: Pointer; Value: integer;
begin
  if Symbol = Numeral1 then
    Constant(Value, Typex, Stop)
  else if Symbol = Name1 then
    begin
      Find(Argument, Object);
      if Object@.Kind = Constantx then
        Constant(Value, Typex, Stop)
      else if Object@.Kind in Variables then
        VariableAccess(Typex, Stop)
      else
        begin KindError(Object);
          Typex := TypeUniversal;
          Expect(Name1, Stop)
        end
    end
  else if Symbol = LeftParenthesis1 then
    begin
      Expect(LeftParenthesis1, . . . );
      Expression(Typex, . . . );
      Expect(RightParenthesis1, . . . )
    end
  else if Symbol = Not1 then
    begin
      Expect(Not1, . . . );
      Factor(Typex, Stop);
      CheckTypes(Typex, TypeBoolean)
    end
  else
    begin SyntaxError(Stop);
      Typex := TypeUniversal
    end
end;
```

Algorithm 7.15

```
{ Term = Factor { MultiplyingOperator Factor } .
  MultiplyingOperator =
    "*" | "div" | "mod" | "and" . }

procedure Term(var Typex: Pointer;
  Stop: Symbols);
var Operator: SymbolType; Type2: Pointer;
begin
  Factor(Typex, . . . );
  while Symbol in MultiplySymbols do
    begin
      Operator := Symbol;
      Expect(Symbol, . . . );
      Factor(Type2, . . . );
      if Typex = TypeInteger then
        begin
          CheckTypes(Typex, Type2);
          if Operator = And1 then TypeError(Typex)
        end
      else if Typex = TypeBoolean then
        begin
          CheckTypes(Typex, Type2);
          if Operator <> And1 then TypeError(Typex)
        end
      else TypeError(Typex)
    end
end;
```

Algorithm 7.16

Algorithm 7.17 replaces an invalid type by the universal type. If the type already is universal, the error message is suppressed.

```
procedure TypeError(var Typex: Pointer);
begin
  if Typex <> TypeUniversal then
    begin Error(Type3);
      Typex := TypeUniversal
    end
end;
```

Algorithm 7.17

There is no reason to go through the rest of the expression procedures here. They are very similar to what you have already seen. You will find them in Appendix A.3.

7.8 STATEMENTS

Statements have the following syntax:

```
Statement =
  AssignmentStatement | ProcedureStatement |
  IfStatement | WhileStatement |
  CompoundStatement | Empty . }
```

Algorithm 7.18 is used to parse statements. This procedure uses the object records to distinguish between different kinds of names. If a statement begins with a variable name, it must be an assignment statement. If it begins with a procedure name, it must be a procedure statement.

```
procedure Statement(Stop: Symbols);
var Object: Pointer;
begin
  if Symbol = Name1 then
    begin
      Find(Argument, Object);
      if Object@.Kind in Variables then
        AssignmentStatement(Stop)
      else if Object@.Kind in Procedures then
        ProcedureStatement(Stop)
      else
        begin KindError(Object);
          Expect(Name1, Stop)
        end
    end
  else if Symbol = If1 then
    IfStatement(Stop)
  else if Symbol = While1 then
    WhileStatement(Stop)
  else if Symbol = Begin1 then
    CompoundStatement(Stop)
  else {Empty}
    SyntaxCheck(Stop)
end;
```

Algorithm 7.18

There are two kinds of procedures: (1) standard procedures, and (2) procedures that are defined in the program text:

```
Procedures = Classes[Procedur, StandardProc]
```

The remaining statements are either empty or begin with unique word symbols.

We will discuss procedure statements in Section 7.9. In the following, we will use assignment and while statements to illustrate type analysis of statements.

In an assignment statement, the variable and the expression must be of the same type (Algorithm 7.19). The types are determined by two procedures discussed earlier (see Algorithms 7.8 and Section 7.7).

```
{ AssignmentStatement =
  VariableAccess ":=" Expression . }

procedure AssignmentStatement(Stop: Symbols);
var VarType, ExprType: Pointer;
begin
  VariableAccess(VarType, . . . );
  Expect(Becomes1, . . . );
  Expression(ExprType, Stop);
  CheckTypes(VarType, ExprType)
end;
```

Algorithm 7.19

The parser checks that the expression in a while statement is of type Boolean (Algorithm 7.20).

```
{ WhileStatement =
    "while" Expression "do" Statement . }

procedure WhileStatement(Stop: Symbols);
var ExprType: Pointer;
begin
  Expect(While1, . . . );
  Expression(ExprType, . . . );
  CheckTypes(ExprType, TypeBoolean);
  Expect(Do1, . . . );
  Statement(Stop)
end;
```

Algorithm 7.20

7.9 PROCEDURES

Figure 7.7 shows the data representation of a procedure P with two formal parameters x and y:

```
procedure P(x: integer; var y: Boolean);
begin . . . end;
```

The objects P, x, and y are described by three records. The procedure record is linked to the record that describes the last parameter y. This parameter record is linked to another record that describes the previous parameter x. The parameter records are also linked to the records that describe their types (Boolean and integer).

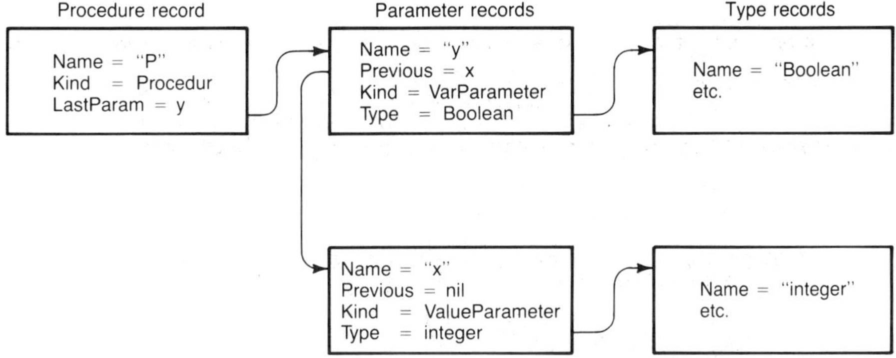

Fig. 7.7 Data representation of a procedure and its formal parameter list.

In general, a procedure definition is described by an object record of the following kind:

```
type
  ObjectRecord =
    record
      Name: integer; Previous: Pointer;
      case Kind: Class of
        . . .
        Procedur:
          (LastParam: Pointer)
    end;
```

The variant part points to the record that describes the last parameter of the procedure. The parameters are described as variables (see Section 7.4).

A procedure definition has the following syntax:

```
ProcedureDefinition =
  "procedure" ProcedureName ProcedureBlock ";" .
ProcedureBlock =
  [ "(" FormalParameterList ")" ] ";" BlockBody .
```

Algorithm 7.21 shows how the parser creates a procedure record.

```
procedure ProcedureDefinition(Stop: Symbols);
var Name: integer; Proc: Pointer;
begin
  Expect(Procedure1, . . . );
  ExpectName(Name, . . . );
  Define(Name, Procedur, Proc);
  NewBlock;
  if Symbol = LeftParenthesis1 then
    begin
      Expect(LeftParenthesis1, . . . );
      FormalParameterList(Proc@.LastParam, . . . );
      Expect(RightParenthesis1, . . . )
    end
  else {no parameter list}
    Proc@.LastParam := nil Pointer;
  Expect(Semicolon1, . . . );
  BlockBody( . . . );
  Expect(Semicolon1, Stop);
  EndBlock
end;
```

Algorithm 7.21

Notice the following:

(1) The procedure record is created at the beginning of the procedure definition to permit recursive calls in the procedure block (Scope Rule 6.2).

(2) The procedure block is treated as a separate block. The formal parameters are local to the procedure block, while the procedure itself is local to the surrounding block. That is why the procedure name is defined before the new block is parsed.

(3) If the procedure has no parameters, the pointer to its last parameter is set to nil. If the procedure has a parameter list, the first parameter is also the first object defined in the procedure block. Consequently, the record of this parameter does not point to any previous object, but has the value nil assigned to the field named Previous. The net result is that the formal parameters of a procedure are always linked by a chain of pointers that begins in the procedure record and ends with a nil pointer. Later, we will use this chain to perform type analysis of procedure statements.

The procedure that parses a formal parameter list

```
{ FormalParameterList =
    ParameterDefinition { ";" ParameterDefinition } . }

procedure FormalParameterList(
  var LastParam: Pointer; Stop: Symbols);
```

returns a pointer to the last parameter record. The parameter records are created one at a time by another procedure named ParameterDefinition. We discussed this procedure earlier (Algorithm 7.7).

The last step in the compilation of a procedure definition is to parse the block body. The procedure that does this was also defined earlier (Algorithm 5.13).

The parser uses the description of a procedure to analyze calls of the procedure. The following example shows a call of the previous procedure P:

```
var a: integer; b: Boolean;
. . . P(a + 1, b) . . .
```

First, the compiler finds the record that describes the procedure (see Fig. 7.7). Then it follows the chain of parameter records and checks the following:

(1) The number of actual parameters in the procedure statement must equal the number of formal parameters in the procedure definition (two).

(2) The actual parameter "a + 1" must be an expression of the same type as the value parameter x (type integer).

(3) The actual parameter "b" must be a variable access of the same type as the variable parameter y (type Boolean).

A procedure statement has the following syntax:

```
ProcedureStatement = IOStatement |
  ProcedureName [ "(" ActualParameterList ")" ] .
```

Statements that invoke standard procedures are known as I/O statements in Pascal—. First, we will discuss statements that refer to procedure definitions. Then we will talk about standard procedures.

The parsing of a procedure statement is simple enough (Algorithm 7.22). When this procedure is called, it assumes that the parser already has determined elsewhere that the statement begins with a procedure name (see Algorithm 7.18).

```
procedure ProcedureStatement(Stop: Symbols);
var Proc: Pointer;
begin {Symbol = (Procedure) Name1}
  Find(Argument, Proc);
  if Proc@.Kind = StandardProc then
    IOStatement(Stop)
  else if Proc@.LastParam <> nil Pointer then
    begin
      Expect(Name1, . . . );
      Expect(LeftParenthesis1, . . . );
      ActualParameterList(Proc@.LastParam, . . . );
      Expect(RightParenthesis1, . . . )
    end
  else {no parameter list}
    Expect(Name1, Stop)
end;
```

Algorithm 7.22

The tricky part of a procedure statement is the type analysis of the actual parameters. Since the actual parameters are input from left to right, we must examine the formal parameters in the same order. Like all other objects, the formal parameters are, however, described by records that are linked in the reverse order starting with the last parameter (Section 6.4).

To get around this problem, we redefine the actual parameter list by a recursive rule:

```
ActualParameterList =
  [ ActualParameterList "," ] ActualParameter .
ActualParameter =
  Expression | VariableAccess .
```

and analyze it by means of a recursive procedure (Algorithm 7.23).

This procedure follows the chain of parameter records and calls itself until it has reached the first parameter record. Each parameter is now handled by a separate call of the procedure. At the end, each procedure call inputs an actual parameter and compares its type to the type of the corresponding formal parameter. We are now going through the parameter records one more time in reverse order. Since the records were reversed to begin with, the net effect of the second reversal is to go through them in the right order!

What makes this procedure even more daring is that it uses the forbidden *left recursion* (Section 5.6). But in this case, the depth of the recursion is controlled by the chain of parameter records (and not by the input symbols). Since a formal parameter list is of finite length, the recursion must eventually reach the end of it and terminate.

```
procedure ActualParameterList(
  LastParam: Pointer; Stop: Symbols);
var Typex: Pointer;
begin {LastParam <> nil Pointer}
  if LastParam@.Previous <> nil Pointer then
    begin
      ActualParameterList(LastParam@.Previous,
        ...);
      Expect(Comma1, ...)
    end;
  if LastParam@.Kind = ValueParameter then
    Expression(Typex, Stop)
  else {LastParam@.Kind = VarParameter}
    VariableAccess(Typex, Stop);
  CheckTypes(Typex, LastParam@.VarType)
end;
```

Algorithm 7.23

Finally, we come to the *standard procedures*

read(x)   write(e)

(Section 2.1).

In Chapter 8 you will see that standard procedures and procedure definitions are implemented differently. The difference between them is even more apparent in Standard Pascal, where standard procedures do not follow the same rules as other procedures [Jensen and Wirth, 1974]. The most blatant example of this is the standard procedure "write," which can be applied to a variable number of arguments of different types:

write(x + 100)   write('$', x + 100)

By contrast, a procedure defined in a program can be applied only to a fixed number of operands of fixed types.

Since standard procedures are very different from other procedures, it is often necessary to compile them by ad hoc methods. We will do the same in the Pascal— compiler.

The standard procedures are described by object records. The variant part of these records consists of a kind field only with the value StandardProc.

The standard procedures have fixed name indices denoted Read0 and Write0 (Section 4.2). The corresponding records are created before the program text is parsed (Section 6.5):

```
var Proc: Pointer;
Define(Read0, StandardProc, Proc);
Define(Write0, StandardProc, Proc)
```

The standard procedures are invoked by I/O statements:

```
IOStatement =
  "read" "(" VariableAccess ")" |
  "write" "(" Expression ")" .
```

which are analyzed by means of Algorithm 7.24.

```
procedure IOStatement(Stop: Symbols);
var Name: integer; Typex: Pointer;
begin
  {Symbol = (Standard Procedure) Name1}
  Name := Argument;
  Expect(Name1, . . . );
  Expect(LeftParenthesis1, . . . );
  if Name = Read0 then
    VariableAccess(Typex, . . . )
  else {Name = Write0}
    Expression(Typex, . . . );
  CheckTypes(Typex, TypeInteger);
  Expect(RightParenthesis1, Stop)
end;
```

Algorithm 7.24

7.10 OBJECT RECORDS

Now that we have discussed the type analysis of different kinds of objects, it may be helpful to show the complete definition of object records including all the variants:

```
type
  Pointer = @ ObjectRecord;

ObjectRecord =
  record
    Name: integer; Previous: Pointer;
    case Kind: Class of
      Constantx:
        (ConstValue: integer;
          ConstType: Pointer);
      ArrayType:
        (LowerBound, UpperBound: integer;
          IndexType, ElementType: Pointer);
      RecordType:
        (LastField: Pointer);
      Field:
        (FieldType: Pointer);
      Variable, ValueParameter, VarParameter:
        (VarType: Pointer);
      Procedur:
        (LastParam: Pointer)
  end;
```

Appendix A.3 contains the complete program text of the parser extended with scope analysis, type analysis, and code generation.

7.11 TESTING

The type analysis is tested by means of three test programs known as Tests 6, 7, and 8. These programs are included in Appendix A.6.

Test 6 shows whether the parser can perform type analysis of *correct sentences.* To illustrate how this program was constructed we will examine the procedure that parses a factor (Algorithm 7.15). To test the statements of this procedure systematically we must use factors of the following kinds:

(1) A numeral

(2) A constant name

(3) A variable access

(4) An expression in parentheses

(5) A negated Boolean expression

Test 6 includes the following examples of these test cases:

```
const a = 10; b = false;
var x, y: integer; z: Boolean;
begin
  x := 1;
  x := a;
  x := y;
  x := (x + 1);
  z := not b
end
```

Test 7 contains *type errors.* To illustrate this test, we will again look at factors. The procedure Factor reports a type error only when a *not* operator is applied to a nonBoolean operand; for example,

```
var y: Boolean;
y := not 1 and 2 and
  3
```

After reporting a type error, the parser assigns the universal type to the negated factor. The **and** operators are added to this example to verify that the universal type prevents further error messages in the same expression. Since the compiler never outputs more than one error message per line, part of the expression must be written on a separate line to see if it produces another error message (Section 3.5).

Test 8 covers *kind errors* detected by the parser. The procedure Factor reports a kind error if the name of an operand does not refer to a constant or a variable; for example,

```
var x: integer;

procedure P( . . . );
begin . . . end;

begin . . . x := P . . . end
```

These test programs are complete tests of the type analysis only. They do not systematically test that the parser can perform syntax and scope analysis. We have already tested that (see Sections 5.7 and 6.6).

When you are testing such a complicated program as a compiler, it is not good enough just to sit down at a terminal and try some program examples chosen without much thought. It is very unlikely that you will find all the programming errors by such an unsystematic method.

The testing of a compiler must proceed as an integral part of the programming process by writing test programs that systematically invoke all parts of the compiler. This method lets you gradually develop the compiler in stages. At each stage, you can be confident that the algorithms developed during the previous stages already work, so you can concentrate on testing the most recent extension of the compiler.

8

A PASCAL COMPUTER

This chapter describes the instruction set of an ideal Pascal computer. The Pascal— compiler generates code for this computer.

8.1 AN IDEAL COMPUTER

The purpose of a program is to describe how a computer accepts well-defined input and produces well-defined output. So you cannot write a program unless you know exactly how its input and output are defined.

Up to this point, we have ignored this obvious requirement and have succeeded in writing the major part of a compiler without knowing anything about its output. We could do that only because the most complicated task of a compiler is to analyze the syntax and semantics of its input. When that has been done, the output of code is a fairly simple task.

In this chapter we define the code produced by the compiler as concisely as we have defined the program text input by the compiler. In Chapter 9 we complete the compiler by adding code generation.

First, we must decide for which computer we will generate code. Let's assume that we are writing the compiler for an IBM Personal Computer with an Intel 8088 microprocessor [Intel, 1978]. If it is essential to obtain the most efficient code for the IBM-PC, the compiler must obviously emit 8088 instructions. Unfortunately, the instruction set of the 8088 is not well suited for compilation. Most traditional computers have the same problem. For historical reasons, they are all very similar, and with few exceptions, they were not designed to support programming languages. At the end of the chapter, I will say more about traditional computers.

Instead of making a compiler for an inconvenient computer, we will do the opposite and invent a new computer that is ideal for our compiler. This new computer is called the *Pascal Computer.* The code generated for this computer is known as *Pascal code.*

The Pascal Computer is ideal in the following sense:

(1) The Pascal instructions correspond directly to the concepts of the Pascal language.

(2) The Pascal code of a program has practically the same syntax as the program itself. Consequently, the code generator is a trivial extension of the parser.

(3) A Pascal Computer implemented in hardware can execute Pascal programs faster than most traditional computers.

The idea of building *language-based computers* goes back to the early 1960s. Eventually this superior idea will be widely used. But in the meantime, what do we do with traditional computers? We pretend that they are Pascal computers! This means that the Pascal code produced by the compiler must be interpreted by a small program written in microcode or assembly language. This program is called a *Pascal interpreter.*

The technique of interpreting Pascal code is surprisingly practical. It has been used successfully to implement the programming languages Concurrent Pascal and Edison on the PDP 11 and the IBM-PC [Brinch Hansen, 1977 and 1983]. The Edison interpreter for the IBM-PC is an assembly language program of 1100 lines only.

An added advantage of code interpretation is *portability*: Software can be moved from one computer to another just by rewriting the interpreter in the assembly language of the target machine. Using this technique, I moved 10,000 lines of Edison programs from the PDP 11 to the IBM-PC in less than two weeks.

Since the focus of this book is the compiler (not the interpreter), I will reduce the effort of programming the interpreter by writing it in Pascal. It will be slow, but at least you will know that a programmer can rewrite it in assembly language in less than a month.

Even if you plan to implement a Pascal computer in hardware (or assembly language), it is still an excellent idea first to write an interpreter in Pascal. This interpreter will serve as a concise algorithmic specification of the

Pascal Computer for hardware designers, assembly language programmers, and compiler writers. By writing this interpreter, you will discover the advantage of using Pascal as a *hardware specification* language.

8.2 THE STACK

The memory of the Pascal Computer is an array of integers called the *store*. The store elements and their indices are known as *words* and *addresses*.

The store holds the code and variables of a single Pascal program (Fig. 8.1). The *code*, which is of fixed length, is placed at the beginning of the store. The rest of the store is used as a *stack* of variables. During the execution of statements, the stack also holds temporary results. The stack grows from low toward high addresses (that is, from the top of the figure toward the bottom).

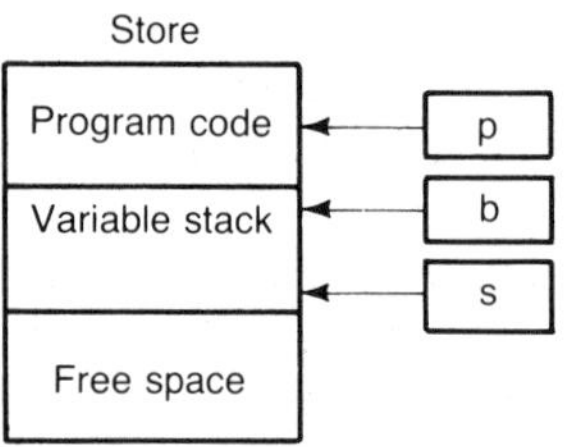

Fig. 8.1 Store and registers.

The computer has three index registers, named p, b, and s. The *program register p* contains the address of the current instruction. The *base register b* is used to access variables. The *stack register s* holds the address of the top of the stack.

In Pascal, the store and index registers are defined as follows:

```
const Min = 0; Max = 8191;
type Store = array [Min . . Max] of integer;
var St: Store; p, b, s: integer;
```

With these definitions, a store location with the address x is denoted St[x].

Initially, the stack is empty. When program execution begins, the computer allocates space in the stack for the variables defined in the program block. These variables exist until the program execution ends.

When the program activates a procedure, the computer allocates space in the stack for the variables defined in the procedure block. These variables are removed from the stack when the procedure execution ends.

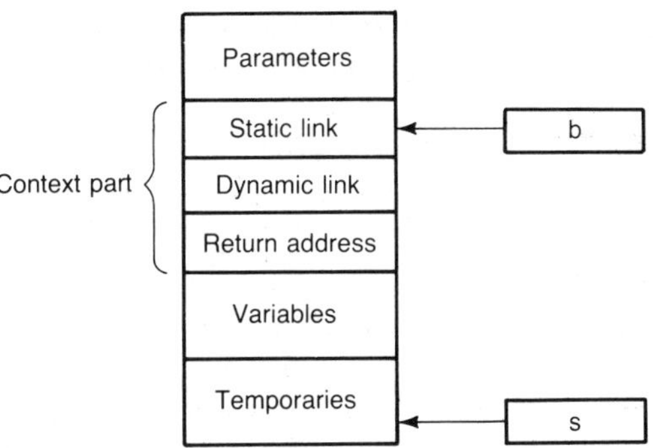

Fig. 8.2 Structure of an activation record.

The variables of a single block are kept in a stack segment known as an *activation record* (Fig. 8.2). This record consists of four parts:

(1) The parameter part

(2) The context part

(3) The variable part

(4) The temporary part

Figure 8.3 shows the activation record of the following procedure:

```
procedure Quicksort(m, n: integer);
var i, j: integer;
begin . . . end;
```

The parameter part contains storage for the formal parameters m and n.
The context part contains three addresses, called the static link, the dynamic link, and the return address. These addresses define the context in

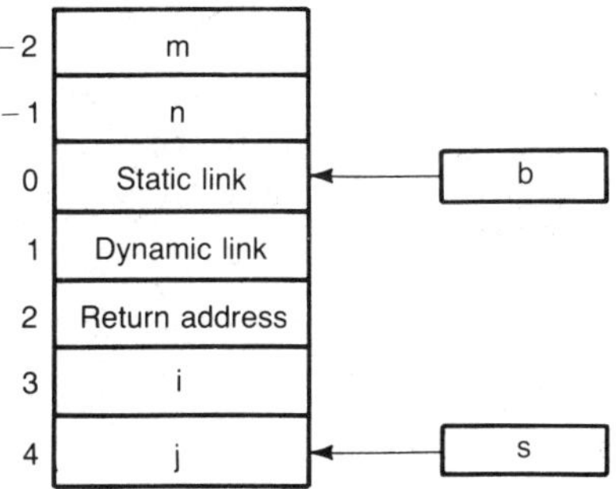

Fig. 8.3 Example of an activation record.

which the procedure was activated. I will explain that later. The b register contains the address of the static link. This address is called the *base address* of the activation record.

The variable part contains storage for the local variables i and j.

These three parts of fixed length are created when the procedure is activated.

The temporary part holds operands and results during the execution of statements. The temporary part is empty at the beginning and end of every statement.

Within an activation record, the parameters and local variables are placed in the order in which they are defined in the procedure.

If a procedure is activated recursively, every activation creates another instance of the activation record in the stack. The compiler is therefore unable to predict the exact addresses of variables. Instead, the following method is used to access variables.

In Pascal—, every variable is of a fixed type. The type is either a standard type, an array type, or a record type. A variable of a standard type occupies a single word. Since arrays and records are combinations of a fixed number of elements of standard types, it follows that every variable occupies a fixed number of words. We will call this the *length* of the variable.

Parameter and variable definitions show the order in which variables will be placed within an activation record. Type definitions enable the compiler to determine the length of these variables. By combining this information, the compiler can compute the relative address of every variable in an activation record. The relative addresses are *displacements* relative to the base address of the activation record (see Fig. 8.3).

In the example above, the variables have the following displacements:

Variable	*Displacement*
m	−2
n	−1
i	3
j	4

When a procedure is activated, the computer creates an activation record and makes the b register point to the base address of the record. Any variable in the record can now be accessed by adding its displacement to the value of the b register:

Variable	*Address*
m	b − 2
n	b − 1
i	b + 3
j	b + 4

The following program (Test 10) includes the previous procedure Quicksort. This program is a good example of the use of nested blocks and recursion. Appendix A.6 contains the complete text of this program.

```
program Test10;
const max = 10;
type T = array [1 . . max] of integer;
var A: T; k: integer;

  procedure Quicksort(m, n: integer);
  var i, j: integer;

    procedure Partition;
    var r, w: integer;
    begin . . . end;

  begin
    if m < n then
      begin
        Partition;
        Quicksort(m, j);
        Quicksort(i, n)
      end
  end;

begin . . . Quicksort(1, max) . . . end.
```

Test 10

Let's look at the stack when the following blocks have been activated:

(1) The program block

(2) The Quicksort procedure (1st activation)

(3) The Quicksort procedure (2nd activation)

(4) The Quicksort procedure (3rd activation)

(5) The Partition procedure

Figure 8.4 shows the corresponding activation records. The program block is treated as a procedure without parameters. When a procedure terminates, the computer must remove the corresponding activation record from the stack. To make this possible, every activation record is linked to the previous one. More precisely, the *dynamic link* of an activation record contains the base address of the previous activation record (see Fig. 8.2). When a procedure terminates, the dynamic link stored in the current activation record is

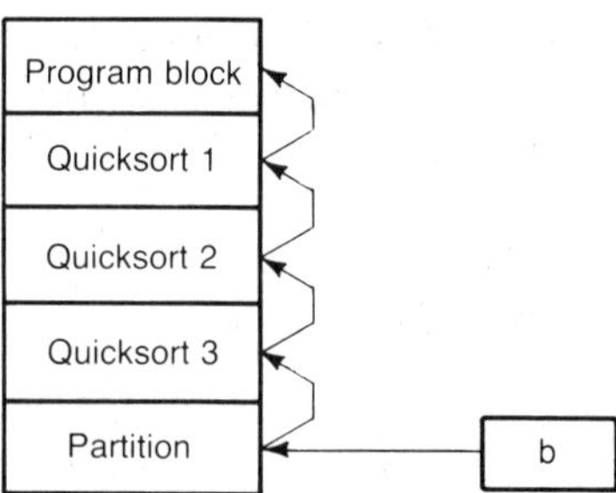

Fig. 8.4 The dynamic chain.

assigned to the b register. The chain of dynamic links is known as the *dynamic chain.* It is called "dynamic" because it defines the dynamic sequence in which blocks have been activated.

The *static links* serve another purpose. They define the set of variables that are accessible within the current block. This set of variables is called the current *context* of the program. In the previous situation, the current context consists of the variables created during the following activations:

(1) The most recent activation of Partition

(2) The most recent activation of Quicksort.

(3) The most recent activation of the program block

The activation records that contain these variables are linked together by static links (Fig. 8.5). The activation record of Partition includes a static link that points to the third activation record of Quicksort. The static link of this activation record, in turn, points to the activation record of the program block. This chain of links is known as the current *static chain.* It is called "static" because it represents the static block structure of the program text.

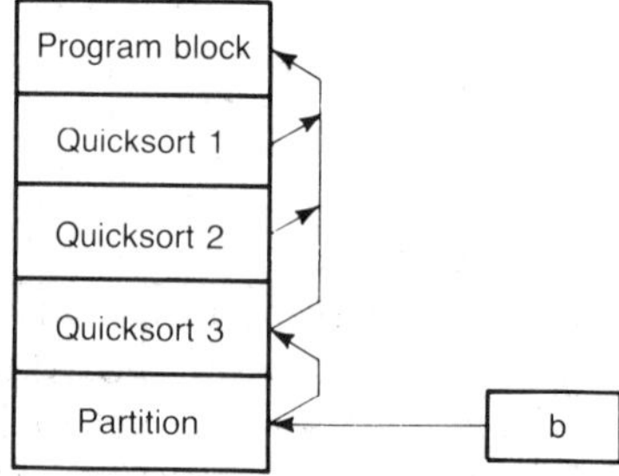

Fig. 8.5 The static chains.

In general, every activation of a block may take place in a different context. Consequently, every activation record is the start of a separate static chain. In the previous situation, every activation record of Quicksort points to the activation record of the program block.

At any given moment, however, the current context is defined by a single static chain that starts with the b register. Figure 8.6 shows only those activation records that are accessible in the current context.

Later, we will discuss how activation records are created and linked together. But in the following, we will just assume that it has been done somehow.

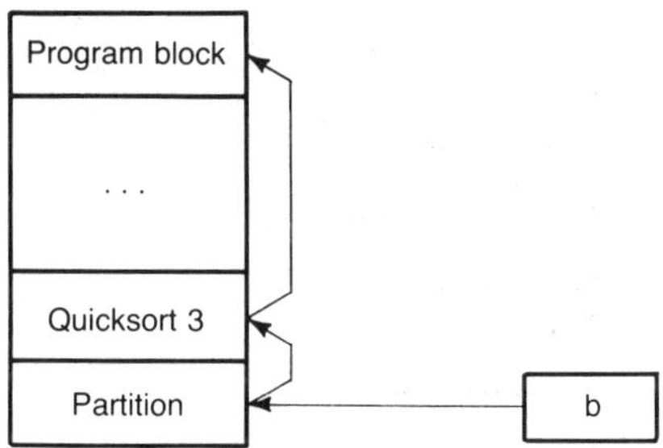

Fig. 8.6 Current context.

8.3 VARIABLE ACCESS

Figure 8.7 is a more detailed picture of the context shown in Fig. 8.6. To access a variable in this context, the program code must specify (1) the activation record that contains the variable, and (2) the displacement of the variable within the record.

The compiler assigns a *level number* to every block in a program (Section 6.4). In the previous program example, the blocks have the following level numbers:

Block	*Level Number*
Program block	1
Quicksort	2
Partition	3

During code generation, the compiler assigns a level number and a displacement to every variable. In this example, the variables will be described as follows:

Variable	*Level*	*Displacement*
A	1	3
k	1	13
m	2	−2
n	2	−1
i	2	3
j	2	4
r	3	3
w	3	4

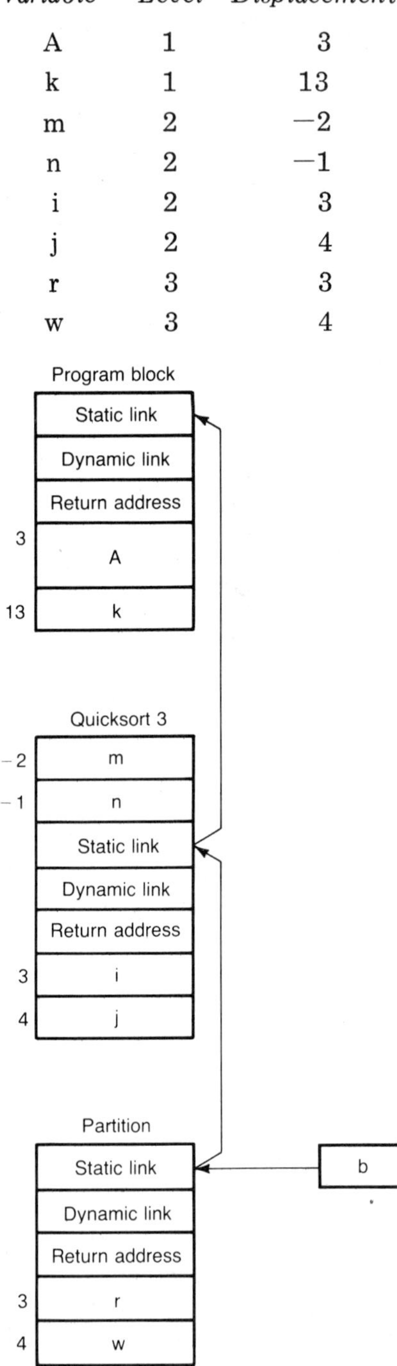

Fig. 8.7 Current context in detail.

During a variable access it is more convenient to identify a variable by a level number that is relative to the current block. This number is obtained by subtracting the level number of the variable from the level number of the current block. Here are some examples of how variables are identified within the Partition procedure:

Variable	*Relative Level*	*Displacement*
A	2	3
m	1	−2
w	0	4

Figure 8.7 shows that the relative level is the number of links the computer must follow along the static chain to reach the activation record that contains a variable. The variable w is at relative level 0 and is therefore addressed relative to the b register. The variable m is at relative level 1 and is therefore addressed relative to the previous base address St[b], and so on. So the previous variables have the following absolute addresses:

Variable	*Address*
A	St[St[b]] + 3
m	St[b] − 2
w	b + 4

Where a program refers to a variable by its name, the corresponding code refers to it by an *instruction* of the form

Variable(Level, Displacement)

The instruction consists of two parts:

(1) An operation part that tells the computer to compute the absolute address of a variable.

(2) Two arguments that define the (relative) level and the displacement of the variable.

The operation part and the arguments occupy one word each (Fig. 8.8). During the execution of the instruction, the *program register p* points to the operation part.

In the Partition procedure, references to the variables A, m, and w are compiled into these instructions:

Variable	*Instruction*
A	Variable(2, 3)
m	Variable(1, −2)
w	Variable(0, 4)

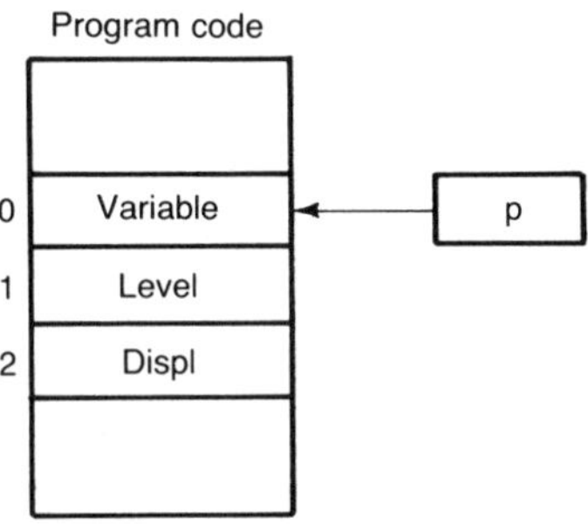

Fig. 8.8 Pascal instruction.

The computer locates the variable A in five steps:

(1) The stack register s is increased by one to create a new temporary location at the top of the stack.

(2) The base address of the variable is found two levels down in the static chain.

(3) The absolute address of the variable is computed by adding the base address and the displacement 3.

(4) The absolute address is stored in the new temporary location.

(5) The program register p is incremented by 3 to make it point at the next instruction.

Figure 8.9 shows the result of these actions. The address of the array variable A is the address of its first word. This address is denoted @A. It remains in the stack until it has been used for its intended purpose. It may, for example, be used by another instruction to assign a value to the variable. When the address has served its purpose, it will be removed from the stack by decreasing the s register by one.

If you look at this explanation of the Variable instruction, you will see that it describes an *algorithm* in *English.* Although the description is correct, it is not nearly as concise as an algorithm written in a formal language. The obvious conclusion must be that *we should define the Pascal computer by algorithms written in Pascal*!

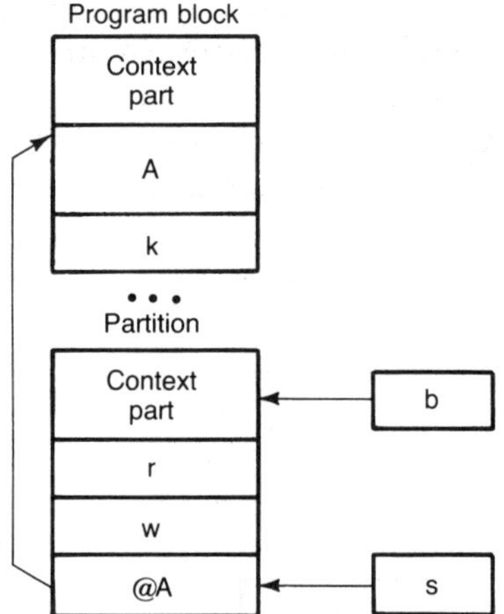

Fig. 8.9 Result of a variable access.

Algorithm 8.1 defines the Variable instruction. The formal parameters of this procedure denote the arguments of the instruction. The local variable x represents a working register used during the execution of the instruction.

```
procedure Variable(Level, Displ: integer);
var x: integer;
begin
  s := s + 1;
  x := b;
  while Level > 0 do
     begin
       x := St[x];
       Level := Level - 1
     end;
  St[s] := x + Displ;
  p := p + 3
end;
```

Algorithm 8.1

Variable instructions are used only to access value parameters and local variables. *Variable parameters* are accessed differently. The following program includes a variable parameter x (in a procedure Q):

```
program P;
var v: integer;
  procedure Q(var x: integer);
  begin . . . x . . . end;
begin . . . Q(v) . . . end.
```

The program block includes a procedure statement Q(v) which binds the parameter x to the variable v while the procedure Q is executed. This means that all operations on x actually are performed on v. In the activation record of the procedure the parameter x is represented by a word that contains the absolute address of the variable v (Fig. 8.10).

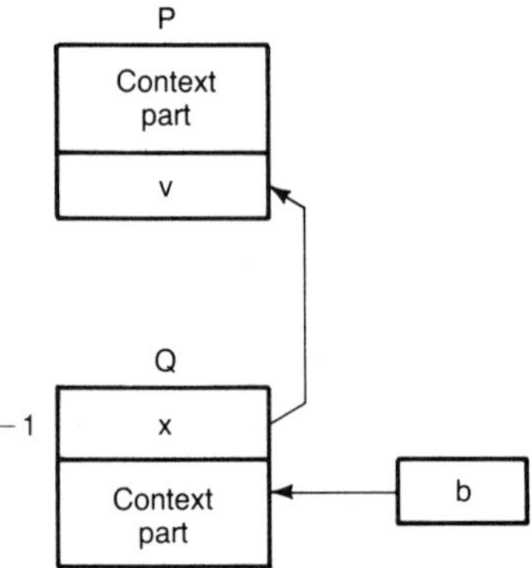

Fig. 8.10 Variable parameter.

A reference within Q to the parameter x is really a reference to the variable v. The effect of executing the instruction

Variable(0, −1)

is to push the address of the parameter location x on top of the stack. But we need the address of the variable to which this location points. So we must introduce another instruction:

VarParam(0, −1)

which is defined by Algorithm 8.2.

```
procedure VarParam(Level, Displ: integer);
var x: integer;
begin
  s := s + 1;
  x := b;
  while Level > 0 do
    begin
      x := St[x];
      Level := Level − 1
    end;
  St[s] := St[x + Displ];
  p := p + 3
end;
```

Algorithm 8.2

As we have just seen, different kinds of variables are accessed by different kinds of instructions. There are many other cases, where different instances of the same language concept generate different instructions. How do we describe that formally? Well, we will again borrow ideas from the programming language itself. When a Pascal sentence can be expressed in many different ways, we characterize all possible forms of the sentence by a *grammar*.

To apply this powerful idea to code generation we must view the Pascal code as a *language*. The symbols of this language are computer instructions, such as Variable and VarParam. The sentences of the code language are sequences of instructions that represent Pascal sentences. The possible sequences of instructions must be defined by syntax rules written in the BNF notation. These syntax rules will be called *code rules*.

To apply this idea systematically, we must follow a few rules:

Rule 8.1:

For every syntax rule in Pascal, we must write a code rule that defines the corresponding sequences of instructions.

Rule 8.2:

Every instruction should preferably have the same name as the Pascal symbol it represents.

Rule 8.3:

A code rule should preferably have the same syntactic structure as the corresponding syntax rule in Pascal.

As an example, a variable access has the following syntax in Pascal—:

VariableAccess = VariableName { Selector } .
Selector = "[" Expression "]" | "." FieldName .

The corresponding code rules are very similar:

VariableAccess = VariableName { Selector } .
VariableName = "**Variable**" | "**VarParam**" .
Selector = Expression "**Index**" | "**Field**" .

The meaning of these rules is the following:

(1) The code for a variable access consists of the code for a variable name possibly followed by the code for one or more selectors.

(2) The code for a variable name is either a Variable instruction or a VarParam instruction.

(3) The code for a selector is either the code for an expression followed by an Index instruction or just a Field instruction.

The Index and Field instructions will be explained in the following.

You will now appreciate what I said at the beginning of the chapter:

(1) The Pascal instructions correspond directly to the concepts of the Pascal language.

(2) The Pascal code of a program has practically the same syntax as the program itself.

In retrospect, the conclusion seems obvious enough: *The input and output of a compiler should both be defined by syntax rules.*

We still need to look at arrays and records. The previous program example includes an array variable A:

type T = **array** [1 . . 10] **of** integer;
var A: T;

The Partition procedure uses a variable i to access an element of this array:

A[i]

This variable access generates the following code:

(1) Variable(2, 3)

(2) Variable(1, 3)

(3) Value(1)

(4) Index(1, 10, 1, 18)

Instructions 2 and 3 are the code for the index expression "i". We will discuss the Value instruction in Section 8.4.

The execution of these instructions has the following effect: Instruction 1 pushes the address of variable A on the stack. Instruction 2 pushes the address of variable i on top of that. Instruction 3 replaces the address of variable i by its value. Figure 8.11a shows the stack at this point. Instruction 4 removes the index value from the top of the stack, checks that it is within the range 1 . . 10, and replaces the address of the variable A by the address of the indexed variable A[i] (see Fig. 8.11b). As you can see, it does not matter if a variable access refers to a whole variable, such as A, or an indexed variable, such as A[i]. The net effect of a variable access is always to push the address of the given variable on the stack.

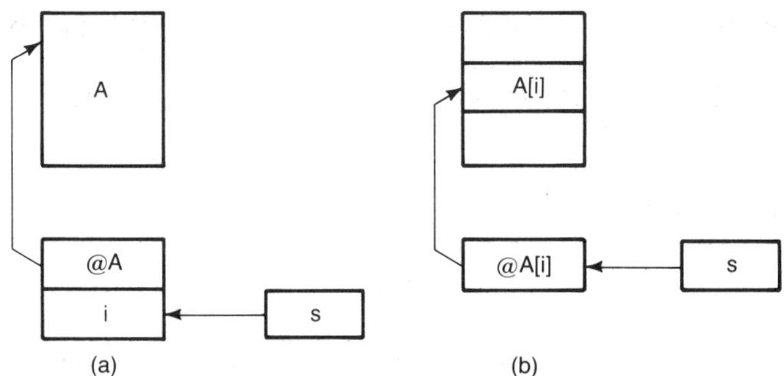

Fig. 8.11 Indexed access.

Algorithm 8.3 defines the *Index instruction.* The arguments define the index range, the length of a single array element, and the program line in which the array element is accessed.

```
procedure Index(Lower, Upper,
  Length, LineNo: integer);
var i: integer;
begin
  i := St[s]; s := s − 1;
  if (i < Lower) or (i > Upper) then
    Error(LineNo, 'Range Error')
  else
    St[s] := St[s] + (i − Lower) * Length;
  p := p + 5
end;
```

Algorithm 8.3

If the index is out of bounds, the computer reports a range error, say

Line 18 Range Error

and stops the program execution by assigning the value false to a Boolean named Running (Algorithm 8.4). When a program has been loaded into the store, Running is set to true. The computer executes the program until Running becomes false.

```
var Running: Boolean;

procedure Error(LineNo: integer; Text: String);
begin
  WriteStr('Line'); WriteInt(LineNo, 5);
  Write(SP); WriteStr(Text); Write(NL);
  Running := false
end;
```

Algorithm 8.4

The following example shows a variable x of a record type R:

type R = **record** f, g: integer; h: Boolean **end**;
var x: R;

A variable access of the form

x.g

refers to the field g of the variable x. This generates the following code:

Variable(0, 3)
Field(1)

The Variable instruction pushes the address of the variable x on top of the stack as shown in Fig. 8.12a. (The address of a record variable is the address of its first word.) The field instruction adds the displacement of the field g to the address of the variable x to obtain the address of the field variable x.g (see Fig. 8.12b).

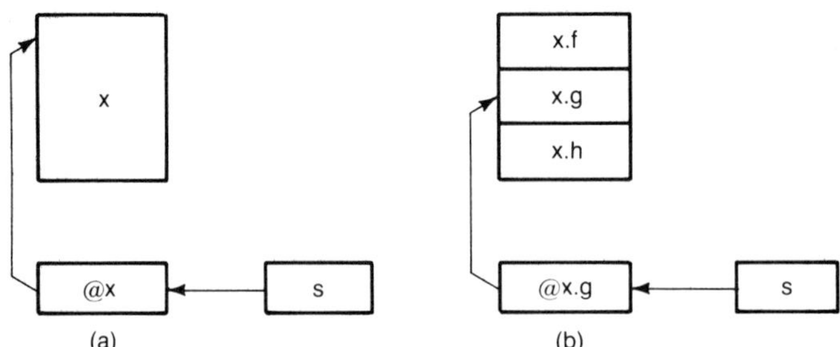

Fig. 8.12 Field access.

The *Field instruction* is very simple (Algorithm 8.5).

procedure Field(Displ: integer);
begin St[s] := St[s] + Displ; p := p + 2 **end**;

Algorithm 8.5

8.4 EXPRESSION EVALUATION

The Pascal Computer evaluates an expression in the temporary part of the current activation record. The stack operands are accessed by means of the s register (Fig. 8.2).

Expressions are composed of factors, terms, and simple expressions. Factors have the following syntax:

Factor = Constant | VariableAccess |
"(" Expression ")" | "**not**" Factor .

and produce the following code:

Factor = "**Constant**" | VariableAccess "**Value**" |
Expression | Factor "**Not**" .

A constant operand, say "5", is represented by a *Constant instruction;* for example,

Constant(5)

This instruction pushes the value of the constant on the stack (Algorithm 8.6).

```
procedure Constant(Value: integer);
begin s := s + 1; St[s] := Value; p := p + 2 end;
```

Algorithm 8.6

A variable operand A produces code that pushes the value of the whole array A on the stack (Fig. 8.7):

Variable(2, 3)
Value(10)

The Variable instruction pushes the address of the variable A on the stack (Fig. 8.9). The *Value instruction* removes the address from the stack and pushes the value of the variable on the stack instead. This instruction is defined by Algorithm 8.7. The argument defines the length of the variable (in words).

```
procedure Value(Length: integer);
var x, i: integer;
begin
  x := St[s]; i := 0;
  while i < Length do
      begin
        St[s + i] := St[x + i];
        i := i + 1
      end;
  s := s + Length - 1;
  p := p + 2
end;
```

Algorithm 8.7

The third part of the code rule for factors says only that parentheses do not exist in the code. An expression enclosed in parentheses produces only the code for the expression itself.

The last part of the rule says that a negated factor, such as

not x

is compiled into code that evaluates the factor followed by a *Not instruction* that negates the result:

```
Variable(xLevel, xDispl)
Value(1)
Not
```

The Not instruction is defined by Algorithm 8.8.

```
procedure Notx;
begin
  if St[s] = ord(true)
    then St[s] := ord(false)
    else St[s] := ord(true);
  p := p + 1
end;
```

Algorithm 8.8

Since the store is defined as an array of integers, Boolean values must be represented by the corresponding ordinal values:

ord(false) = 0 **ord**(true) = 1

Negated factors illustrate an important characteristic of expressions. In the program text, an expression is written in the conventional *infix* notation. In this notation, an operator, such as "**not**," which has a single operand, appears *before* the operand; for example,

not x

An operator with one operand is called a *monadic* operator (The word *monad* means "a single entity") [IFIP, 1971].

The code is, however, compiled as if the expression was written in *postfix* notation where a monadic operator appears *after* the operand:

x **not**

Postfix notation is ideal for a stack computer. The computer scans a compiled expression from left to right. When an operand is referenced, its value is immediately pushed on the stack. When a monadic operator occurs, the computer applies it to the operand in the top of the stack.

In the programming language, a term is written in the infix notation:

```
Term = Factor { MultiplyingOperator Factor } .
MultiplyingOperator =
  "*" | "div" | "mod" | "and" .
```

The multiplying operators have two operands. They are called *dyadic* operators (The word *dyad* means "a pair") [IFIP, 1971].

In the code language, the corresponding instructions appear in postfix order (that is, after the operands):

```
Term = Factor { Factor MultiplyingOperator } .
MultiplyingOperator =
  "Multiply" | "Divide" | "Modulo" | "And" .
```

It may be helpful to look at an example:

y * z **div** 5

In the postfix notation, the same term would be written as

y z * 5 **div**

The corresponding sequence of instructions is as follows:

(1) Variable(yLevel, yDispl)

(2) Value(1)

(3) Variable(zLevel, zDispl)

(4) Value(1)

(5) Multiply

(6) Constant(5)

(7) Divide

Figure 8.13 shows the stack at various stages during the execution of these instructions. As usual, the stack grows from the top of the figure toward the bottom. The figure does not show the s register, which points to the current top of the stack.

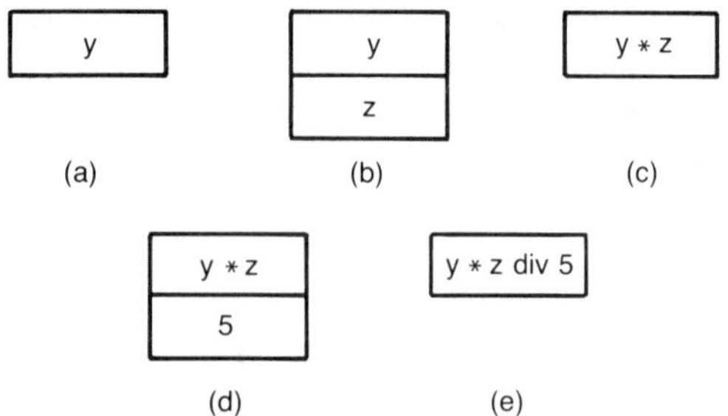

Fig. 8.13 Evaluation of a term.

Instructions 1 and 2 push the value of y on the stack (Fig. 8.13a). Instructions 3 and 4 push the value of z on top of that (Fig. 8.13b). Instruction 5 removes the operands y and z from the stack and replaces them with the product y * z (Fig. 8.13c). Instruction 6 pushes the constant 5 on top of the previous result (Fig. 8.13d). Finally, instruction 7 removes the operands y * z and 5 from the stack and replaces them with the quotient y * z **div** 5 (Fig. 8.13e). Notice that the stack grows and shrinks during the evaluation of the term. At the end, however, the evaluation leaves only the final result in the stack.

Algorithm 8.9 defines the *Multiply instruction.* The *Divide* and *Modulo instructions* are very similar, but use the operators "**div**" and "**mod**" instead of "*".

```
procedure Multiply;
begin
  s := s - 1;
  St[s] := St[s] * St[s + 1];
  p := p + 1
end;
```

Algorithm 8.9

The *And instruction* looks a bit strange at first (Algorithm 8.10). If St[s] is true, the result of the And operation is true if St[s + 1] is true, and false if St[s + 1] is false. In other words, the result is the same as the value of St[s + 1]. But if St[s] is false, the result is also false. So in that case, we may as well leave St[s] unchanged.

```
procedure Andx;
begin
  s := s - 1;
  if St[s] = ord(true) then
    St[s] := St[s + 1];
  p := p + 1
end;
```

Algorithm 8.10

In the infix notation of Pascal−, simple expressions have the following syntax:

```
SimpleExpression =
  [ SignOperator ] Term { AddingOperator Term } .
SignOperator = "+" | "−" .
AddingOperator = "+" | "−" | "or" .
```

The corresponding instructions are output in postfix order:

```
SimpleExpression =
  Term [ SignOperator ] { Term AddingOperator } .
SignOperator = Empty | "Minus" .
AddingOperator = "Add" | "Subtract" | "Or" .
```

The following example shows a simple expression both in the infix notation:

$$-y + z - 7$$

and in the postfix notation:

$$y \underline{-} z + 7 -$$

In the postfix form, the notation must show the difference between the monadic operator "$\underline{-}$" and the dyadic operator "−". We will call these operators "minus" and "subtract."

The postfix notation does not use *parentheses*. Instead, the operators appear in the order in which they must be applied to their operands.

The code rules show that the previous example generates the following instructions:

```
Variable(yLevel, y Displ)
Value(1)
Minus
Variable(zLevel, zDispl)
Value(1)
Add
Constant(7)
Subtract
```

The effect of this code should be obvious.

The *Minus instruction* is trivial (Algorithm 8.11).

```
procedure Minus;
begin St[s] := − St[s]; p := p + 1 end;
```

Algorithm 8.11

The *Add* and *Subtract instructions* are similar to the Multiply instruction but use the operators "+" and "—" instead of "*".

The *Or instruction* is defined by Algorithm 8.12. If St[s] is false, the Or operation has the same value as the other operand St[s + 1]. If St[s] is true, the result of the operation is also true. So St[s] is left unchanged.

```
procedure Orx;
begin
  s := s − 1;
  if St[s] = ord(false) then
    St[s] := St[s + 1];
  p := p + 1
end;
```

Algorithm 8.12

A complete Pascal— expression has the following syntax:

```
Expression = SimpleExpression
  [ RelationalOperator SimpleExpression ] .
RelationalOperator = "<" | "=" | ">" |
  "<=" | "<>" | ">=" .
```

The corresponding code rules are

```
Expression = SimpleExpression
  [ SimpleExpression RelationalOperator ] .
RelationalOperator = "Less" | "Equal" | "Greater" |
  "NotGreater" | "NotEqual" | "NotLess" .
```

A *Less instruction* replaces two values in the stack with a Boolean result. The result is true if the first value is less than the second one; otherwise, it is false (Algorithm 8.13). The other relational instructions use the operators "=", ">", "<=", "<>", and ">=" instead of "<".

```
procedure Less;
begin
  s := s − 1;
  St[s] := ord(St[s] < St[s + 1]);
  p := p + 1
end;
```

Algorithm 8.13

We will now use the code rules to derive the code of a complete expression. The Partition procedure in Section 8.2 contains the following while statement:

while r < A[j] **do** j := j − 1

Let's look at the Boolean expression

r < A[j]

and compile it manually in small steps:

(1) First, we use the code rule for expressions to find a first approximation of the code

```
r       (SimpleExpression)
A[j]    (SimpleExpression)
Less    (RelationalOperator)
```

(2) In this case, each of the simple expressions consists of a single term:

```
r       (Term)
A[j]    (Term)
Less
```

(3) In fact, the terms are just factors:

```
r       (Factor)
A[j]    (Factor
Less
```

(4) The code rule for factors enables us to outline the code in more detail:

```
r           (VariableAccess)
Value(1)
A[j]        (VariableAccess)
Value(1)
Less
```

(5) The next step is to compile the variable accesses (see Fig. 8.7):

```
Variable(0, 3)          (r)
Value(1)
Variable(2, 3)          (A)
j                       (Expression)
Index(1, 10, 1, 19)
Value(1)
Less
```

(6) The index expression is a factor that refers to the variable j. After inserting the corresponding instructions, we finally obtain the complete code of the Boolean expression:

```
Variable(0, 3)
Value(1)
Variable(2, 3)
Variable(1, 4)
Value(1)
Index(1, 10, 1, 19)
Value(1)
Less
```

Figure 8.14 shows the contents of the stack after the execution of each of these instructions.

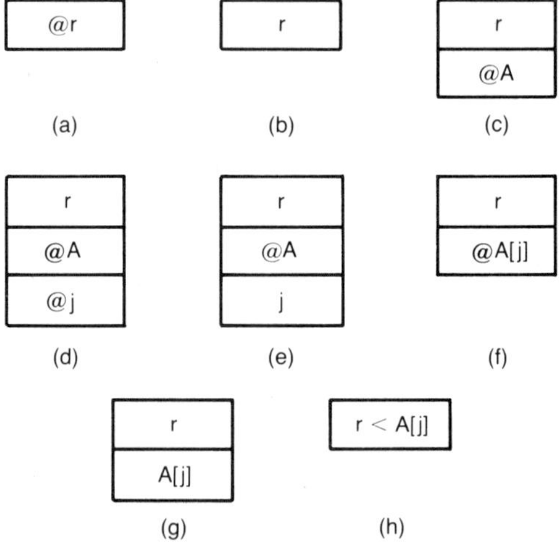

Fig. 8.14 Evaluation of an expression.

8.5 STATEMENT EXECUTION

An *assignment statement* produces the following code:

AssignmentStatement =
  VariableAccess Expression "**Assign**" .

The variable access code pushes the address of a variable on the stack. The expression code pushes the value of an expression on top of the variable address. The *Assign instruction* removes both operands from the stack and assigns the value to the variable.

The following example defines two variables A and B of the same type T:

type T = **array** [1 . . 10] **of** integer;
var A, B: T;

The assignment statement

A := B

produces the following code:

Variable(0, 3)
Variable(0, 13)
Value(10)
Assign(10)

Figure 8.15 shows the stack just before the execution of the Assign instruction. The instruction is defined by Algorithm 8.14.

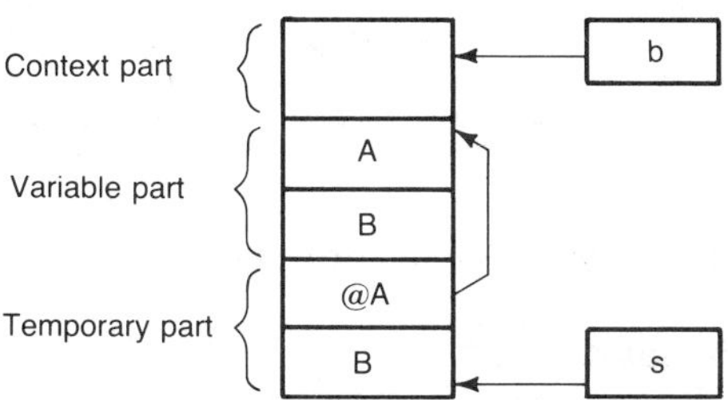

Fig. 8.15 The stack immediately before an assignment.

```
procedure Assign(Length: integer);
var x, y, i: integer;
begin
  s := s - Length - 1;
  x := St[s + 1];
  y := s + 2;
  i := 0;
  while i < Length do
    begin
      St[x + i] := St[y + i];
      i := i + 1
    end;
  p := p + 2
end;
```

Algorithm 8.14

A *while statement*

while B **do** S

produces code of the form

```
L1: B
    Do(L2)
    S
    Goto(L1)
L2:
```

The code is executed in the following steps:

(1) The expression code B is evaluated to obtain a Boolean value in the stack.

(2) The Do instruction removes the Boolean value from the stack. If the value is true, the computer proceeds to step 3. Otherwise, the execution of the while statement is finished by jumping to the point labeled L2.

(3) The statement code S is executed and step 1 is repeated by jumping to L1.

The following rule describes the code above:

```
WhileStatement =
   Expression "Do" Statement "Goto" .
```

The BNF notation is not flexible enough to show the jump addresses.

The Pascal Computer always loads program code at the beginning of the store (Fig. 8.1). Since the compiler knows the address and length of every instruction, it could output jump instructions with absolute addresses. But in most other systems, the address of a program is unknown until it has been loaded by an operating system. Since a compiler must expect to deal with this uncertainty, we will design the Pascal— compiler to produce code that can be placed anywhere in memory. This is called *relocatable code.*

The simplest way to make code relocatable is to let every jump instruction define its destination by a displacement relative to the instruction itself. When a jump instruction is executed, the destination address is obtained by adding the displacement to the program register p.

This is exactly what the *Goto instruction* does (Algorithm 8.15).

```
procedure Gotox(Displ: integer);
begin p := p + Displ end;
```

Algorithm 8.15

The *Do instruction* either proceeds to the next instruction or jumps to another instruction, depending on a Boolean value found in the stack (Algorithm 8.16).

```
procedure Dox(Displ: integer);
begin
  if St[s] = ord(true)
    then p := p + 2
    else p := p + Displ;
  s := s - 1
end;
```

Algorithm 8.16

The simplest kind of *if statement,*

if B **then** S

is compiled into the following code:

```
        B
        Do(L)
        S
     L:
```

If the expression code B yields the value false, the Do instruction jumps to L at the end of the if statement. Otherwise, the statement code S is executed.

An if statement of the form

if B **then** S1 **else** S2

is compiled into the following code:

```
     B
     Do(L1)
     S1
     Goto(L2)
L1:  S2
L2:
```

If B is true, the statement code S1 is executed before the Goto instruction jumps to L2 at the end of the if Statement. Otherwise, the Do instruction jumps to L1, where the statement code S2 is executed.

The following code rule describes both forms of the if statement:

```
IfStatement = Expression "Do" Statement
  [ "Goto" Statement ] .
```

The code rule for an arbitrary statement is as follows:

```
Statement =
  AssignmentStatement | ProcedureStatement |
  IfStatement | WhileStatement |
  CompoundStatement | Empty .
```

It says that a statement of a certain kind, for example an assignment statement, produces code defined by another rule, which in this case is named AssignmentStatement.

The empty statement produces no code. We will discuss procedure statements in Section 8.6.

The code for a compound statement

begin S1; S2; . . . Sn **end**

consists of the code for the statements S1, S2, . . . , Sn. In other words, the code rule is simply

```
CompoundStatement = Statement { Statement } .
```

8.6 PROCEDURE ACTIVATION

Earlier we looked at a program with the following block structure:

```
program Test10;
const max = 10;
  . . .
  procedure Quicksort(m, n:  integer);
  var i, j:  integer;

    procedure Partition;
    begin . . . end;

  begin . . . Quicksort(m, j) . . . end;

begin . . . Quicksort(1, max) . . . end.
```

Figure 8.16 shows the stack in two situations: (a) after the first activation of Quicksort, and (b) after the second activation of Quicksort. The following is a detailed explanation of how the stack changes from (a) to (b) during execution of the procedure statement

Quicksort(m, j)

The activation of Quicksort creates new instances of the formal parameters m and n.

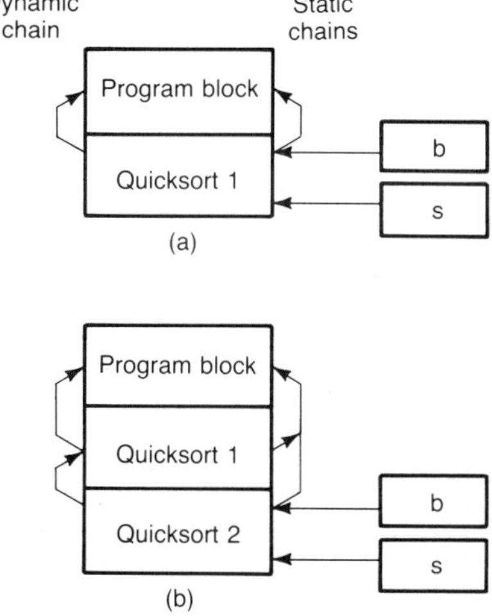

Fig. 8.16 Procedure activation.

The actual parameter m generates the following code:

```
Variable(0, −2)
Value(1)
```

These instructions create a new location in the temporary part of the stack and assign the value of the previous instance of m to that location.

Similarly, the actual parameter j generates the following code:

```
Variable(0, 4)
Value(1)
```

which creates another location in the stack and assigns it the value of the variable j. This is how the formal parameters m and n are created and initialized (Fig. 8.17a).

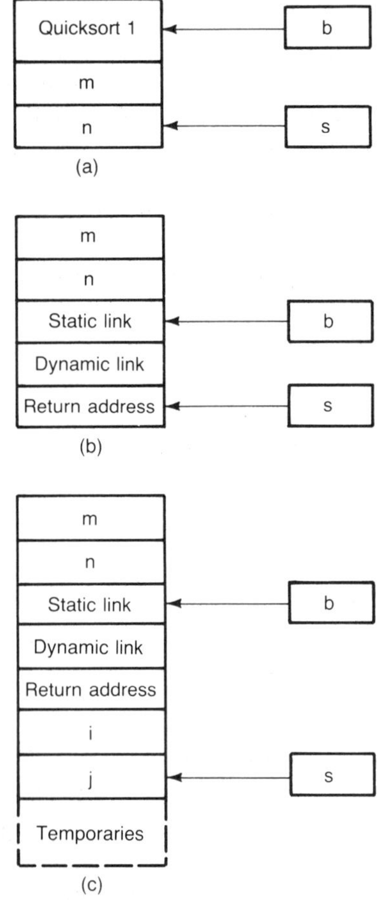

Fig. 8.17 Creation of an activation record.

The code for the actual parameters is followed by a *ProcCall instruction*:

ProcCall(Level, Displ)

This instruction creates the context part of the activation record (Fig. 8.17b). The context part consists of three addresses:

(1) The static link points to the activation record of the block that surrounds the procedure (Fig. 8.16b). This link is found in the current context shown in Fig. 8.16a. The ProcCall instruction defines the (relative) level at which the new static link is found. In this example, the Quicksort procedure is surrounded by the program block. This block is at level 1 relative to the current block (which is Quicksort itself).

(2) The dynamic link is the base address of the previous activation record (Fig. 8.16b).

(3) The return address is the address of the first instruction after the ProcCall instruction. When the procedure execution ends, the computer jumps to the return address.

After creating the context part of the activation record, the ProcCall instruction jumps to the procedure code. To make the code relocatable, the procedure code is defined by a displacement relative to the ProcCall instruction.

The ProcCall instruction is defined by Algorithm 8.17.

```
procedure ProcCall(Level, Displ: integer);
var x: integer;
begin
  s := s + 1;
  x := b;
  while Level > 0 do
    begin
      x := St[x];
      Level := Level - 1
    end;
  St[s] := x;           {Static link}
  St[s + 1] := b;       {Dynamic link}
  St[s + 2] := p + 3;   {Return address}
  b := s;
  s := b + 2;
  p := p + Displ
end;
```

Algorithm 8.17

After the ProcCall instruction, the computer executes the first instruction of the procedure, which is a *Procedure instruction* (Algorithm 8.18). The VarLength is the total length of the local variables defined in the procedure. The TempLength is the maximum extent of the temporary part of the stack during the execution of the procedure. The Displacement is the address of the statement part of the procedure relative to the Procedure instruction. (The computer uses this argument to jump around the local procedure Partition inside Quicksort.) The LineNo shows where the procedure is defined in the program text.

```
procedure Procedurex(VarLength, TempLength,
  Displ, LineNo: integer);
begin
  s := s + VarLength;
  if s + TempLength > Max then
    Error(LineNo, 'Stack Limit')
  else
    p := p + Displ
end;
```

Algorithm 8.18

The computer allocates space for the local variables of the procedure by incrementing the s register by the variable length (Fig. 8.17c). It then checks that there is sufficient room in the stack for the temporaries and jumps to the statement part of the procedure.

At the end of the procedure, the computer executes an *EndProc instruction.* This instruction uses the dynamic link to remove the activation record of the procedure. It then jumps to the return address (Algorithm 8.19). The ParamLength is the total length of the formal parameters.

```
procedure EndProc(ParamLength: integer);
begin
  s := b - Paramlength - 1;
  p := St[b + 2]; {Return address}
  b := St[b + 1]  {Dynamic link}
end;
```

Algorithm 8.19

The availability of temporary storage is checked at the beginning of every block. When that has been done, the rest of the block can increment the stack register s without checking the available storage space.

The code for a procedure activation is defined concisely by the following rules:

ProcedureStatement = IOStatement |
  [ActualParameterList] "**ProcCall**" .
ActualParameterList =
  ActualParameter { ActualParameter } .
ActualParameter = Expression | VariableAccess .

An actual parameter that corresponds to a value parameter is an expression. An actual parameter that corresponds to a variable parameter is a variable access.

We will discuss I/O statements shortly.

A procedure definition produces the following code:

ProcedureDefinition =
  "**Procedure**" BlockBody "**EndProc**" .
BlockBody =
  { ProcedureDefinition } CompoundStatement .

I/O statements have the form

Read(x)   Write(e)

where x is a variable and e is an expression of type integer. These statements produce the following code:

IOStatement =
  VariableAccess "**Read**" | Expression "**Write**" .

The *Read instruction* inputs an integer and assigns it to a variable x. The *Write instruction* outputs an integer e.

The implementation of Read and Write is system dependent. Appendix A.5 shows how they are defined in the Pascal− interpreter written for the Pascal* system.

8.7 PROGRAM EXECUTION

A complete program generates the following code:

Program = "**Program**" BlockBody "**EndProg**" .

After loading the program, the computer sets the Boolean Running to true and executes the first instruction of the program (Algorithm 8.20). The arguments have the same meaning as the arguments of a Procedure instruction (Algorithm 8.18).

```
procedure Programx(VarLength, TempLength,
  Displ, LineNo: integer);
begin
  b := StackBottom;
  s := b + 2 + VarLength;
  if s + TempLength > Max then
    Error(LineNo, 'StackLimit')
  else
    p := p + Displ
end;
```

Algorithm 8.20

The stack begins right after the program code (Fig. 8.1). A register named StackBottom holds the start address of the stack. The *Program Instruction* creates an activation record with a dummy context part and jumps to the statement part of the program block.

The last instruction of the program is an *EndProg instruction*, which sets Running to false to make the computer stop the program execution (Algorithm 8.21).

```
procedure EndProg;
begin Running := false end;
```

Algorithm 8.21

8.8 CODE SYNTAX

The following is a list of the code rules defined in this chapter. These rules correspond to the syntax rules of Pascal— (Section 2.4).

```
Program = "Program" BlockBody "EndProg" .
BlockBody =
  { ProcedureDefinition } CompoundStatement .
ProcedureDefinition = "Procedure" BlockBody "EndProc" .
Statement =
  AssignmentStatement | ProcedureStatement |
  IfStatement | WhileStatement |
  CompoundStatement | Empty .
AssignmentStatement =
  VariableAccess Expression "Assign" .
ProcedureStatement = IOStatement |
  [ ActualParameterList ] "ProcCall" .
IOStatement = VariableAccess "Read" |
  Expression "Write" .
```

```
ActualParameterList =
  ActualParameter { ActualParameter } .
ActualParameter = VariableAccess | Expression .
IfStatement = Expression "Do" Statement
  [ "Goto" Statement ] .
WhileStatement = Expression "Do" Statement "Goto" .
CompoundStatement = Statement { Statement } .
Expression = SimpleExpression
  [ SimpleExpression RelationalOperator ] .
RelationalOperator = "Less" | "Equal" | "Greater" |
  "NotGreater" | "NotEqual" | "NotLess" .
SimpleExpression =
  Term [ SignOperator ] { Term AddingOperator }.
SignOperator = Empty | "Minus" .
AddingOperator = "Add" | "Subtract" | "Or" .
Term = Factor { Factor MultiplyingOperator } .
MultiplyingOperator =
  "Multiply" | "Divide" | "Modulo" | "And" .
Factor = "Constant" | VariableAccess "Value" |
  Expression | Factor "Not" .
VariableAccess = VariableName { Selector } .
VariableName = "Variable" | "VarParam" .
Selector = Expression "Index" | "Field" .
```

8.9 TESTING

It is important to test the compiler, but it is even more important to test the instructions of the Pascal Computer. Once you build this computer in hardware, it is too late to correct errors in the instruction set. Fortunately, we can use the interpreter to test the instructions before the computer is built.

The instruction algorithms are tested by means of a test program written in Pascal—. When the interpreter follows the compiled code of this program, it will execute every instruction algorithm at least once.

Appendices A.5 and A.6 contain the text of the interpreter and the test program (Test 9). Since the compiler cannot translate the test program yet, we must run it later.

8.10 A TRADITIONAL COMPUTER

After designing the instruction set of an ideal computer, we will look at a traditional processor, the Intel 8088, which is a 16-bit processor [Intel, 1978].

The 8088 supports a stack. The stack and base registers are called sp and bp. But the operations on the stack are very limited indeed.

Local variables can be addressed relative to the base register bp; for example,

```
push(st[bp + 3])
```

This instruction pushes the value of a local variable on the stack. The instruction is written in the assembly language Alva for the IBM-PC [Brinch Hansen, 1983].

So far, so good. Now for the bad news. Although you can push the value of a local variable on the stack, you cannot push the address of the variable on the stack unless you move it to a register first.

By means of a single instruction, you can access a variable in the current activation record, but not in a previous activation record. To achieve the same effect as the Pascal instruction

```
Variable(2, 3)
```

the 8088 must execute five instructions:

```
move(bp, bx)
move(st[bx], bx)
move(st[bx], bx)
add(3, bx)
push(bx)
```

These instructions use an index register called bx.

The processor has none of the instructions that are used to access variables (Variable, VarParam, Index, and Field). To do the same as the Pascal instruction

```
Index(2, 100, 3, 28)
```

the 8088 needs 15 words of code (!):

```
     pop(ax)
     move(sp, bx)
     compare(100, ax)
     ifgreater(L1)
     subtract(2, ax)
     ifnotless(L2)
L1:  push(28)
     call(rangeerror)
L2:  multiply(3)
     add(ax, st[bx])
```

How about expression evaluation? Well, if you need to push a constant on the stack, it must first be moved to a register:

```
move(5, ax)
push(ax)
```

There is no Not instruction. Instead, you must compute the ordinal value of "**not** x" as "1 − x":

```
move(sp, bx)
negate(st[bx])
increment(st[bx])
```

The 8088 cannot address temporaries relative to the stack register sp. So you must assign the value of sp to another index register, such as bx, before you can access the operands.

A subtraction of two stack operands with overflow testing is even more complicated:

```
    pop(ax)
    move(sp, bx)
    subtract(ax, st[bx])
    ifnotoverflow(L)
    move(lineno, ax)
    push(ax)
    call(rangeerror)
L:
```

The multiplication instruction is particularly strange. It leaves a 32-bit result in two fixed registers (ax and dx). A 32-bit product may be useful to a programmer who writes procedures for double-length arithmetic in assembly language. But for a Pascal implementer, it complicates matters since integer variables can hold single-length values only.

The division instruction has the same problem. A 16-bit operand must first be moved to the ax register and extended to 32 bits before the division can be performed.

The arithmetic instructions are unsystematic in another respect. Addition, subtraction, and multiplication indicate overflow in a flag register, but division causes an interrupt instead!

The Boolean result of a relational instruction is left in the flag register (not in the stack, where it belongs). To make matters worse, there is no instruction that can move a particular flag bit to the stack. There are, however, instructions that test flag bits and branch if they are zero (or one). So the only way you can compare two stack operands, say for equality, is by means of the following instructions:

```
       pop(ax)
       move(sp, bx)
       move(1, dx)
       compare(ax, st[bx])
       ifequal(L)
       decrement(dx)
    L: move(dx, st[bx])
```

When you look at if and while statements, you will find that the 8088 has no less than 29 conditional jump instructions, but not one of them works like the Do instruction. Instead, you must do this:

```
          pop(ax)
          compare(1, ax)
          ifequal(L1)
          jump(L2)
    L1:     . . .
    L2:     . . .
```

Procedure activations are not supported very well either. The call instruction of the 8088 pushes the return address on the stack but not the static and dynamic links. There is no Procedure instruction that checks whether there is enough memory left to execute a procedure. Also, the return instruction assumes that the return address is at the top of the stack. So another instruction is required to remove the local variables from the stack.

These examples show that a traditional computer often complicates the task of a compiler writer considerably. Although we have looked at one processor only, I must add that I have never worked with a computer that simplifies the compilation of code. However, considering the number of programmers who now use Pascal-like languages, it is only a matter of time before most microprocessors will be language-based.

9

CODE GENERATION

This chapter explains how the compiler generates code for the Pascal Computer. The code generator is divided into two parts: (1) an extension of the parser, which outputs Pascal code; and (2) an assembler, which defines forward references and optimizes the code a bit.

9.1 OPERATION PARTS

Every instruction output by the compiler consists of an operation part followed by zero or more arguments (Section 8.3). In the compiler, the operation parts are represented by values of the following type:

```
type
  OperationPart = (Add2, And2, Assign2,
    Constant2, Divide2, Do2, EndProc2, EndProg2,
    Equal2, Field2, Goto2, Greater2, Index2,
    Less2, Minus2, Modulo2, Multiply2, Not2,
    NotEqual2, NotGreater2, NotLess2, Or2,
    ProcCall2, Procedure2, Program2, Subtract2,
    Value2, Variable2, VarParam2, Read2,
    Write2, DefAddr2, DefArg2);
```

DefAddr and DefArg are pseudoinstructions which are used during code generation only, not during program execution.

The parser emits an instruction of the form

Variable(Level, Displ)

by means of a procedure statement

Emit3(Variable2, Level, Displ)

The procedure Emit3 calls the compiler administration to output the operation part and the arguments (see Algorithm 9.1 and Section 3.4).

```
procedure Emit3(Op: OperationPart;
  Arg1, Arg2: integer);
begin
  Emit(ord(Op)); Emit(Arg1);
  Emit(Arg2)
end;
```

Algorithm 9.1

The parser includes three other output procedures, named Emit1, Emit2, and Emit5.

9.2 VARIABLE ADDRESSING

The most difficult aspect of code generation is the addressing of variables by relative level numbers and displacements. We will use an example from Section 8.2 to show how it is done:

```
procedure Quicksort(m, n: integer);
var i, j: integer;

  procedure Partition;
  begin . . . j := n . . . end;
```

The Quicksort procedure has two formal parameters m and n and two local variables i and j. Partition is a local procedure of Quicksort.

When Quicksort is activated, a fresh instance of its parameters and local variables is created in the form of an activation record (see Fig. 8.3).

A reference within Partition to the global variable j generates the instruction

Variable(1, 4)

The first argument of the instruction shows that the variable j is stored one level below the variables of Partition (Fig. 8.7). The second argument shows that j is stored four words above the base address of the activation record.

To compile this instruction, we must extend the object record of a variable with an absolute level number and a displacement:

```
type
  ObjectRecord =
    record
      Name: integer; Previous: Pointer;
      case Kind: Class of
        . . .
        Variable, ValueParameter, VarParameter:
          (VarLevel, VarDispl: integer;
            VarType: Pointer);
        . . .
    end;
```

(Compare this variant with the version defined in Section 7.4.)

The procedure that parses the variable group

```
i, j: integer
```

stores the names and type of the variables i and j in two object records. The procedure also counts the number of variables in the group and returns pointers to the records that describe the last variable j and the type integer (Algorithm 7.4):

```
procedure VariableGroup(
  Kind: Class; var Number: integer;
  var LastVar, Typex: Pointer;
  Stop: Symbols);
```

The procedure VariableDefinition uses this information to compute the length of the variable group (Algorithm 9.2). The dots . . . represent a set of stop symbols defined in the previous version of the procedure (Algorithm 7.6).

```
procedure VariableDefinition(
  var Lastvar: Pointer; var Length: integer;
  Stop: Symbols);
var Number: integer; Typex: Pointer;
begin
  VariableGroup(Variable, Number, Lastvar,
    Typex, . . . );
  Length := Number * TypeLength(Typex);
  Expect(Semicolon1, Stop)
end;
```

Algorithm 9.2

The length of a single variable is computed by a recursive function (Algorithm 9.3).

```
function TypeLength(Typex: Pointer): integer;
begin
  if Typex@.Kind = StandardType then
    TypeLength := 1
  else if Typex@.Kind = ArrayType then
    TypeLength :=
      (Typex@.UpperBound − Typex@.LowerBound + 1)
        * TypeLength(Typex@.ElementType)
  else {Typex@.Kind = RecordType}
    TypeLength := Typex@.RecordLength
end;
```

Algorithm 9.3

A standard value has the length one. The length of an array value is found by multiplying the number of array elements with the length of a single element (Section 7.5). The length of a record value is stored in the variant part of the object record that describes the record type:

```
RecordType:
  (RecordLength: integer; LastField: Pointer)
```

The procedure that parses the variable definition part

```
var i, j: integer;
```

is defined by Algorithm 9.4.

```
procedure VariableDefinitionPart(
  var Length: integer; Stop: Symbols);
var LastVar: Pointer; More: integer;
begin
  Expect(Var1, . . . );
  VariableDefinition(LastVar, Length, . . . );
  while Symbol = Name1 do
     begin
       VariableDefinition(LastVar, More, . . . );
       Length := Length + More
     end;
  VariableAddressing(Length, LastVar)
end;
```

Algorithm 9.4

At the end of the variable definition part, the parser calls a procedure that goes through the variables in reverse order and assigns them the displacements shown in Fig. 8.3 (Algorithm 9.5). The variables are offset by the context part of the activation record, which occupies three words.

```
procedure VariableAddressing(
  VarLength: integer; Lastvar: Pointer);
var Displ: integer;
begin
  Displ := 3 + VarLength;
  while Displ > 3 do
     begin
       Displ := Displ −
         TypeLength(LastVar@.VarType);
       LastVar@.VarLevel := BlockLevel;
       LastVar@.VarDispl := Displ;
       LastVar := LastVar@.Previous
     end
end;
```

Algorithm 9.5

The addressing of formal parameters is slightly different. The Quicksort procedure has the following parameter list:

m, n: integer

When the parser finds a reference in the Partition procedure to the value parameter n, it outputs the instruction

Variable(1, −1)

The level number 1 shows that n is stored one level below the variables of Partition (Fig. 8.7). The displacement −1 shows that n is stored one word below the base address of the activation record.

When the parser scans the formal parameter list of Quicksort, it stores the names and type of the parameters m and n in two object records. The parser also computes the total length of the parameter list and keeps a pointer to the last parameter n. At the end of the parameter list, the parser goes through the parameters in reverse order and gives them negative displacements (Algorithm 9.6). A variable parameter occupies one word (Section 8.3). The length of a value parameter is determined by its type.

```
procedure ParameterAddressing(
  ParamLength: integer; LastParam: Pointer);
var Displ: integer;
begin
  Displ := 0;
  while Displ > - ParamLength do
    begin
      if LastParam@.Kind = VarParameter then
        Displ := Displ - 1
      else {LastParam@.Kind = ValueParameter}
        Displ := Displ -
          TypeLength(LastParam@.VarType);
      LastParam@.VarLevel := BlockLevel;
      LastParam@.VarDispl := Displ;
      LastParam := LastParam@.Previous
    end
end;
```

Algorithm 9.6

When the parser finds a variable name in a statement, it calls a procedure named VariableAccess (Algorithm 7.8). This procedure retrieves the object record of the variable, computes its level number relative to the current block, and outputs a Variable instruction as follows:

```
var Object: Pointer; Level: integer;
Level := BlockLevel - Object@.VarLevel;
if Object@.Kind = VarParameter then
  Emit3(VarParam2, Level, Object@.VarDispl)
else
  Emit3(Variable2, Level, Object@.VarDispl)
```

When the parser encounters a reference to an *indexed variable* x[e], it produces code for addressing x and evaluating e. Afterward, the parser uses the description of the array type of x to output an Index instruction (Sections 7.5 and 8.3):

```
var Typex: Pointer;
Emit5(Index2, Typex@.LowerBound,
  Typex@.UpperBound,
  TypeLength(Typex@.ElementType),
  LineNo);
```

The addressing of record fields is very similar to the addressing of variables (except that fields do not have level numbers). The fields of a record type are assigned consecutive displacements starting at zero. The displacement of a field is stored in the variant part of its object record (Section 7.6):

```
Field:
  (FieldDispl: integer; FieldType: Pointer)
```

You will find the details in Appendix A.3, which contains the complete program text of the parser.

When the parser recognizes a reference to a *field variable* x.f, it finds the object record of the field f and emits a Field instruction (Sections 7.6 and 8.3):

```
var Fieldx: Pointer;
Emit2(Field2, Fieldx@.FieldDispl)
```

9.3 EXPRESSION CODE

Consider a block with two local variables

```
var y, z: integer;
```

and the expression

```
y * z div 5
```

This expression is compiled into the following instructions (Section 8.4):

```
Variable(0, 3)
Value(1)
Variable(0, 4)
Value(1)
Multiply
Constant(5)
Divide
```

We will follow the compilation of the expression step by step.

(1) When the parser encounters the expression, it calls four procedures, named Expression, SimpleExpression, Term, and Factor, in that order. Factor recognizes the variable name y and executes the following statements:

```
VariableAccess(Typex, Stop)
Length := TypeLength(Typex);
Emit2(Value2, Length)
Push(Length — 1)
```

The call of VariableAccess generates the first instruction:

```
Variable(0, 3)
```

The Factor procedure produces the next one:

```
Value(1)
```

(I will explain the meaning of the Push operation later.)

(2) When the Term procedure recognizes the multiplication operator, it enters the following loop, which stores the operator temporarily and calls Factor again:

```
Factor(Typex, . . . );
while Symbol in MultiplySymbols do
  begin
    Operator := Symbol;
    Expect(Symbol, . . . );
    Factor(Type2, . . . );
      . . .
  end
```

(3) This time, Factor recognizes the variable name z and generates the next two instructions:

```
Variable(0, 4)
Value(1)
```

(4) Afterward, the Term procedure executes the following statements in the previous loop:

```
if Typex = TypeInteger then
  begin
    CheckTypes(Typex, Type2);
    if Operator = Asterisk1 then
      Emit1(Multiply2)
    else if Operator = Div1 then
      Emit1(Divide2)
    else if Operator = Mod1 then
      Emit1(Modulo2)
    else { Operator = And1 }
      TypeError(Typex);
    Pop(1)
```

The effect of this is to output the multiply operator as an instruction

```
Multiply
```

(I will explain the Pop operation shortly.)

(5) When Term encounters the division operator, it stores it temporarily and calls Factor again. The Factor procedure now recognizes the constant 5:

```
Constant(Value, Typex, Stop)
Emit2(Constant2, Value)
Push(1)
```

and emits the instruction

```
Constant(5)
```

(6) Finally, Term outputs the division operator as an instruction

```
Divide
```

After looking at bits and pieces of the Term procedure, you may want to see it as a whole (Algorithm 9.7).

The other expression procedures are very similar to this one (see Appendix A.3).

The compiler determines how much temporary storage the computer needs to execute every block in a program. The computer uses this information at the beginning of a block to check whether there is enough memory to execute the block. Once that has been done, it is unnecessary to check the available memory space in the rest of the block (Section 8.6).

During scope analysis, the parser maintains a stack of block records (Section 6.4). This stack describes all objects that are known in the current block. When the parser enters a block in the program text, a new block record is pushed on the compilation stack. At the end of the block, the record is removed from the stack. During code generation, the same stack is used to keep track of the *temporary storage* of every block.

A block record is extended with two new fields named TempLength and MaxTemp:

```
type
  BlockRecord =
    record
      TempLength, MaxTemp: integer;
      LastObject: Pointer
    end;
  BlockTable =
    array [0 . . MaxLevel] of BlockRecord;
var
  Block: BlockTable; BlockLevel: integer;
```

When the compiler outputs an instruction, it predicts how much the size of the stack will change when the instruction is executed. The parser stores the current length of the temporary area in the TempLength field. The maximum number of temporary locations used by the current block is stored in the MaxTemp field.

```
procedure Term(var Typex: Pointer;
  Stop: Symbols);
var Operator: SymbolType; Type2: Pointer;
begin
  Factor(Typex, . . . );
  while Symbol in MultiplySymbols do
     begin
       Operator := Symbol;
       Expect(Symbol, . . . );
       Factor(Type2, . . . );
       if Typex = TypeInteger then
         begin
           CheckTypes(Typex, Type2);
           if Operator = Asterisk1 then
             Emit1(Multiply2)
           else if Operator = Div1 then
             Emit1(Divide2)
           else if Operator = Mod1 then
             Emit1(Modulo2)
           else { Operator = And1 }
             TypeError(Typex);
           Pop(1)
         end
       else if Typex = TypeBoolean then
         begin
           CheckTypes(Typex, Type2);
           if Operator = And1 then
             Emit1(And2)
           else { Arithmetic Operator }
             TypeError(Typex);
           Pop(1)
         end
       else TypeError(Typex)
     end
end;
```

Algorithm 9.7

At the beginning of a block both fields are zero. When the parser emits a Variable instruction, it calls a procedure named Push to indicate that the execution of this instruction will increase the stack by one word:

Push(1)

The Push procedure increments the TempLength of the current block and changes MaxTemp if necessary (Algorithm 9.8).

```
procedure Push(Length: integer);
begin
  Block[BlockLevel].TempLength :=
    Block[BlockLevel].TempLength + Length;
  if Block[BlockLevel].MaxTemp <
    Block[BlockLevel].TempLength then
      Block[BlockLevel].MaxTemp :=
        Block[BlockLevel].TempLength
end;
```

Algorithm 9.8

After emitting a Multiply instruction, the parser calls a procedure named Pop to indicate that the execution of this instruction will decrease the stack by one word:

Pop(1)

The Pop procedure decrements the TempLength of the current block (Algorithm 9.9).

```
procedure Pop(Length: integer);
begin
  BlockLevel[BlockLevel].TempLength :=
    Block[BlockLevel].TempLength − Length
end;
```

Algorithm 9.9

9.4 STATEMENT CODE

The code of an *assignment statement* has the form

```
AssignmentStatement =
  VariableAccess Expression "Assign" .
```

(Section 8.5).

Earlier, we discussed type analysis of assignment statements (Section 7.8). Algorithm 9.10 shows the parsing procedure extended with code generation. The added lines are marked * to illustrate how easy it is to add code generation to a recursive-descent parser (when the instruction set is designed right!). Notice how the parser produces postfix code by delaying the output of the assign operator until the code of the operands has been generated (Section 8.4).

```
   procedure AssignmentStatement(Stop: Symbols);
   var VarType, ExprType: Pointer;
*    Length: integer;
   begin
     VariableAccess(VarType, . . . );
     Expect(Becomes1, . . . );
     Expression(ExprType, Stop);
     CheckTypes(VarType, ExprType)
*    Length := TypeLength(ExprType);
*    Emit2(Assign2, Length);
*    Pop(1 + Length)
   end;
```

Algorithm 9.10

An assignment statement has an important property which we will call the *Temp property*: *If the temporary part of the stack is empty before the execution of the statement, it is also empty after the execution of the statement.*

During the execution of an assignment statement, the computer pushes two temporaries on the stack: (1) the address of a variable, and (2) the value of an expression. The temporaries are then removed by the Assign instruction.

It turns out that all statements in Pascal— have the Temp property. As we shall see, this property makes it possible for the compiler to predict the maximum extent of the temporaries during a block activation.

The code for a *while statement*

while B **do** S

includes two jump instructions:

```
L1: B
    Do(L2)
    S
    Goto(L1)
L2:
```

The Do instruction refers to the program point labeled L2. The Goto instruction refers to L1.

The parser scans the program text from left to right and outputs code directly to the disk. When the parser is ready to emit the Do instruction, it has not yet compiled the statement S. It is therefore unable to output the address of L2.

This problem of *forward references* is solved in three steps:

(1) The parser (pass 2) assigns a *numeric label* to every jump destination. The labels are distinct integers 1, 2, 3, ... Let's say that the program points L1 and L2 are assigned the labels 17 and 18. In that case, the parser outputs the following intermediate code for the while statement:

```
DefAddr(17)
B code
Do(18)
S code
Goto(17)
DefAddr(18)
```

(2) The *assembler* (pass 3) scans the intermediate code and keeps track of the address of the current instruction. The instruction address is computed relative to the beginning of the program.

Suppose that the instructions of the while statement have the following addresses:

Address	*Code*
279	DefAddr(17)
279	B code
287	Do(18)
289	S code
320	Goto(17)
322	DefAddr(18)

The assembler stores the address of every jump destination in a table. When the assembler inputs the instruction

DefAddr(17)

it stores the current address in table entry number 17:

Table[17] = 279

When it encounters the instruction

DefAddr(18)

it stores the current address in entry number 18:

Table[18] = 322

During this scan of the code, the assembler defines the addresses of all labels but does not output code. The DefAddr instructions serve only to define jump addresses. When these pseudoinstructions are input, the current address remains unchanged and nothing is output.

(3) Afterward, the assembler scans the same code again and uses the table to output final code.

When the assembler inputs the instruction

Do(18)

it computes the displacement of label 18 relative to the Do instruction itself:

$$\text{DoDispl} = \text{Table}[18] - 287 = 322 - 287 = 35$$

and outputs the instruction with this displacement:

Do(35)

The displacement of the Goto instruction is computed in the same way:

$$\text{GotoDispl} = \text{Table}[17] - 320 = 279 - 320 = -41$$

The final code is as follows:

```
B code
Do(35)
S code
Goto(-41)
```

Let us examine some of the algorithms that compile jump instructions. The parser uses a variable to count the number of labels created so far:

```
var LabelNo: integer;
```

When the parser needs a new label, it executes Algorithm 9.11.

```
procedure NewLabel(var No: integer);
begin
  TestLimit(LabelNo, MaxLabel);
  LabelNo := LabelNo + 1;
  No := LabelNo
end;
```

Algorithm 9.11

The procedure checks that the number of labels does not exceed the limit of the assembly table (Section 3.5).

The parsing of a while statement is now straightforward (Algorithm 9.12).

```
procedure WhileStatement(Stop: Symbols);
var Label1, Label2: integer;
  ExprType: Pointer;
begin
  NewLabel(Label1);
  Emit2(DefAddr2, Label1);
  Expect(While1, . . . );
  Expression(ExprType, . . . );
  CheckTypes(ExprType, TypeBoolean);
  Expect(Do1, . . . );
  NewLabel(Label2);
  Emit2(Do2, Label2);
  Pop(1);
  Statement(Stop);
  Emit2(Goto2, Label1);
  Emit2(DefAddr2, Label2)
end;
```

Algorithm 9.12

The assembler keeps the address of the current instruction in a variable:

```
var Address: integer;
```

The address is incremented after the output of an instruction (Algorithm 9.13).

```
procedure Emit2(Op: OperationPart;
  Arg: integer);
begin
  Emit(ord(Op)); Emit(Arg);
  Address := Address + 2
end;
```

Algorithm 9.13

The addresses of labels are stored in a table:

```
const MaxLabel = 1000;
type AssemblyTable =
  array [1 . . MaxLabel] of integer;
var Table: AssemblyTable;
```

After inputting a *DefAddr instruction*, the assembler stores the current address in the table and inputs the next instruction (Algorithm 9.14).

```
procedure DefAddr(LabelNo: integer);
begin
  Table[LabelNo] := Address;
  NextInstruction
end;
```

Algorithm 9.14

When the parser encounters a *jump instruction*, it outputs the instruction with a displacement (Algorithm 9.15). During the first phase of the assembly, the compiler administration suppresses the output of code (Algorithm 3.1).

```
procedure Jump(Op: OperationPart;
  LabelNo: integer);
begin
  {Op in Operations[Do2, Goto2]}
  Emit2(Op, Table[LabelNo] − Address);
  NextInstruction
end;
```

Algorithm 9.15

The compilation of if statements is very similar (see Appendix A.3).

When the parser estimates the *temporaries* of a block, it takes advantage of the Temp property of statements. The grammar of Pascal− shows that some statements are elementary, whereas others are composed of substatements (Section 2.4). The elementary statements are assignment statements, procedure statements, and empty statements. The composite statements are if statements, while statements, and compound statements.

To prove that all statements have the Temp property we will use a proof method known as *structural induction*. This method applies to recursively defined structures, such as Pascal statements. The basis step of the induction is to show that the elementary statements have the property. The inductive step is to prove that the composite statements have the property if the substatements have it. We may then conclude that all statements have the property.

The empty statement obviously has the Temp property. The temporaries created by an assignment statement are removed by the Assign instruction. The temporaries of a procedure statement are removed at the end of the procedure. This completes the basis step.

Let us assume that there are no temporaries in the stack before the execution of an if statement:

if B **then** S1 **else** S2

The evaluation of B leaves a Boolean value in the stack which is removed by the Do instruction. This leaves the stack empty at the beginning of the chosen substatement (which is either S1 or S2). If both S1 and S2 leave the stack empty, there are no temporaries left at the end of the if statement. So if S1 and S2 have the Temp property, the if statement also has it.

If there are no temporaries at the beginning of a while statement

while B **do** S

there are also none at the beginning of the statement S. If S has the Temp property, there are no temporaries left at the end of S either. So when the while statement terminates, there are still no temporaries left. In short, the while statement has the Temp property if the statement S has it.

Finally, it is obvious that if S1, S2, . . . , Sn leave no temporaries behind, neither does the compound statement

begin S1; S2; . . . ; Sn **end**

This completes the inductive step of the proof.

Since there are no temporaries at the beginning of a program, and, since all statements have the Temp property, we may conclude that *there are no temporaries in the stack before and after the execution of any statement.*

An if statement

if B **then** S1 **else** S2

consists of three components B, S1, and S2. We do not know whether the computer will execute S1 or S2. But since each component creates and removes its own temporaries, the compiler can analyze them one at a time from left to right and find out which one needs the largest temporary space. That is exactly what the parser does. It analyzes instructions as they are being generated and remembers the maximum extent of the temporaries after any one of them. The parser is really ignoring the conditional nature of an if statement and is treating it as a sequential piece of code:

B; S1; S2

In other words, the parser is using the following rule:

MaxTemp(**if** B **then** S1 **else** S2) = MaxTemp(B; S1; S2)

Every repetition of a while statement

while B **do** S

also creates and removes its own temporaries. It is therefore possible to estimate the extent of the temporaries during a single repetition. This is done by analyzing B and S from left to right during code generation. The parser, in effect, ignores the iterative nature of the while statement and treats it as a sequential piece of code according to the following rule:

MaxTemp(**while** B **do** S) = MaxTemp(B; S)

9.5 PROCEDURE CODE

The code of the Quicksort procedure

procedure Quicksort(m, n: integer);
var i, j: integer;

  procedure Partition;
  begin . . . **end**;

begin SL **end**;

has the following form (Section 8.6):

```
Procedure(VarLength, TempLength,
  Displ, LineNo)
Partition code
SL code
EndProc(ParamLength)
```

When the parser reaches the Quicksort procedure, it must output a Procedure instruction. But at this point, the parser is not yet able to compute the arguments of the instruction:

(1) The VarLength is the combined length of the local variables i and j. This argument is known only after parsing of the variable definition part:

var i, j: integer;

(2) The TempLength is the maximum extent of the temporaries in the statement list SL. It is known only at the end of the Quicksort procedure.

(3) The Displacement is the address of the statement list relative to the Procedure instruction. It is known only at the beginning of SL. These *forward references* are resolved by the assembler. The parser assigns a numeric *label* to each of the arguments above and outputs the Procedure instruction with these labels:

```
Procedure(VarLabel, TempLabel,
  BeginLabel, LineNo)
```

When the parser reaches a point where the value of an argument is known, it outputs the value (and the corresponding label) in the form of a pseudo-instruction:

```
DefArg(VarLabel, VarLength)
```

During its first phase, the assembler uses the DefArg instruction to enter the argument in a table:

```
Table[VarLabel] := Varlength
```

In the second phase, the assembler replaces the VarLabel in the Procedure instruction by the corresponding table value.

The following shows the intermediate form of the procedure code output by the parser:

```
DefAddr(ProcLabel)
Procedure(VarLabel, TempLabel,
  BeginLabel, LineNo)
Partition code
DefAddr(BeginLabel)
SL code
DefArg(VarLabel, VarLength)
DefArg(TempLabel, MaxTemp)
EndProc(ParamLength)
```

The parser also assigns a label to the Procedure instruction (the ProcLabel). Every call of Quicksort uses this label to refer to the procedure code. As an example, the statement

```
Quicksort(m, j)
```

is compiled into code that pushes the actual parameters m and j on the stack followed by a ProcCall instruction:

```
m code
j code
ProcCall(Level, ProcLabel)
```

The level of the procedure is defined relative to the block in which it is called (Section 8.6). The assembler replaces the procedure label with the displacement of the procedure code.

During parsing, the level number and label of a procedure are stored in the variant part of the corresponding object record:

```
Procedur:
  (ProcLevel, ProcLabel: integer;
    LastParam: Pointer)
```

In Chapter 7 we discussed the parsing of a procedure definition (Algorithm 7.21). Algorithm 9.16 is the final version of this parsing procedure. The added lines are marked *.

```
   procedure ProcedureDefinition(Stop: Symbols);
   var Name: integer; Proc: Pointer;
*    ProcLabel, ParamLength, VarLabel,
*    TempLabel, BeginLabel: integer;
   begin
     Expect(Procedure1, . . . );
     ExpectName(Name, . . . );
     Define(Name, Procedur, Proc);
*    Proc@.ProcLevel := BlockLevel;
*    NewLabel(Proc@.ProcLabel);
     NewBlock;
     if Symbol = LeftParenthesis1 then
       begin
         Expect(LeftParenthesis1, . . . );
         FormalParameterList(Proc@.LastParam,
*           ParamLength, . . . );
         Expect(RightParenthesis1, . . . )
       end
     else {no parameter list}
       begin
         Proc@.LastParam := nil Pointer;
*        ParamLength := 0
       end;
*    NewLabel(VarLabel);
*    NewLabel(TempLabel);
*    NewLabel(BeginLabel);
*    Emit2(DefAddr2, Proc@.ProcLabel);
*    Emit5(Procedure2, VarLabel, TempLabel,
*      BeginLabel, LineNo);
     Expect(Semicolon1, . . . );
     Blockbody(
*      BeginLabel, VarLabel, TempLabel, . . . );
     Expect(Semicolon1, . . . );
*    Emit2(EndProc2, ParamLength);
     EndBlock
   end;
```

Algorithm 9.16

The arguments of the Procedure instruction are defined at the end of the block body (compare Algorithms 5.13 and 9.17).

```
    procedure BlockBody(
*     BeginLabel, VarLabel, TempLabel: integer;
      Stop: Symbols);
*   var VarLength: integer;
    begin
      SyntaxCheck(BlockSymbols + Stop);
      if Symbol = Const1 then
        ConstantDefinitionPart( . . . );
      if Symbol = Type1 then
        TypeDefinitionPart( . . . );
      if Symbol = Var1 then
        VariableDefinitionPart(
*         VarLength, . . . )
*     else VarLength := 0;
      while Symbol = Procedure1 do
         ProcedureDefinition( . . . );
*     Emit2(DefAddr2, BeginLabel);
      CompoundStatement(Stop);
*     Emit3(DefArg2, VarLabel, VarLength);
*     Emit3(DefArg2, TempLabel,
*       Block[BlockLevel].MaxTemp)
    end;
```

Algorithm 9.17

If we ignore standard procedures, a procedure statement is parsed as defined by Algorithm 9.18 (compare this with Algorithm 7.22). When the code of a procedure statement is executed, the temporary part of the current activation record is increased by the actual parameters and the context part of the new activation record (Fig. 8.2). The context part occupies three words. Upon return from the procedure, the parameters and context part have been removed from the stack.

When the assembler inputs a ProcCall instruction, it replaces the procedure label with the address of the procedure code (relative to the current address) (see Algorithm 9.19).

```
    procedure ProcedureStatement(Stop: Symbols);
    var Proc: Pointer;
*     ParamLength: integer;
    begin {Symbol = (Procedure) Name1}
      Find(Argument, Proc);
      if Proc@.LastParam <> nil Pointer then
        begin
          Expect(Name1, . . . );
          Expect(LeftParenthesis1, . . . );
          ActualParameterList(Proc@.LastParam,
*            ParamLength, . . . );
          Expect(RightParenthesis1, . . . )
        end
      else {no parameter list}
*       begin
          Expect(Name1, Stop);
*         ParamLength := 0
*       end;
*     Emit3(ProcCall2,
*       BlockLevel - Proc@.ProcLevel,
*       Proc@.ProcLabel);
*     Push(3); Pop(ParamLength + 3)
    end;
```

Algorithm 9.18

```
procedure ProcCall(Level, LabelNo: integer);
begin
  Emit3(ProcCall2, Level,
      Table[LabelNo] - Address);
  NextInstruction
end;
```

Algorithm 9.19

9.6 CODE OPTIMIZATION

Although Pascal code is simple to generate, it occupies more space than it needs to. As an example, the assignment statement

$$k := k + 1$$

produces 13 words of code:

```
Variable(0, 13)
Variable(0, 13)
Value(1)
Constant(1)
Add
Assign(1)
```

This code can be reduced to 8 words if we extend the *standard instructions* of the Pascal Computer with a few *extra instructions*:

```
*  LocalVar(13)
*  LocalValue(13)
   Constant(1)
   Add
*  SimpleAssign
```

The extra instructions are marked *. They represent special cases that occur frequently in Pascal programs. The resulting code is called *optimized* Pascal code.

Experimental studies show that a block mostly uses its own *local variables* and (to a lesser extent) *global variables* defined in the immediately surrounding block. In other words, a block tends to access variables at (relative) levels 0 and 1. The LocalVar and LocalValue instructions take advantage of this.

A *LocalVar instruction* replaces a Variable instruction referring to level zero. We will express the relationship between the new instruction and the standard instruction by means of a parameterized code rule:

LocalVar(Displ) = Variable(0, Displ) .

We will call this an *optimization rule.*

When the computer executes a LocalVar instruction, it pushes the address of a local variable on the stack (Algorithm 9.20).

```
procedure LocalVar(Displ: integer);
begin
  s := s + 1; St[s] := b + Displ;
  p := p + 2
end;
```

Algorithm 9.20

A *LocalValue instruction* replaces two instructions:

Variable(0, Displ) Value(1)

We can express this by another optimization rule:

LocalValue(Displ) = Variable(0, Displ) Value(1) .

We can make this rule more elegant by appealing to the previous optimization rule:

LocalValue(Displ) = LocalVar(Displ) Value(1) .

The execution of a LocalValue instruction pushes the value of a local, simple variable on the stack (Algorithm 9.21).

```
procedure LocalValue(Displ: integer);
begin
  s := s + 1; St[s] := St[b + Displ];
  p := p + 2
end;
```

Algorithm 9.21

The corresponding instructions for global variables are defined by the following optimization rules:

GlobalVar(Displ) = Variable(1, Displ) .
GlobalValue(Displ) = GlobalVar(Displ) Value(1) .

The instruction algorithms are derived from the previous ones by replacing "b" with "St[b]".

A *SimpleValue instruction* replaces the address of a simple variable by its value (Algorithm 9.22).

```
{ SimpleValue = Value(1) . }

procedure SimpleValue;
begin St[s] := St[St[s]]; p := p + 1 end;
```

Algorithm 9.22

A *SimpleAssign instruction* assigns a value to a simple variable (Algorith 9.23).

```
{ SimpleAssign = Assign(1) . }

procedure SimpleAssign;
begin
  St[St[s - 1]] := St[s];
  s := s - 2; p := p + 1
end;
```

Algorithm 9.23

The extra instruction

GlobalCall(Displ) = ProcCall(1, Displ) .

represents the case where a procedure Q defined in a block calls another procedure P defined in the same block:

```
procedure P;
begin . . . end;

procedure Q;
begin . . . P . . . end;
```

The interpreter includes the algorithms of the extra instructions (Appendix A.5).

It should also be mentioned that a Variable instruction followed by a Field instruction:

Variable(Level, VarDispl) Field(FieldDispl)

are replaced by a modified Variable instruction:

Variable(Level, VarDispl + FieldDispl)

A Field instruction with the displacement zero is, of course, skipped wherever it occurs.

The use of syntax rules to describe code optimization has an interesting interpretation: *The extra instructions can be regarded as syntactic units recognized in the standard code.*

To put it differently, code generation is defined by a two-pass algorithm:

(1) During the first phase, the parser scans a program and outputs standard code that corresponds closely to the syntax of the program itself.

(2) In the second phase, the assembler scans the standard code and replaces some code sequences by optimized code.

Let's see how the assembler optimizes the standard code. First, we must extend the instruction set with the extra instructions

```
type OperationPart = ( . . . GlobalCall2,
  GlobalValue2, GlobalVar2, LocalValue2,
  LocalVar2, SimpleAssign2, SimpleValue2);
```

The assembler uses a procedure to input the next standard instruction and store it in a set of variables (Algorithm 9.24).

```
var Op: OperationPart;
  Arg1, Arg2, Arg3, Arg4: integer;

procedure NextInstruction;
begin
  Read(Op:integer);
  if Op in NoArguments then { skip }
  else if Op in OneArgument then
    Read(Arg1)
  else if Op in TwoArguments then
    begin Read(Arg1); Read(Arg2) end
  else if Op in FourArguments then
    begin
      Read(Arg1); Read(Arg2);
      Read(Arg3); Read(Arg4)
    end
end;
```

Algorithm 9.24

The procedure uses sets to define the number of arguments that follow an operation part:

```
type Operations = set of OperationPart;
var NoArguments, OneArgument, TwoArguments,
  FourArguments: Operations;
```

The sets are defined at the beginning of the assembly.

After inputting a Variable instruction, the assembler calls a procedure of the same name:

```
Variable(Arg1, Arg2)
```

and passes the arguments of the instruction as parameters to the procedure.

Algorithm 9.25 defines the Variable instruction.

```
procedure Variable(Level, Displ: integer);
begin
  NextInstruction;
  while Op = Field2 do
    begin
      Displ := Displ + Arg1;
      NextInstruction
    end;
  if Level = 0 then
    if (Op = Value2) and (Arg1 = 1) then
      begin
        Emit2(LocalValue2, Displ);
        NextInstruction
      end
    else Emit2(LocalVar2, Displ)
  else if Level = 1 then
    if (Op = Value2) and (Arg1 = 1) then
      begin
        Emit2(GlobalValue2, Displ);
        NextInstruction
      end
    else Emit2(GlobalVar2, Displ)
  else Emit3(Variable2, Level, Displ)
end;
```

Algorithm 9.25

The assembler uses the *single-symbol look-ahead* method (Section 4.3). As soon as it has recognized the Variable instruction and called the procedure above, it reads the next instruction to see if it can be combined with the Variable instruction.

A sample Pascal program of 515 lines was originally compiled into 3419 words of standard code. When the code was optimized, its length dropped to 2321 words. The following table shows the contribution of every new instruction to the code reduction. The table also shows the effect of the field optimization:

LocalValue	10%
GlobalValue	7%
Field optimization	3%
LocalVar	3%
GlobalCall	3%
SimpleAssign	3%
GlobalVar	2%
SimpleValue	1%
Code reduction	32%

9.7 TESTING

We must test the compiler both when it generates standard code and when it produces optimized code. To simplify this dual test, it is convenient to make the code optimization conditional. Instead of writing an optimization condition like this:

if Level = 0 **then** . . .

it is expressed as a parameter of a function:

if Optimize(Level = 0) **then** . . .

If the code must be optimized, the function returns the Boolean value of the optimization condition:

```
function Optimize(SpecialCase: Boolean): Boolean;
begin Optimize := SpecialCase end;
```

But the optimization can also be suppressed by making the function always return the value false.

The code generation was tested by compiling Test 9 (Appendix A.6) with and without code optimization. The output code was printed as a sequence of integers and studied in detail.

10

PERFORMANCE

This chapter presents performance figures for the Pascal— compiler. The performance was measured on the Compaq Portable Computer, which is compatible with the IBM Personal Computer.

10.1 COMPILER SIZE

The compiler consists of four programs written in Pascal:

Administration	100 lines	(5%)
Scanner	300 lines	(14%)
Parser	1400 lines	(67%)
Assembler	300 lines	(14%)
Compiler text	2100 lines	(100%)

Although the parser is much larger than the scanner, it uses the same amount of memory when the variables are included.

The following shows the number of program lines devoted to each of the major compilation tasks:

Administration	100 lines	(5%)
Lexical analysis	300 lines	(14%)
Syntax analysis	600 lines	(29%)
Scope analysis	100 lines	(5%)
Type analysis	400 lines	(18%)
Code generation	600 lines	(29%)
Compiler text	2100 lines	(100%)

It is interesting that two-thirds of the compiler is dedicated to program analysis and one-third only is concerned with code generation. The error recovery accounts for 200 of the 600 lines used for syntax analysis.

The code of the compiler has the following size:

Administration	700 words
Scanner	1700 words
Parser	5000 words
Assembler	1000 words
Compiler code	8400 words

The Pascal— compiler was designed to compile programs of the order of 2000 lines with up to 500 names (Section 4.4). When the *scanner* analyzes a program text of this size, it uses the memory as follows:

Spelling table (5,000 characters)	5,000 words
Hash table (631 lists)	631 words
Word records (500 names)	2,500 words
Other variables	600 words
Variables	8,700 words
Code (administration + scanner)	2,400 words
Scanner space	11,100 words

The 11,100 words used during scanning leaves almost 9,000 words unused (Section 3.2).

When the *parser* analyzes a program with 500 names, it uses the following amount of memory:

Object records (500 objects)	3,500 words
Other variables	1,100 words
Variables	4,600 words
Code (administration + parser)	5,700 words
Parser space	10,300 words

The "other variables" include the local variables of the parsing procedures. It is surprising how deeply the procedure calls can be nested. For example, when the parser scans the statement

w := A[i]

in Test 10, it is in the middle of 31 incomplete procedure activations:

	Procedure Activation	*Program Sentence*
14	Programx	**program** Test 10
15	BlockBody	. . .
18	ProcedureDefinition	**procedure** Quicksort
15	BlockBody	. . .
18	ProcedureDefinition	**procedure** Partition
15	BlockBody	. . .
11	CompoundStatement	**begin**
12	Statement	. . .
14	WhileStatement	**while** i <= j **do**
12	Statement	
11	CompoundStatement	**begin**
12	Statement	. . .
14	IfStatement	**if** i <= j **then**
12	Statement	
11	CompoundStatement	**begin**
12	Statement	
14	AssignmentStatement	w := A[i]
14	Expression	
22	SimpleExpression	
22	Term	
15	Factor	
22	VariableAccess	A[i]
13	IndexedSelector	[i]
14	Expression	
22	SimpleExpression	
22	Term	
15	Factor	
22	VariableAccess	i
6	Emit3	
4	Emit	
4	Write	

The numbers shown on the left are the lengths of the activation records. They add up to 447 words.

The *assembler* uses very little memory:

Variables (1,000 labels)	1,200 words
Code (administration + assembler)	1,700 words
Assembler space	2,900 words

If the compiler had been written as a single-pass program, it would not have been able to work in the available space of 20,000 words:

Code	8,400 words
Variables	14,500 words
Single-pass compiler	22,900 words

The multipass compiler generates about 4 words of code per line. A compiled program that occupies the entire memory of 20,000 words would therefore be about 5000 lines long and would probably use about 1000 different names. The compiler has enough memory available to compile such a program.

10.2 COMPILATION SPEED

While discussing *lexical analysis*, we compared different search methods by looking at the number of comparisons per word (Section 4.4). We will now compare the same methods by measuring how long it takes to scan a sample program of 2,000 lines (or 55,000 characters). Here are the results:

Linear search	2,700 sec
Letter indexing	475 sec
Hashing (linear probing)	363 sec
Hashing (direct chaining)	353 sec

Linear searching reduces the scan rate to less than one line per second. A scanner that uses hashing with direct chaining is almost eight times faster.

In Section 4.4 we found direct chaining to be 31 percent faster than linear probing. But the measurements above show that it is only 3 percent faster. The discrepancy occurs because the earlier estimate focused on the search time only (measured in terms of the number of comparisons). In practice, the scanner is limited by other factors also. A closer analysis reveals that the final scanner spends its time as follows:

Disk input	2.5 msec/char	(40%)
Word scanning	2.2 msec/char	(35%)
Other symbols	0.9 msec/char	(14%)
Disk output	0.7 msec/char	(11%)
Scanning	6.3 msec/char	(100%)

From these figures, we can draw several conclusions:

(1) Scanning is a time-consuming process that has a decisive influence on the performance of the whole compiler.

(2) The validity of theoretical performance estimates should always be verified by real measurements.

(3) The most time-consuming part of scanning is inputting the source text from disk. This process can be optimized only by careful design of the operating system.

(4) The time used for disk output is of much less importance since the intermediate code occupies less than a third of the space of the source text (Section 4.2).

(5) It is crucial to use an efficient algorithm to search for words, but it makes almost no difference whether you use hashing with linear probing or direct chaining.

(6) The scanning time of all other symbols is so small that there is no need to look for faster methods of recognizing these symbols. It makes absolutely no difference whether you use an if statement or a case statement to recognize the first characters of special symbols and numerals (Section 4.3).

(7) The overall processing speed of the scanner is 159 characters per second.

The performance of the whole compiler was tested by compiling a program of 515 lines (or 11,000 characters). The individual passes performed as follows:

Scanner	6.3 msec/char	(45%)
Parser	4.8 msec/char	(34%)
Assembler	2.9 msec/char	(21%)
Compiler	14.0 msec/char	(100%)

The parser does not input a program as a sequence of characters, but as a sequence of symbol values. Similarly, the assembler inputs a sequence of instructions. But to make it easier to compare the performance of the compiler passes, all processing times are expressed in terms of the source text (in milliseconds per character).

After an initial time of 10 sec, the compiler translates 71 characters per second (or 3.3 lines per second). The compilation time of the sample program of 515 lines is 2.8 min.

The compilation time is distributed as follows among the major compilation tasks:

Disk input/output	7.2 msec/char	(52%)
Lexical analysis	3.1 msec/char	(22%)
Syntax analysis	0.8 msec/char	(6%)
Scope analysis	0.9 msec/char	(6%)
Type analysis	0.9 msec/char	(6%)
Code generation	1.1 msec/char	(8%)
Compilation	14.0 msec/char	(100%)

The compilation time is obviously dominated by disk input/output and lexical analysis.

At this point, it is reasonable to ask what price we pay for the extensive error recovery during *syntax analysis* (Section 5.8). The overhead is mainly in the procedure Expect, which checks whether every single symbol is followed by a correct stop symbol (see Algorithm 5.9). An experiment with a parser without error recovery shows that it uses 0.6 milliseconds per character less than a parser with error recovery. So the error recovery increases the compilation time by 4 percent only.

During *scope analysis*, the parser uses linear searching to determine if names refer to known objects (Section 6.5). You may wonder why linear searching of names is too slow for lexical analysis but acceptable for scope analysis.

During lexical analysis, names are represented by text strings. Since names can be fairly long, they waste too much space if they are stored as strings of fixed length. The simplest way of storing them as strings of variable length is by keeping all of them in the same table (the spelling table described in Section 4.5). The price we pay for this economy of storage is that names must be compared character by character. This is such a slow process that we are forced to use hashing to reduce the number of comparisons.

The situation is very different during scope analysis. Names are now represented by integer values which can be compared directly. Within a block, most sentences tend to refer to objects that are defined in the same block. Since the binding algorithm starts by examining the local objects of the current block, the search is often confined to a small subset of all objects defined in a program. Although the sample program defines 139 objects, the average binding only involves comparing a name to 25 other names. Since the scope analysis takes 6 percent of the compilation time only, there is very little to gain by trying to speed it up.

A

A COMPLETE COMPILER

A.1 ADMINISTRATION

```
        {   PASCAL- COMPILER: ADMINISTRATION
                     20 April 1984
          Copyright (c) 1984 Per Brinch Hansen }

program Compile;
type
  ErrorKind = (Ambiguous3, Comment3, Kind3, Numeral3,
    Range3, Syntax3, Type3, Undefined3);
var
  Source, Code: String; LineNo: integer;
  Emitting, Errors, CorrectLine: Boolean;

procedure Emit(Value: integer);
begin if Emitting then Write(chr(Value))
end;

procedure ReRun;
begin Reset('temp2'); Emitting := true end;

procedure NewLine(Number: integer);
begin LineNo := Number; CorrectLine := true end;

procedure Error(Kind: ErrorKind);
var Text: String;
begin
  if not Errors then
    begin Close; Rewrite('notes');
      Emitting := false; Errors := true
    end;
  if Kind = Ambiguous3 then
    Text := 'Ambiguous Name'
  else if Kind = Comment3 then
    Text := 'Invalid Comment'
  else if Kind = Kind3 then
    Text := 'Invalid Name Kind'
  else if Kind = Numeral3 then
    Text := 'Invalid Numeral'
  else if Kind = Range3 then
    Text := 'Invalid Index Range'
  else if Kind = Syntax3 then
    Text := 'Invalid Syntax'
  else if Kind = Type3 then
    Text := 'Invalid Type'
  else if Kind = Undefined3 then
    Text := 'Undefined Name';
  if CorrectLine then
    begin
```

```
      WriteStr('Line ');
      WriteInt(LineNo, 4);
      WriteStr('  '); WriteStr(Text);
      Write(NL); CorrectLine := false
    end
end;

procedure TestLimit(Length, Maximum: integer);
begin
  if Length >= Maximum then
    begin Rewrite('screen');
      Write(NL);
      WriteStr('Program Too Big');
      Write(NL);
      Assume(false, '  ')
    end
end;

begin
  WriteStr('  Source name = ');
  ReadStr(Source);
  WriteStr('  Code name = ');
  ReadStr(Code);
  Delete('notes');
  Errors := false; Emitting := true;
  Reset(Source); Rewrite('temp1');
  call Descriptor('pass1'), Read, EOF, Emit,
    NewLine, Error, TestLimit;
  Close;
  if not Errors then
    begin
      Reset('temp1'); Rewrite('temp2');
      call Descriptor('pass2'), Read, Emit,
        NewLine, Error, TestLimit;
      Close
    end;
  Delete('temp1');
  if not Errors then
    begin
      Reset('temp2'); Rewrite(Code);
      Emitting := false;
      call Descriptor('pass3'), Read, Emit,
        Rerun;
      Close
    end;
  Delete('temp2');
  if Errors then
    begin Rewrite('screen'); Write(NL);
      WriteStr('Compilation Errors');
      Write(NL)
    end
```

```
end.
```

A.2 SCANNER

```
*       {       PASCAL- COMPILER: SCANNER
                      20 April 1984
          Copyright (c) 1984 Per Brinch Hansen }

const
  MaxChar = 5000; MaxKey = 631; MaxInt = 32767;
  Integer0 = 1; Boolean0 = 2; False0 = 3;
  True0 = 4; Read0 = 5; Write0 = 6;

type
  SymbolType = (And1, Array1, Asterisk1, Becomes1,
    Begin1, Colon1, Comma1, Const1, Div1, Do1,
    DoubleDot1, Else1, End1, EndText1, Equal1,
    Greater1, If1, LeftBracket1, LeftParenthesis1,
    Less1, Minus1, Mod1, Name1, NewLine1, Not1,
    NotEqual1, NotGreater1, NotLess1, Numeral1,
    Of1, Or1, Period1, Plus1, Procedure1, Program1,
    Record1, RightBracket1, RightParenthesis1,
    Semicolon1, Then1, Type1, Var1, While1,
    Unknown1);

  ErrorKind = (Ambiguous3, Comment3, Kind3, Numeral3,
    Range3, Syntax3, Type3, Undefined3);

procedure Read(var Value: char);
function EOF: Boolean;
procedure Emit(Value: integer);
procedure NewLine(LineNo: integer);
procedure Error(Kind: ErrorKind);
procedure TestLimit(Length, Maximum: integer);

program Pass1;

const
  ETX = 3C; NL = 10C; SP = ' ';
  LeftBrace = 123C; RightBrace = 125C;
  LastStandardName = Write0;

type
  CharSet = set of char;

  SpellingTable = array [1..MaxChar] of char;

  WordPointer = @ WordRecord;

  WordRecord =
    record
```

```
      NextWord: WordPointer;
      IsName: Boolean;
      Index, Length, LastChar: integer
    end;

  HashTable = array [1..MaxKey] of WordPointer;

var
  LineNo: integer; ch: char;
  AlphaNumeric, CapitalLetters, Digits,
    EndComment, Invisible, Letters,
    Separators, SmallLetters: CharSet;
  Spelling: SpellingTable; Characters: integer;
  Hash: HashTable; Names: integer;

                                  { INPUT }

procedure NextChar;
begin
  if EOF then ch := ETX
  else
    begin Read(ch);
      if ch in Invisible then NextChar
    end
end;

                                 { OUTPUT }

procedure Emit1(Symbol: SymbolType);
begin Emit(ord(Symbol)) end;

procedure Emit2(Symbol: SymbolType;
  Argument: integer);
begin Emit(ord(Symbol)); Emit(Argument) end;

                         { WORD SYMBOLS AND NAMES }

function Key(Text: String; Length: integer)
  : integer;
const W = 32641 {32768 - 127}; N = MaxKey;
var Sum, i: integer;
begin Sum := 0; i := 1;
  while i <= Length do
    begin
      Sum := (Sum  + ord(Text[i])) mod W;
      i := i + 1
    end;
  Key := Sum mod N + 1
end;

procedure Insert(IsName: Boolean; Text: String;
```

```
  Length, Index, KeyNo: integer);
var Pointer: WordPointer; M, N: integer;
begin
  {Insert the word in the spelling table}
  Characters := Characters + Length;
  TestLimit(Characters, MaxChar);
  M := Length; N := Characters - M;
  while M > 0 do
    begin Spelling[M + N] := Text[M];
      M := M - 1
    end;
  {Insert the word in a word list}
  New(Pointer);
  Pointer@.NextWord := Hash[KeyNo];
  Pointer@.IsName := IsName;
  Pointer@.Index := Index;
  Pointer@.Length := Length;
  Pointer@.LastChar := Characters;
  Hash[KeyNo] := Pointer
end;

function Found(Text: String; Length: integer;
  Pointer: WordPointer): Boolean;
var Same: Boolean; M, N: integer;
begin
  if Pointer@.Length <> Length then
    Same := false
  else
    begin Same := true; M := Length;
      N := Pointer@.LastChar - M;
      while Same and (M > 0) do
        begin
          Same := Text[M] = Spelling[M + N];
          M := M - 1
        end
    end;
  Found := Same
end;

procedure Define(IsName: Boolean; Text: String;
  Length, Index: integer);
begin
  Insert(IsName, Text, Length, Index,
    Key(Text, Length))
end;

procedure Search(Text: String; Length: integer;
  var IsName: Boolean; var Index: integer);
var KeyNo: integer; Pointer: WordPointer;
  Done: Boolean;
begin
```

```
  KeyNo := Key(Text, Length);
  Pointer := Hash[KeyNo]; Done := false;
  while not Done do
    if Pointer = nil WordPointer then
      begin IsName := true;
        Names := Names + 1; Index := Names;
        Insert(true, Text, Length, Index, KeyNo);
        Done := true
      end
    else if Found(Text, Length, Pointer) then
      begin IsName := Pointer@.IsName;
        Index := Pointer@.Index; Done := true
      end
    else Pointer := Pointer@.NextWord
end;

function SubSet(First, Last: char): CharSet;
var Value: CharSet; ch: char;
begin Value := CharSet[]; ch := First;
  while ch <= Last do
    begin Value := Value + CharSet[ch];
      ch := chr(ord(ch) + 1)
    end;
  SubSet := Value
end;

procedure Initialize;
var KeyNo: integer;
begin
  Digits := SubSet('0', '9');
  CapitalLetters := SubSet('A', 'Z');
  SmallLetters := SubSet('a', 'z');
  Letters := CapitalLetters + SmallLetters;
  AlphaNumeric := Letters + Digits;
  EndComment := CharSet[RightBrace, ETX];
  Invisible := SubSet(0C, 31C) +
    CharSet[127C] - CharSet[NL, ETX];
  Separators := CharSet[SP, NL, LeftBrace];
  KeyNo := 1;
  while KeyNo <= MaxKey do
    begin Hash[KeyNo] := nil WordPointer;
      KeyNo := KeyNo + 1
    end;
  Characters := 0;
  {Insert the word symbols}
  Define(false, 'and', 3, ord(And1));
  Define(false, 'array', 5, ord(Array1));
  Define(false, 'begin', 5, ord(Begin1));
  Define(false, 'const', 5, ord(Const1));
  Define(false, 'div', 3, ord(Div1));
  Define(false, 'do', 2, ord(Do1));
```

```
  Define(false, 'else', 4, ord(Else1));
  Define(false, 'end', 3, ord(End1));
  Define(false, 'if', 2, ord(If1));
  Define(false, 'mod', 3, ord(Mod1));
  Define(false, 'not', 3, ord(Not1));
  Define(false, 'of', 2, ord(Of1));
  Define(false, 'or', 2, ord(Or1));
  Define(false, 'procedure', 9, ord(Procedure1));
  Define(false, 'program', 7, ord(Program1));
  Define(false, 'record', 6, ord(Record1));
  Define(false, 'then', 4, ord(Then1));
  Define(false, 'type', 4, ord(Type1));
  Define(false, 'var', 3, ord(Var1));
  Define(false, 'while', 5, ord(While1));
  {Insert the standard names}
  Define(true, 'integer', 7, Integer0);
  Define(true, 'boolean', 7, Boolean0);
  Define(true, 'false', 5, False0);
  Define(true, 'true', 4, True0);
  Define(true, 'read', 4, Read0);
  Define(true, 'write', 5, Write0);
  Names := LastStandardName
end;

                    { LEXICAL ANALYSIS }

procedure BeginLine(Number: integer);
begin LineNo := Number;
  NewLine(LineNo);
  Emit2(NewLine1, LineNo)
end;

procedure EndLine;
begin BeginLine(LineNo + 1) end;

procedure Comment;
begin {ch = LeftBrace} NextChar;
  while not (ch in EndComment) do
    if ch = LeftBrace then Comment
    else
      begin
        if ch = NL then EndLine;
        NextChar
      end;
  if ch = RightBrace then NextChar
  else Error(Comment3)
end;

procedure NextSymbol;
var IsName: Boolean; Text: String;
  Length, Index, Value, Digit: integer;
```

```
begin
  while ch in Separators do
    if ch = SP then NextChar
    else if ch = NL then
      begin EndLine; NextChar end
    else {ch = LeftBrace} Comment;
  if ch in Letters then
    begin Length := 0;
      while ch in AlphaNumeric do
        begin
          if ch in CapitalLetters then
            ch := chr(ord(ch) + ord('a') - ord('A'));
          Length := Length + 1;
          Text[Length] := ch; NextChar
        end;
      Search(Text, Length, IsName, Index);
      if IsName then Emit2(Name1, Index)
      else Emit(Index)
    end
  else if ch in Digits then
    begin Value := 0;
      while ch in Digits do
        begin
          Digit := ord(ch) - ord('0');
          if Value <= (MaxInt - Digit) div 10 then
            begin
              Value := 10 * Value + Digit;
              NextChar
            end
          else
            begin Error(Numeral3);
              while ch in Digits do NextChar
            end
        end;
      Emit2(Numeral1, Value)
    end
  else if ch = '+' then
    begin Emit1(Plus1); NextChar end
  else if ch = '-' then
    begin Emit1(Minus1); NextChar end
  else if ch = '*' then
    begin Emit1(Asterisk1); NextChar end
  else if ch = '<' then
    begin NextChar;
      if ch = '=' then
        begin Emit1(NotGreater1); NextChar end
      else if ch = '>' then
        begin Emit1(NotEqual1); NextChar end
      else Emit1(Less1)
    end
  else if ch = '=' then
```

```
    begin Emit1(Equal1); NextChar end
  else if ch = '>' then
    begin NextChar;
      if ch = '=' then
        begin Emit1(NotLess1); NextChar end
      else Emit1(Greater1)
    end
  else if ch = ':' then
    begin NextChar;
      if ch = '=' then
        begin Emit1(Becomes1); NextChar end
      else Emit1(Colon1)
    end
  else if ch = '(' then
    begin Emit1(LeftParenthesis1); NextChar end
  else if ch = ')' then
    begin Emit1(RightParenthesis1); NextChar end
  else if ch = '[' then
    begin Emit1(LeftBracket1); NextChar end
  else if ch = ']' then
    begin Emit1(RightBracket1); NextChar end
  else if ch = ',' then
    begin Emit1(Comma1); NextChar end
  else if ch = '.' then
    begin NextChar;
      if ch = '.' then
        begin Emit1(DoubleDot1); NextChar end
      else Emit1(Period1)
    end
  else if ch = ';' then
    begin Emit1(Semicolon1); NextChar end
  else if ch <> ETX then
    begin Emit1(Unknown1); NextChar end
end;

begin
  Initialize; BeginLine(1); NextChar;
  while ch <> ETX do NextSymbol;
  Emit1(EndText1)
end.
```

A.3 PARSER

```
*       {        PASCAL- COMPILER: PARSER
                      20 April 1984
          Copyright (c) 1984 Per Brinch Hansen }

const
  MaxLabel = 1000; MaxLevel = 10;
  Integer0 = 1; Boolean0 = 2; False0 = 3;
  True0 = 4; Read0 = 5; Write0 = 6;

type
  SymbolType = (And1, Array1, Asterisk1, Becomes1,
    Begin1, Colon1, Comma1, Const1, Div1, Do1,
    DoubleDot1, Else1, End1, EndText1, Equal1,
    Greater1, If1, LeftBracket1, LeftParenthesis1,
    Less1, Minus1, Mod1, Name1, NewLine1, Not1,
    NotEqual1, NotGreater1, NotLess1, Numeral1,
    Of1, Or1, Period1, Plus1, Procedure1, Program1,
    Record1, RightBracket1, RightParenthesis1,
    Semicolon1, Then1, Type1, Var1, While1,
    Unknown1);

  OperationPart = (Add2, And2, Assign2,
    Constant2, Divide2, Do2, EndProc2, EndProg2,
    Equal2, Field2, Goto2, Greater2, Index2,
    Less2, Minus2, Modulo2, Multiply2, Not2,
    NotEqual2, NotGreater2, NotLess2, Or2,
    ProcCall2, Procedure2, Program2, Subtract2,
    Value2, Variable2, VarParam2, Read2,
    Write2, DefAddr2, DefArg2);

  ErrorKind = (Ambiguous3, Comment3, Kind3, Numeral3,
    Range3, Syntax3, Type3, Undefined3);

procedure Read(var Value: integer);
procedure Emit(Value: integer);
procedure NewLine(LineNo: integer);
procedure Error(Kind: ErrorKind);
procedure TestLimit(Length, Maximum: integer);

program Pass2;

const
  NoName = 0;

type
  Symbols = set of SymbolType;
```

```
  Class = (Constantx, StandardType, ArrayType,
    RecordType, Field, Variable, ValueParameter,
    VarParameter, Procedur, StandardProc,
    Undefined);

  Classes = set of Class;

  Pointer = @ ObjectRecord;

  ObjectRecord =
    record
      Name: integer; Previous: Pointer;
      case Kind: Class of
        Constantx:
          (ConstValue: integer;
            ConstType: Pointer);
        ArrayType:
          (LowerBound, UpperBound: integer;
            IndexType, ElementType: Pointer);
        RecordType:
          (RecordLength: integer;
            LastField: Pointer);
        Field:
          (FieldDispl: integer;
            FieldType: Pointer);
        Variable, ValueParameter, VarParameter:
          (VarLevel, VarDispl: integer;
            VarType: Pointer);
        Procedur:
          (ProcLevel, ProcLabel: integer;
            LastParam: Pointer)
    end;

  BlockRecord =
    record
      TempLength, MaxTemp: integer;
      LastObject: Pointer
    end;

  BlockTable =
    array [0..MaxLevel] of BlockRecord;

var
  LineNo: integer; Symbol: SymbolType;
    Argument: integer;
  AddSymbols, BlockSymbols, ConstantSymbols,
    ExpressionSymbols, FactorSymbols,
    LongSymbols, MultiplySymbols,
    ParameterSymbols, RelationSymbols,
    SelectorSymbols, SignSymbols,
    SimpleExprSymbols, StatementSymbols,
```

```
    TermSymbols: Symbols;
  Block: BlockTable; BlockLevel: integer;
  Types, Variables, Procedures: Classes;
  TypeUniversal, TypeInteger,
    TypeBoolean: Pointer;
  LabelNo: integer;

                       { INPUT }

procedure NextSymbol;
begin Read(Symbol:integer);
  while Symbol = NewLine1 do
    begin
      Read(LineNo); NewLine(LineNo);
      Read(Symbol:integer)
    end;
  if Symbol in LongSymbols then
    Read(Argument)
end;

                      { OUTPUT }

procedure Emit1(Op: OperationPart);
begin Emit(ord(Op)) end;

procedure Emit2(Op: OperationPart;
  Arg: integer);
begin Emit(ord(Op)); Emit(Arg) end;

procedure Emit3(Op: OperationPart;
  Arg1, Arg2: integer);
begin
  Emit(ord(Op)); Emit(Arg1);
  Emit(Arg2)
end;

procedure Emit5(Op: OperationPart;
  Arg1, Arg2, Arg3, Arg4: integer);
begin
  Emit(ord(Op)); Emit(Arg1);
  Emit(Arg2); Emit(Arg3);
  Emit(Arg4)
end;

                  { SCOPE ANALYSIS }

procedure Search(Name, LevelNo: integer;
  var Found: Boolean; var Object: Pointer);
var More: Boolean;
begin
  More := true;
```

```
    Object := Block[LevelNo].LastObject;
    while More do
      if Object = nil Pointer then
        begin More := false; Found := false end
      else if Object@.Name = Name then
        begin More := false; Found := true end
      else
        Object := Object@.Previous
  end;

  procedure Define(Name: integer; Kind: Class;
    var Object: Pointer);
  var Found: Boolean; Other: Pointer;
  begin
    if Name <> NoName then
      begin
        Search(Name, BlockLevel, Found, Other);
        if Found then Error(Ambiguous3)
      end;
    New(Object);
    Object@.Name := Name;
    Object@.Previous :=
      Block[BlockLevel].LastObject;
    Object@.Kind := Kind;
    Block[BlockLevel].LastObject := Object
  end;

  procedure Find(Name: integer;
    var Object: Pointer);
  var More, Found: Boolean; LevelNo: integer;
  begin
    More := true; LevelNo := BlockLevel;
    while More do
      begin
        Search(Name, LevelNo, Found, Object);
        if Found or (LevelNo = 0) then More := false
        else LevelNo := LevelNo - 1
      end;
    if not Found then
      begin Error(Undefined3);
        Define(Name, Undefined, Object)
      end
  end;

  procedure NewBlock;
  var Current: BlockRecord;
  begin
    TestLimit(BlockLevel, MaxLevel);
    BlockLevel := BlockLevel + 1;
    Current.TempLength := 0;
    Current.MaxTemp := 0;
```

```
  Current.LastObject := nil Pointer;
  Block[BlockLevel] := Current
end;

procedure EndBlock;
begin BlockLevel := BlockLevel - 1 end;

procedure StandardBlock;
var Constx, Proc: Pointer;
begin
  BlockLevel := - 1;
  NewBlock;
  Define(NoName, StandardType, TypeUniversal);
  Define(Integer0, StandardType, TypeInteger);
  Define(Boolean0, StandardType, TypeBoolean);
  Define(False0, Constantx, Constx);
  Constx@.ConstValue := ord(false);
  Constx@.ConstType := TypeBoolean;
  Define(True0, Constantx, Constx);
  Constx@.ConstValue := ord(true);
  Constx@.ConstType := TypeBoolean;
  Define(Read0, StandardProc, Proc);
  Define(Write0, StandardProc, Proc)
end;

                    { TYPE ANALYSIS }

procedure CheckTypes(
  var Type1: Pointer; Type2: Pointer);
begin
  if Type1 <> Type2 then
    begin
      if (Type1 <> TypeUniversal) and
        (Type2 <> TypeUniversal) then
          Error(Type3);
      Type1 := TypeUniversal
    end
end;

procedure TypeError(var Typex: Pointer);
begin
  if Typex <> TypeUniversal then
    begin Error(Type3);
      Typex := TypeUniversal
    end
end;

procedure KindError(Object: Pointer);
begin
  if Object@.Kind <> Undefined then
    Error(Kind3)
```

```
end;

                    { VARIABLE ADDRESSING }

function TypeLength(Typex: Pointer): integer;
begin
  if Typex@.Kind = StandardType then
    TypeLength := 1
  else if Typex@.Kind = ArrayType then
    Typelength :=
      (Typex@.UpperBound - Typex@.LowerBound + 1)
        * TypeLength(Typex@.ElementType)
  else { Typex@.Kind = RecordType }
    TypeLength := Typex@.RecordLength
end;

procedure FieldAddressing(
  RecordLength: integer; LastField: Pointer);
var Displ: integer;
begin
  Displ := RecordLength;
  while Displ > 0 do
    begin
      Displ := Displ -
        TypeLength(LastField@.FieldType);
      LastField@.FieldDispl := Displ;
      LastField := LastField@.Previous
    end
end;

procedure VariableAddressing(
  VarLength: integer; LastVar: Pointer);
var Displ: integer;
begin
  Displ := 3 + VarLength;
  while Displ > 3 do
    begin
      Displ := Displ -
        TypeLength(LastVar@.VarType);
      LastVar@.VarLevel := BlockLevel;
      LastVar@.VarDispl := Displ;
      LastVar := LastVar@.Previous
    end
end;

procedure ParameterAddressing(
  ParamLength: integer; LastParam: Pointer);
var Displ: integer;
begin
  Displ := 0;
  while Displ > - ParamLength do
```

```
    begin
      if LastParam@.Kind = VarParameter then
        Displ := Displ - 1
      else {LastParam@.Kind = ValueParameter}
        Displ := Displ -
          TypeLength(LastParam@.VarType);
      LastParam@.VarLevel := BlockLevel;
      LastParam@.VarDispl := Displ;
      LastParam := LastParam@.Previous
    end
end;

                    { LABELS }

procedure NewLabel(var No: integer);
begin
  TestLimit(LabelNo, MaxLabel);
  LabelNo := LabelNo + 1;
  No := LabelNo
end;

                  { TEMPORARIES }

procedure Push(Length: integer);
begin
  Block[BlockLevel].TempLength :=
    Block[BlockLevel].TempLength + Length;
  if Block[BlockLevel].MaxTemp <
    Block[BlockLevel].TempLength then
      Block[BlockLevel].MaxTemp :=
        Block[BlockLevel].TempLength
end;

procedure Pop(Length: integer);
begin
  Block[BlockLevel].TempLength :=
    Block[BlockLevel].TempLength - Length
end;

                { INITIALIZATION }

procedure Initialize;
begin
  AddSymbols := Symbols[Minus1, Or1, Plus1];
  BlockSymbols := Symbols[Begin1, Const1,
    Procedure1, Type1, Var1];
  ConstantSymbols := Symbols[Name1, Numeral1];
  ExpressionSymbols := Symbols[LeftParenthesis1,
    Minus1, Name1, Not1, Numeral1, Plus1];
  FactorSymbols := Symbols[LeftParenthesis1,
    Name1, Not1, Numeral1];
```

```
  LongSymbols := Symbols[Name1, Numeral1];
  MultiplySymbols :=
    Symbols[And1, Asterisk1, Div1, Mod1];
  ParameterSymbols := Symbols[Name1, Var1];
  RelationSymbols := Symbols[Equal1, Greater1,
    Less1, NotEqual1, NotGreater1, NotLess1];
  SelectorSymbols :=
    Symbols[LeftBracket1, Period1];
  SignSymbols := Symbols[Minus1, Plus1];
  StatementSymbols := Symbols[Begin1, If1,
    Name1, While1];
  TermSymbols := FactorSymbols;
  SimpleExprSymbols := SignSymbols + TermSymbols;
  Types := Classes[StandardType, ArrayType,
    RecordType];
  Variables := Classes[Variable, ValueParameter,
    VarParameter];
  Procedures := Classes[Procedur, StandardProc];
  LabelNo := 0
end;

                    { SYNTAX ANALYSIS }

procedure SyntaxError(Stop: Symbols);
begin Error(Syntax3);
  while not (Symbol in Stop) do
    NextSymbol
end;

procedure SyntaxCheck(Stop: Symbols);
begin
  if not (Symbol in Stop) then
    SyntaxError(Stop)
end;

procedure Expect(s: SymbolType; Stop: Symbols);
begin
  if Symbol = s then NextSymbol
  else SyntaxError(Stop);
  SyntaxCheck(Stop)
end;

procedure ExpectName(var Name: integer;
  Stop: Symbols);
begin
  if Symbol = Name1 then
    begin Name := Argument; NextSymbol end
  else
    begin Name := NoName; SyntaxError(Stop) end;
  SyntaxCheck(Stop)
end;
```

```
{ TypeName = Name . }

procedure TypeName(var Typex: Pointer;
  Stop: Symbols);
var Object: Pointer;
begin
  if Symbol = Name1 then
    begin
      Find(Argument, Object);
      if Object@.Kind in Types then
        Typex := Object
      else
        begin KindError(Object);
          Typex := TypeUniversal
        end
    end
  else Typex := TypeUniversal;
  Expect(Name1, Stop)
end;

{ Constant = Numeral | ConstantName . }

procedure Constant(var Value: integer;
  var Typex: Pointer; Stop: Symbols);
var Object: Pointer;
begin
  if Symbol = Numeral1 then
    begin
      Value := Argument;
      Typex := TypeInteger;
      Expect(Numeral1, Stop)
    end
  else if Symbol = Name1 then
    begin
      Find(Argument, Object);
      if Object@.Kind = Constantx then
        begin
          Value := Object@.ConstValue;
          Typex := Object@.ConstType
        end
      else
        begin KindError(Object);
          Value := 0;
          Typex := TypeUniversal
        end;
      Expect(Name1, Stop)
    end
  else
    begin SyntaxError(Stop);
      Value := 0;
```

```
      Typex := TypeUniversal
    end
end;

{ ConstantDefinition =
    ConstantName "=" Constant ";" . }

procedure ConstantDefinition(Stop: Symbols);
var Name, Value: integer;
  Constx, Typex: Pointer;
begin
  ExpectName(Name, Symbols[Equal1, Semicolon1]
    + ConstantSymbols + Stop);
  Expect(Equal1, ConstantSymbols
    + Symbols[Semicolon1] + Stop);
  Constant(Value, Typex, Symbols[Semicolon1]
    + Stop);
  Define(Name, Constantx, Constx);
  Constx@.ConstValue := Value;
  Constx@.ConstType := Typex;
  Expect(Semicolon1, Stop)
end;

{ ConstantDefinitionPart =
    "const" ConstantDefinition
      { ConstantDefinition } . }

procedure ConstantDefinitionPart(Stop: Symbols);
var Stop2: Symbols;
begin
  Stop2 := Symbols[Name1] + Stop;
  Expect(Const1, Stop2);
  ConstantDefinition(Stop2);
  while Symbol = Name1 do
    ConstantDefinition(Stop2)
end;

{ NewArrayType =
    "array" "[" IndexRange "]" "of" TypeName .
  IndexRange = Constant ".." Constant . }

procedure NewArrayType(Name: integer;
  Stop: Symbols);
var NewType, LowerType, UpperType,
  ElementType: Pointer;
  LowerBound, UpperBound: integer;
begin
  Expect(Array1, Symbols[LeftBracket1,
    RightBracket1, Of1, Name1]
      + ConstantSymbols + Stop);
  Expect(LeftBracket1, Symbols[RightBracket1,
```

```
    Of1, Name1] + ConstantSymbols + Stop);
  Constant(LowerBound, LowerType,
    Symbols[DoubleDot1, RightBracket1, Of1,
      Name1] + ConstantSymbols + Stop);
  Expect(DoubleDot1, Symbols[RightBracket1,
    Of1, Name1] + ConstantSymbols + Stop);
  Constant(UpperBound, UpperType,
    Symbols[RightBracket1, Of1, Name1] + Stop);
  CheckTypes(LowerType, UpperType);
  if LowerBound > UpperBound then
    begin Error(Range3);
      LowerBound := UpperBound
    end;
  Expect(RightBracket1, Symbols[Of1, Name1]
    + Stop);
  Expect(Of1, Symbols[Name1] + Stop);
  TypeName(ElementType, Stop);
  Define(Name, ArrayType, NewType);
  NewType@.LowerBound := LowerBound;
  NewType@.UpperBound := UpperBound;
  NewType@.IndexType := LowerType;
  NewType@.ElementType := ElementType
end;

{ RecordSection = FieldName SectionTail .
  SectionTail =
    "," RecordSection ¦ ":" TypeName . }

procedure RecordSection(
  var Number: integer;
  var LastField, Typex: Pointer;
  Stop: Symbols);
var Name: integer; Fieldx: Pointer;
begin
  ExpectName(Name, Symbols[Comma1, Colon1]
    + Stop);
  Define(Name, Field, Fieldx);
  if Symbol = Comma1 then
    begin
      Expect(Comma1, Symbols[Name1] + Stop);
      RecordSection(Number, LastField,
        Typex, Stop);
      Number := Number + 1
    end
  else
    begin
      Expect(Colon1, Symbols[Name1] + Stop);
      TypeName(Typex, Stop);
      LastField := Fieldx;
      Number := 1
    end;
```

```
  Fieldx@.FieldType := Typex
end;

{ FieldList =
    RecordSection { ";" RecordSection } . }

procedure FieldList(var LastField: Pointer;
  var Length: integer; Stop: Symbols);
var Stop2: Symbols; Number: integer;
  Typex: Pointer;
begin
  Stop2 := Symbols[Semicolon1] + Stop;
  RecordSection(Number, LastField,
    Typex, Stop2);
  Length := Number * TypeLength(Typex);
  while Symbol = Semicolon1 do
    begin
      Expect(Semicolon1, Symbols[Name1] + Stop2);
      RecordSection(Number, LastField,
        Typex, Stop2);
      Length :=
        Length + Number * TypeLength(Typex)
    end;
  FieldAddressing(Length, LastField)
end;

{ NewRecordType = "record" FieldList "end" . }

procedure NewRecordType(Name: integer;
  Stop: Symbols);
var NewType, LastField: Pointer;
  Length: integer;
begin
  NewBlock;
  Expect(Record1, Symbols[Name1, End1] + Stop);
  FieldList(LastField, Length,
    Symbols[End1] + Stop);
  Expect(End1, Stop);
  EndBlock;
  Define(Name, RecordType, NewType);
  NewType@.RecordLength := Length;
  NewType@.LastField := LastField
end;

{ TypeDefinition = TypeName "=" NewType ";" .
  NewType = NewArrayType | NewRecordType . }

procedure TypeDefinition(Stop: Symbols);
var Stop2: Symbols; Name: integer; Object: Pointer;
begin
  Stop2 := Symbols[Semicolon1] + Stop;
```

```
  ExpectName(Name, Symbols[Equal1, Array1,
    Record1] + Stop2);
  Expect(Equal1, Symbols[Array1, Record1]
    + Stop2);
  if Symbol = Array1 then
    NewArrayType(Name, Stop2)
  else if Symbol = Record1 then
    NewRecordType(Name, Stop2)
  else
    begin
      Define(Name, Undefined, Object);
      SyntaxError(Stop2);
    end;
  Expect(Semicolon1, Stop)
end;

{ TypeDefinitionPart = "type" TypeDefinition
    { TypeDefinition } . }

procedure TypeDefinitionPart(Stop: Symbols);
var Stop2: Symbols;
begin
  Stop2 := Symbols[Name1] + Stop;
  Expect(Type1, Stop2);
  TypeDefinition(Stop2);
  while Symbol = Name1 do
    TypeDefinition(Stop2)
end;

{ VariableGroup = VariableName GroupTail .
  GroupTail =
    "," VariableGroup | ":" TypeName . }

procedure VariableGroup(
  Kind: Class; var Number: integer;
  var LastVar, Typex: Pointer;
  Stop: Symbols);
var Name: integer; Varx: Pointer;
begin
  ExpectName(Name, Symbols[Comma1, Colon1]
    + Stop);
  Define(Name, Kind, Varx);
  if Symbol = Comma1 then
    begin
      Expect(Comma1, Symbols[Name1] + Stop);
      VariableGroup(Kind, Number, LastVar,
        Typex, Stop);
      Number := Number + 1
    end
  else
    begin
```

```
      Expect(Colon1, Symbols[Name1] + Stop);
      TypeName(Typex, Stop);
      LastVar := Varx;
      Number := 1
    end;
  Varx@.VarType := Typex
end;

{ VariableDefinition = VariableGroup ";" . }

procedure VariableDefinition(
  var LastVar: Pointer; var Length: integer;
  Stop: Symbols);
var Number: integer; Typex: Pointer;
begin
  VariableGroup(Variable, Number, LastVar,
    Typex, Symbols[Semicolon1] + Stop);
  Length := Number * TypeLength(Typex);
  Expect(Semicolon1, Stop)
end;

{VariableDefinitionPart = "var" VariableDefinition
  { VariableDefinition } . }

procedure VariableDefinitionPart(
  var Length: integer; Stop: Symbols);
var Stop2: Symbols; LastVar: Pointer;
  More: integer;
begin
  Stop2 := Symbols[Name1] + Stop;
  Expect(Var1, Stop2);
  VariableDefinition(LastVar, Length, Stop2);
  while Symbol = Name1 do
    begin
      VariableDefinition(LastVar, More, Stop2);
      Length := Length + More
    end;
  VariableAddressing(Length, LastVar)
end;

{ ParameterDefinition =
    [ "var" ] VariableGroup . }

procedure ParameterDefinition(
  var LastParam: Pointer; var Length: integer;
  Stop: Symbols);
var Number: integer; Typex: Pointer;
begin
  SyntaxCheck(Symbols[Var1, Name1] + Stop);
  if Symbol = Var1 then
    begin
```

```
      Expect(Var1, Symbols[Name1] + Stop);
      VariableGroup(VarParameter, Length,
        Lastparam, Typex, Stop)
    end
  else
    begin
      VariableGroup(ValueParameter, Number,
        LastParam, Typex, Stop);
      Length := Number * TypeLength(Typex)
    end
end;

{ FormalParameterList = ParameterDefinition
    { ";" ParameterDefinition } . }

procedure FormalParameterList(
  var LastParam: Pointer; var Length: integer;
  Stop: Symbols);
var Stop2: Symbols; More: integer;
begin
  Stop2 := Symbols[Semicolon1] + Stop;
  ParameterDefinition(LastParam,
    Length, Stop2);
  while Symbol = Semicolon1 do
    begin
      Expect(Semicolon1,
        ParameterSymbols + Stop2);
      ParameterDefinition(LastParam,
        More, Stop2);
      Length := Length + More
    end;
  ParameterAddressing(Length, LastParam);
end;

{ ProcedureDefinition =
    "procedure" ProcedureName ProcedureBlock  ";" .
  ProcedureBlock = [ "(" FormalParameterList ")" ]
    ";" BlockBody . }

procedure BlockBody(BeginLabel, VarLabel,
  Templabel: integer; Stop: Symbols); forward;

procedure ProcedureDefinition(Stop: Symbols);
var Name: integer; Proc: Pointer;
  ProcLabel, ParamLength, VarLabel,
  TempLabel, BeginLabel: integer;
begin
  Expect(Procedure1, Symbols[Name1,
    LeftParenthesis1, Semicolon1]
      + BlockSymbols + Stop);
  ExpectName(Name, Symbols[LeftParenthesis1,
```

```
    Semicolon1] + BlockSymbols + Stop);
  Define(Name, Procedur, Proc);
  Proc@.ProcLevel := BlockLevel;
  NewLabel(Proc@.ProcLabel);
  NewBlock;
  if Symbol = LeftParenthesis1 then
    begin
      Expect(LeftParenthesis1, ParameterSymbols +
        Symbols[RightParenthesis1, Semicolon1] +
          BlockSymbols + Stop);
      FormalParameterList(Proc@.LastParam,
        ParamLength, Symbols[RightParenthesis1,
          SemiColon1] + BlockSymbols + Stop);
      Expect(RightParenthesis1, Symbols[Semicolon1]
        + BlockSymbols + Stop)
    end
  else {no parameter list}
    begin
      Proc@.LastParam := nil Pointer;
      ParamLength := 0
    end;
  NewLabel(VarLabel);
  NewLabel(TempLabel);
  NewLabel(BeginLabel);
  Emit2(DefAddr2, Proc@.ProcLabel);
  Emit5(Procedure2, VarLabel, TempLabel,
    BeginLabel, LineNo);
  Expect(Semicolon1, Symbols[Semicolon1]
    + BlockSymbols + Stop);
  BlockBody(BeginLabel, VarLabel, TempLabel,
    Symbols[Semicolon1] + Stop);
  Expect(Semicolon1, Stop);
  Emit2(EndProc2, ParamLength);
  EndBlock
end;

{ IndexedSelector = "[" Expression "]" . }

procedure Expression(var Typex: Pointer;
  Stop: Symbols); forward;

procedure IndexedSelector(var Typex: Pointer;
  Stop: Symbols);
var ExprType: Pointer;
begin
  Expect(LeftBracket1, ExpressionSymbols
    + Symbols[RightBracket1] + Stop);
  Expression(ExprType, Symbols[RightBracket1]
    + Stop);
  if Typex@.Kind = ArrayType then
    begin
```

```
        CheckTypes(ExprType, Typex@.IndexType);
        Emit5(Index2, Typex@.LowerBound,
          Typex@.UpperBound,
          TypeLength(Typex@.ElementType),
          LineNo);
        Pop(1);
        Typex := Typex@.ElementType
      end
    else
      begin KindError(Typex);
        Typex := TypeUniversal
      end;
    Expect(RightBracket1, Stop)
  end;

  { FieldSelector = "." FieldName . }

  procedure FieldSelector(var Typex: Pointer;
    Stop: Symbols);
  var Found: Boolean; Fieldx: Pointer;
  begin
    Expect(Period1, Symbols[Name1] + Stop);
    if Symbol = Name1 then
      begin
        if Typex@.Kind = RecordType then
          begin
            Found := false;
            Fieldx := Typex@.LastField;
            while not Found and
              (Fieldx <> nil Pointer) do
                if Fieldx@.Name <> Argument then
                  Fieldx := Fieldx@.Previous
                else Found := true;
            if Found then
              begin
                Typex := Fieldx@.FieldType;
                Emit2(Field2, Fieldx@.FieldDispl)
              end
            else
              begin Error(Undefined3);
                Typex := TypeUniversal
              end
          end
        else
          begin KindError(Typex);
            Typex := TypeUniversal
          end;
        Expect(Name1, Stop)
      end
    else
      begin SyntaxError(Stop);
```

```
      Typex := TypeUniversal
    end
end;

{ VariableAccess = VariableName { Selector } .
  Selector = IndexedSelector | FieldSelector . }

procedure VariableAccess(var Typex: Pointer;
  Stop: Symbols);
var Stop2: Symbols; Object: Pointer;
  Level, Displ: integer;
begin
  if Symbol = Name1 then
    begin
      Stop2 := SelectorSymbols + Stop;
      Find(Argument, Object);
      Expect(Name1, Stop2);
      if Object@.Kind in Variables then
        begin
          Typex := Object@.VarType;
          Level := BlockLevel - Object@.VarLevel;
          Displ := Object@.VarDispl;
          if Object@.Kind = VarParameter then
            Emit3(VarParam2, Level, Displ)
          else
            Emit3(Variable2, Level, Displ);
          Push(1)
        end
      else
        begin KindError(Object);
          Typex := TypeUniversal
        end;
      while Symbol in SelectorSymbols do
        if Symbol = LeftBracket1 then
          IndexedSelector(Typex, Stop2)
        else {Symbol = Period1}
          FieldSelector(Typex, Stop2)
    end
  else
    begin SyntaxError(Stop);
      Typex := TypeUniversal
    end
end;

{ Factor = Constant | VariableAccess |
    "(" Expression ")" | "not" Factor . }

procedure Factor(var Typex: Pointer;
  Stop: Symbols);
var Object: Pointer; Value, Length: integer;
begin
```

```
  if Symbol = Numeral1 then
    begin
      Constant(Value, Typex, Stop);
      Emit2(Constant2, Value);
      Push(1)
    end
  else if Symbol = Name1 then
    begin
      Find(Argument, Object);
      if Object@.Kind = Constantx then
        begin
          Constant(Value, Typex, Stop);
          Emit2(Constant2, Value);
          Push(1)
        end
      else if Object@.Kind in Variables then
        begin
          VariableAccess(Typex, Stop);
          Length := TypeLength(Typex);
          Emit2(Value2, Length);
          Push(Length - 1)
        end
      else
        begin KindError(Object);
          Typex := TypeUniversal;
          Expect(Name1, Stop)
        end
    end
  else if Symbol = LeftParenthesis1 then
    begin
      Expect(LeftParenthesis1, ExpressionSymbols
        + Symbols[RightParenthesis1] + Stop);
      Expression(Typex, Symbols[RightParenthesis1]
        + Stop);
      Expect(RightParenthesis1, Stop)
    end
  else if Symbol = Not1 then
    begin
      Expect(Not1, FactorSymbols + Stop);
      Factor(Typex, Stop);
      CheckTypes(Typex, TypeBoolean);
      Emit1(Not2)
    end
  else
    begin SyntaxError(Stop);
      Typex := TypeUniversal
    end
end;

{ Term = Factor { MultiplyingOperator Factor } .
  MultiplyingOperator =
```

```
    "*" | "div" | "mod" | "and" . }

procedure Term(var Typex: Pointer;
  Stop: Symbols);
var Stop2: Symbols; Operator: SymbolType;
  Type2: Pointer;
begin
  Stop2 := MultiplySymbols + Stop;
  Factor(Typex, Stop2);
  while Symbol in MultiplySymbols do
    begin
      Operator := Symbol;
      Expect(Symbol, FactorSymbols + Stop2);
      Factor(Type2, Stop2);
      if Typex = TypeInteger then
        begin
          CheckTypes(Typex, Type2);
          if Operator = Asterisk1 then
            Emit1(Multiply2)
          else if Operator = Div1 then
            Emit1(Divide2)
          else if Operator = Mod1 then
            Emit1(Modulo2)
          else { Operator = And1 }
            TypeError(Typex);
          Pop(1)
        end
      else if Typex = TypeBoolean then
        begin
          CheckTypes(Typex, Type2);
          if Operator = And1 then
            Emit1(And2)
          else { Arithmetic Operator }
            TypeError(Typex);
          Pop(1)
        end
      else TypeError(Typex)
    end
end;

{ SimpleExpression =
    [ SignOperator ] Term { AddingOperator Term } .
  SignOperator = "+" | "-" .
  AddingOperator = "+" | "-" | "or" . }

procedure SimpleExpression(var Typex: Pointer;
  Stop: Symbols);
var Stop2: Symbols; Operator: SymbolType;
  Type2: Pointer;
begin
  Stop2 := AddSymbols + Stop;
```

```
  SyntaxCheck(SignSymbols + TermSymbols + Stop2);
  if Symbol in SignSymbols then
    begin
      Operator := Symbol;
      Expect(Symbol, TermSymbols + Stop2);
      Term(Typex, Stop2);
      CheckTypes(Typex, TypeInteger);
      if Operator = Minus1 then Emit1(Minus2)
    end
  else Term(Typex, Stop2);
  while Symbol in AddSymbols do
    begin
      Operator := Symbol;
      Expect(Symbol, TermSymbols + Stop2);
      Term(Type2, Stop2);
      if Typex = TypeInteger then
        begin
          CheckTypes(Typex, Type2);
          if Operator = Plus1 then
            Emit1(Add2)
          else if Operator = Minus1 then
            Emit1(Subtract2)
          else { Operator = Or1 }
            TypeError(Typex);
          Pop(1)
        end
      else if Typex = TypeBoolean then
        begin
          CheckTypes(Typex, Type2);
          if Operator = Or1 then
            Emit1(Or2)
          else { Arithmetic Operator }
            TypeError(Typex);
          Pop(1)
        end
      else TypeError(Typex)
    end
end;

{ Expression = SimpleExpression
    [ RelationalOperator SimpleExpression ] .
  RelationalOperator = "<" | "=" | ">" |
    "<=" | "<>" | ">=" . }

procedure Expression(var Typex: Pointer;
  Stop: Symbols);
var Operator: SymbolType; Type2: Pointer;
begin
  SimpleExpression(Typex, RelationSymbols
    + Stop);
  if Symbol in RelationSymbols then
```

```
    begin
      Operator := Symbol;
      Expect(Symbol, SimpleExprSymbols + Stop);
      SimpleExpression(Type2, Stop);
      if Typex@.Kind = StandardType then
        begin
          CheckTypes(Typex, Type2);
          if Operator = Less1 then
            Emit1(Less2)
          else if Operator = Equal1 then
            Emit1(Equal2)
          else if Operator = Greater1 then
            Emit1(Greater2)
          else if Operator = NotGreater1 then
            Emit1(NotGreater2)
          else if Operator = NotEqual1 then
            Emit1(NotEqual2)
          else { Operator = NotLess1 }
            Emit1(NotLess2);
          Pop(1)
        end
      else TypeError(Typex);
      Typex := TypeBoolean
    end
end;

{ IOStatement =
    "Read" "(" VariableAccess ")" |
    "Write" "(" Expression ")" . }

procedure IOStatement(Stop: Symbols);
var Stop2: Symbols; Name: integer;
  Typex: Pointer;
begin
  {Symbol = (Standard Procedure) Name1}
  Stop2 := Symbols[RightParenthesis1] + Stop;
  Name := Argument;
  Expect(Name1, ExpressionSymbols + Stop2);
  Expect(LeftParenthesis1, ExpressionSymbols
    + Stop2);
  if Name = Read0 then
    begin
      VariableAccess(Typex, Stop2);
      Emit1(Read2)
    end
  else {Name = Write0}
    begin
      Expression(Typex, Stop2);
      Emit1(Write2)
    end;
  Pop(1);
```

```
  CheckTypes(Typex, TypeInteger);
  Expect(RightParenthesis1, Stop)
end;

{ ActualParameterList =
    [ ActualParameterList "," ] ActualParameter .
  ActualParameter =
    Expression | VariableAccess . }

procedure ActualParameterList(
  LastParam: Pointer; var Length: integer;
  Stop: Symbols);
var Typex: Pointer; More: integer;
begin {LastParam <> nil Pointer}
  if LastParam@.Previous <> nil Pointer then
    begin
      ActualParameterList(LastParam@.Previous, More,
        Symbols[Comma1] + ExpressionSymbols + Stop);
      Expect(Comma1, ExpressionSymbols + Stop)
    end
  else More := 0;
  if LastParam@.Kind = ValueParameter then
    begin
      Expression(Typex, Stop);
      Length := TypeLength(Typex) + More
    end
  else {LastParam@.Kind = VarParameter}
    begin
      VariableAccess(Typex, Stop);
      Length := 1 + More
    end;
  CheckTypes(Typex, LastParam@.VarType)
end;

{ ProcedureStatement = IOStatement |
    ProcedureName
      [ "(" ActualParameterList ")" ] . }

procedure ProcedureStatement(Stop: Symbols);
var Stop2: Symbols; Proc: Pointer;
  ParamLength: integer;
begin {Symbol = (Procedure) Name1}
  Find(Argument, Proc);
  if Proc@.Kind = StandardProc then
    IOStatement(Stop)
  else
    begin
      if Proc@.LastParam <> nil Pointer then
        begin
          Stop2 := Symbols[RightParenthesis1]
            + Stop;
```

```
          Expect(Name1, Symbols[LeftParenthesis1]
            + ExpressionSymbols + Stop2);
          Expect(LeftParenthesis1,
            ExpressionSymbols + Stop2);
          ActualParameterList(Proc@.LastParam,
            ParamLength, Stop2);
          Expect(RightParenthesis1, Stop)
        end
      else {no parameter list}
        begin
          Expect(Name1, Stop);
          ParamLength := 0
        end;
      Emit3(ProcCall2,
        BlockLevel - Proc@.ProcLevel,
        Proc@.ProcLabel);
      Push(3); Pop(ParamLength + 3)
    end
end;

{ AssignmentStatement =
    VariableAccess ":=" Expression . }

procedure AssignmentStatement(Stop: Symbols);
var VarType, ExprType: Pointer;
  Length: integer;
begin
  VariableAccess(VarType, Symbols[Becomes1]
    + ExpressionSymbols + Stop);
  Expect(Becomes1, ExpressionSymbols + Stop);
  Expression(ExprType, Stop);
  CheckTypes(VarType, ExprType);
  Length := TypeLength(ExprType);
  Emit2(Assign2, Length);
  Pop(1 + Length)
end;

{ IfStatement = "if" Expression "then" Statement
    [ "else" Statement ] . }

procedure Statement(Stop: Symbols); forward;

procedure IfStatement(Stop: Symbols);
var ExprType: Pointer; Label1, Label2: integer;
begin
  Expect(If1, ExpressionSymbols +
    Symbols[Then1, Else1] +
    StatementSymbols + Stop);
  Expression(ExprType, Symbols[Then1, Else1]
    + StatementSymbols + Stop);
  CheckTypes(ExprType, TypeBoolean);
```

```
  Expect(Then1, StatementSymbols
    + Symbols[Else1] + Stop);
  NewLabel(Label1);
  Emit2(Do2, Label1);
  Pop(1);
  Statement(Symbols[Else1] + Stop);
  if Symbol = Else1 then
    begin
      Expect(Else1, StatementSymbols + Stop);
      NewLabel(Label2);
      Emit2(Goto2, Label2);
      Emit2(DefAddr2, Label1);
      Statement(Stop);
      Emit2(DefAddr2, Label2)
    end
  else Emit2(DefAddr2, Label1)
end;

{ WhileStatement =
    "while" Expression "do" Statement . }

procedure WhileStatement(Stop: Symbols);
var Label1, Label2: integer;
  ExprType: Pointer;
begin
  NewLabel(Label1);
  Emit2(DefAddr2, Label1);
  Expect(While1, ExpressionSymbols +
    Symbols[Do1] + StatementSymbols +
    Stop);
  Expression(ExprType, Symbols[Do1]
    + StatementSymbols + Stop);
  CheckTypes(ExprType, TypeBoolean);
  Expect(Do1, StatementSymbols + Stop);
  NewLabel(Label2);
  Emit2(Do2, Label2);
  Pop(1);
  Statement(Stop);
  Emit2(Goto2, Label1);
  Emit2(DefAddr2, Label2)
end;

{ Statement =
    AssignmentStatement | ProcedureStatement |
    IfStatement | WhileStatement |
    CompoundStatement | Empty . }

procedure CompoundStatement(Stop: Symbols);
  forward;

procedure Statement{Stop: Symbols};
```

```
var Object: Pointer;
begin
  if Symbol = Name1 then
    begin
      Find(Argument, Object);
      if Object@.Kind in Variables then
        AssignmentStatement(Stop)
      else if Object@.Kind in Procedures then
        ProcedureStatement(Stop)
      else
        begin KindError(Object);
          Expect(Name1, Stop)
        end
    end
  else if Symbol = If1 then
    IfStatement(Stop)
  else if Symbol = While1 then
    WhileStatement(Stop)
  else if Symbol = Begin1 then
    CompoundStatement(Stop)
  else {Empty}
    SyntaxCheck(Stop)
end;

{ CompoundStatement =
    "begin" Statement { ";" Statement } "end" . }

procedure CompoundStatement{Stop: Symbols};
begin
  Expect(Begin1, StatementSymbols +
    Symbols[Semicolon1, End1] + Stop);
  Statement(Symbols[Semicolon1, End1]
    + Stop);
  while Symbol = Semicolon1 do
    begin
      Expect(Semicolon1, StatementSymbols +
        Symbols[Semicolon1, End1] + Stop);
      Statement(Symbols[Semicolon1, End1] +
        Stop)
    end;
  Expect(End1, Stop)
end;

{ BlockBody =
    [ ConstantDefinitionPart ] [ TypeDefinitionPart ]
    [ VariableDefinitionPart ] { ProcedureDefinition }
    CompoundStatement . }

procedure BlockBody(BeginLabel, VarLabel,
  TempLabel: integer; Stop: Symbols);
var VarLength: integer;
```

```
begin
  SyntaxCheck(BlockSymbols + Stop);
  if Symbol = Const1 then
    ConstantDefinitionPart(Symbols[Type1, Var1,
      Procedure1, Begin1] + Stop);
  if Symbol = Type1 then
    TypeDefinitionPart(Symbols[Var1, Procedure1,
      Begin1] + Stop);
  if Symbol = Var1 then
    VariableDefinitionPart(VarLength,
      Symbols[Procedure1, Begin1] + Stop)
  else VarLength := 0;
  while Symbol = Procedure1 do
    ProcedureDefinition(Symbols[Procedure1,
      Begin1] + Stop);
  Emit2(DefAddr2, BeginLabel);
  CompoundStatement(Stop);
  Emit3(DefArg2, VarLabel, VarLength);
  Emit3(DefArg2, TempLabel,
    Block[BlockLevel].MaxTemp)
end;

{ Program =
    "program" ProgramName ";" BlockBody "." . }

procedure Programx(Stop: Symbols);
var VarLabel, TempLabel, BeginLabel: integer;
begin
  Expect(Program1, Symbols[Name1, Semicolon1,
    Period1] + BlockSymbols + Stop);
  Expect(Name1, Symbols[Semicolon1, Period1]
    + BlockSymbols + Stop);
  NewLabel(VarLabel);
  NewLabel(TempLabel);
  NewLabel(BeginLabel);
  Emit5(Program2, VarLabel, TempLabel,
    BeginLabel, LineNo);
  Expect(Semicolon1, Symbols[Period1]
    + BlockSymbols + Stop);
  NewBlock;
  BlockBody(BeginLabel, VarLabel, TempLabel,
    Symbols[Period1] + Stop);
  Emit1(EndProg2);
  EndBlock;
  Expect(Period1, Stop)
end;

begin Initialize; NextSymbol;
  StandardBlock;
  Programx(Symbols[EndText1])
end.
```

A.4 ASSEMBLER

```
*         {      PASCAL- COMPILER: ASSEMBLER
                       20 April 1984
             Copyright (c) 1984 Per Brinch Hansen }

const MaxLabel = 1000;

type
  OperationPart = (Add2, And2, Assign2,
    Constant2, Divide2, Do2, EndProc2, EndProg2,
    Equal2, Field2, Goto2, Greater2, Index2,
    Less2, Minus2, Modulo2, Multiply2, Not2,
    NotEqual2, NotGreater2, NotLess2, Or2,
    ProcCall2, Procedure2, Program2, Subtract2,
    Value2, Variable2, VarParam2, Read2,
    Write2, DefAddr2, DefArg2, GlobalCall2,
    GlobalValue2, GlobalVar2, LocalValue2,
    LocalVar2, SimpleAssign2, SimpleValue2);

procedure Read(var Value: integer);
procedure Emit(Value: integer);
procedure Rerun;

program Pass3;

type
  Operations = set of OperationPart;

  AssemblyTable = array [1..MaxLabel] of integer;

var
  NoArguments, OneArgument,
    TwoArguments, FourArguments,
    Blocks, Jumps: Operations;
  Op: OperationPart;
  Arg1, Arg2, Arg3, Arg4: integer;
  Address: integer;
  Table: AssemblyTable;

procedure NextInstruction;
begin
  Read(Op:integer);
  if Op in NoArguments then { skip }
  else if Op in OneArgument then
    Read(Arg1)
  else if Op in TwoArguments then
    begin Read(Arg1); Read(Arg2) end
  else {Op in FourArguments}
```

```
    begin
      Read(Arg1); Read(Arg2);
      Read(Arg3); Read(Arg4)
    end
end;

procedure Emit1(Op: Operationpart);
begin
  Emit(ord(Op));
  Address := Address + 1
end;

procedure Emit2(Op: OperationPart;
  Arg: integer);
begin
  Emit(ord(Op)); Emit(Arg);
  Address := Address + 2
end;

procedure Emit3(Op: OperationPart;
  Arg1, Arg2: integer);
begin
  Emit(ord(Op)); Emit(Arg1); Emit(Arg2);
  Address := Address + 3
end;

procedure Emit5(Op: OperationPart;
  Arg1, Arg2, Arg3, Arg4: integer);
begin
  Emit(ord(op)); Emit(Arg1); Emit(Arg2);
  Emit(Arg3); Emit(Arg4);
  Address := Address + 5
end;

function Optimize(SpecialCase: Boolean): Boolean;
begin Optimize := SpecialCase end;

function JumpDispl(LabelNo: integer): integer;
begin JumpDispl := Table[LabelNo] - Address end;

procedure Assign(Length: integer);
begin
  if Optimize(Length = 1) then
    Emit1(SimpleAssign2)
  else
    Emit2(Assign2, Length);
  NextInstruction
end;

procedure Block(Op: OperationPart;
  VarLabel, TempLabel, BeginLabel,
```

```
  LineNo: integer);
begin
  {Op in Operations[Procedure2, Program2]}
  Emit5(Op, Table[VarLabel], Table[TempLabel],
    JumpDispl(BeginLabel), LineNo);
  NextInstruction
end;

procedure DefAddr(LabelNo: integer);
begin
  Table[LabelNo] := Address;
  NextInstruction
end;

procedure DefArg(LabelNo, Value: integer);
begin
  Table[LabelNo] := Value;
  NextInstruction
end;

procedure Field(Displ: integer);
begin
  if Optimize(Displ = 0) then { Empty }
  else Emit2(Field2, Displ);
  NextInstruction
end;

procedure Jump(Op: OperationPart;
  LabelNo: integer);
begin
  {Op in Operations[Do2, Goto2]}
  Emit2(Op, JumpDispl(LabelNo));
  NextInstruction
end;

procedure ProcCall(Level, LabelNo: integer);
var Displ: integer;
begin
  Displ := JumpDispl(LabelNo);
  if Optimize(Level = 1) then
    Emit2(GlobalCall2, Displ)
  else
    Emit3(ProcCall2, Level, Displ);
  NextInstruction
end;

procedure Value(Length: integer);
begin
  if Optimize(Length = 1) then
    Emit1(SimpleValue2)
  else
```

```
    Emit2(Value2, Length);
  NextInstruction
end;

procedure Variable(Level, Displ: integer);
begin
  NextInstruction;
  while Optimize(Op = Field2) do
    begin
      Displ := Displ + Arg1;
      NextInstruction
    end;
  if Optimize(Level = 0) then
    if (Op = Value2) and (Arg1 = 1) then
      begin
        Emit2(LocalValue2, Displ);
        NextInstruction
      end
    else Emit2(LocalVar2, Displ)
  else if Optimize(Level = 1) then
    if (Op = Value2) and (Arg1 = 1) then
      begin
        Emit2(GlobalValue2, Displ);
        NextInstruction
      end
    else Emit2(GlobalVar2, Displ)
  else Emit3(Variable2, Level, Displ)
end;

procedure CopyInstruction;
begin
  if Op in NoArguments then
    Emit1(Op)
  else if Op in OneArgument then
    Emit2(Op, Arg1)
  else if Op in TwoArguments then
    Emit3(Op, Arg1, Arg2)
  else {Op in FourArguments}
    Emit5(Op, Arg1, Arg2, Arg3, Arg4);
  NextInstruction
end;

procedure Assemble;
begin
  Address := 0;
  NextInstruction;
  while Op <> EndProg2 do
    if Op = Assign2 then
      Assign(Arg1)
    else if Op in Blocks then
      Block(Op, Arg1, Arg2, Arg3, Arg4)
```

```
    else if Op = DefAddr2 then
      DefAddr(Arg1)
    else if Op = DefArg2 then
      DefArg(Arg1, Arg2)
    else if Op = Field2 then
      Field(Arg1)
    else if Op in Jumps then
      Jump(Op, Arg1)
    else if Op = ProcCall2 then
      ProcCall(Arg1, Arg2)
    else if Op = Value2 then
      Value(Arg1)
    else if Op = Variable2 then
      Variable(Arg1, Arg2)
    else
      CopyInstruction;
  Emit1(EndProg2)
end;

procedure Initialize;
var LabelNo: integer;
begin
  NoArguments := Operations[Add2, And2, Divide2,
    EndProg2, Equal2, Greater2, Less2, Minus2,
    Modulo2, Multiply2, Not2, NotEqual2,
    NotGreater2, NotLess2, Or2, Subtract2,
    Read2, Write2];
  OneArgument := Operations[Assign2, Constant2,
    Do2, EndProc2, Field2, Goto2, Value2,
    DefAddr2];
  TwoArguments := Operations[ProcCall2, Variable2,
    VarParam2, DefArg2];
  FourArguments := Operations[Index2, Procedure2,
    Program2];
  Blocks := Operations[Procedure2, Program2];
  Jumps := Operations[Do2, Goto2];
  LabelNo := 1;
  while LabelNo <= MaxLabel do
    begin
      Table[LabelNo] := 0;
      LabelNo := labelNo + 1
    end
end;

begin
  Initialize; Assemble;
  Rerun; Assemble
end.
```

A.5 INTERPRETER

```
          {          PASCAL- INTERPRETER
                        20 April 1984
              Copyright (c) 1984 Per Brinch Hansen }

program Interpret;

const
  Min = 0; Max = 8191;

type
  OperationPart = (Add2, And2, Assign2,
    Constant2, Divide2, Do2, EndProc2, EndProg2,
    Equal2, Field2, Goto2, Greater2, Index2,
    Less2, Minus2, Modulo2, Multiply2, Not2,
    NotEqual2, NotGreater2, NotLess2, Or2,
    ProcCall2, Procedure2, Program2, Subtract2,
    Value2, Variable2, VarParam2, Read2,
    Write2, DefAddr2, DefArg2, GlobalCall2,
    GlobalValue2, GlobalVar2, LocalValue2,
    LocalVar2, SimpleAssign2, SimpleValue2);

  Store = array [Min..Max] of integer;

var
  St: Store; p, b, s: integer;
  StackBottom: integer;
  Running: Boolean;

procedure Error(LineNo: integer; Text: String);
begin
  WriteStr('Line'); WriteInt(LineNo, 5);
  Write(SP); WriteStr(Text); Write(NL);
  Running := false
end;

{ VariableAccess = VariableName { Selector } .
  VariableName = "Variable" | "VarParam" .
  Selector = Expression "Index" | "Field" . }

procedure Variable(Level, Displ: integer);
var x: integer;
begin
  s := s + 1;
  x := b;
  while Level > 0 do
    begin
      x := St[x];
```

```
      Level := Level - 1
    end;
  St[s] := x + Displ;
  p := p + 3
end;

procedure VarParam(Level, Displ: integer);
var x: integer;
begin
  s := s + 1;
  x := b;
  while Level > 0 do
    begin
      x := St[x];
      Level := Level - 1
    end;
  St[s] := St[x + Displ];
  p := p + 3
end;

procedure Index(Lower, Upper,
  Length, LineNo: integer);
var i: integer;
begin
  i := St[s]; s := s - 1;
  if (i < Lower) or (i > Upper) then
    Error(LineNo, 'Range Error')
  else
    St[s] := St[s] + (i - Lower) * Length;
  p := p + 5
end;

procedure Field(Displ: integer);
begin St[s] := St[s] + Displ; p := p + 2 end;

{ Factor = "Constant" | VariableAccess "Value" |
    Expression | Factor "Not" . }

procedure Constant(Value: integer);
begin s := s + 1; St[s] := Value; p := p + 2 end;

procedure Value(Length: integer);
var x, i: integer;
begin
  x := St[s]; i := 0;
  while i < Length do
    begin
      St[s + i] := St[x + i];
      i := i + 1
    end;
  s := s + Length - 1;
```

```
  p := p + 2
end;

procedure Notx;
begin
  if St[s] = ord(true)
    then St[s] := ord(false)
    else St[s] := ord(true);
  p := p + 1
end;

{ Term = Factor { Factor MultiplyingOperator } .
  MultiplyingOperator =
    "Multiply" | "Divide" | "Modulo" | "And" . }

procedure Multiply;
begin
  s := s - 1;
  St[s] := St[s] * St[s + 1];
  p := p + 1
end;

procedure Divide;
begin
  s := s - 1;
  St[s] := St[s] div St[s + 1];
  p := p + 1
end;

procedure Modulo;
begin
  s := s - 1;
  St[s] := St[s] mod St[s + 1];
  p := p + 1
end;

procedure Andx;
begin
  s := s - 1;
  if St[s] = ord(true) then
    St[s] := St[s + 1];
  p := p + 1
end;

{ SimpleExpression =
    Term [ SignOperator ] { Term AddingOperator } .
  SignOperator = Empty | "Minus" .
  AddingOperator = "Add" | "Subtract" | "Or" . }

procedure Minus;
begin St[s] := - St[s]; p := p + 1 end;
```

```
procedure Add;
begin
  s := s - 1;
  St[s] := St[s] + St[s + 1];
  p := p + 1
end;

procedure Subtract;
begin
  s := s - 1;
  St[s] := St[s] - St[s + 1];
  p := p + 1
end;

procedure Orx;
begin
  s := s - 1;
  if St[s] = ord(false) then
    St[s] := St[s + 1];
  p := p + 1
end;

{ Expression = SimpleExpression
    [ SimpleExpression RelationalOperator ] .
  RelationalOperator = "Less" | "Equal" | "Greater" |
    "NotGreater" | "NotEqual" | "NotLess" . }

procedure Less;
begin
  s := s - 1;
  St[s] := ord(St[s] < St[s + 1]);
  p := p + 1
end;

procedure Equal;
begin
  s := s - 1;
  St[s] := ord(St[s] = St[s + 1]);
  p := p + 1
end;

procedure Greater;
begin
  s := s - 1;
  St[s] := ord(St[s] > St[s + 1]);
  p := p + 1
end;

procedure NotGreater;
begin
```

```
  s := s - 1;
  St[s] := ord(St[s] <= St[s + 1]);
  p := p + 1
end;

procedure NotEqual;
begin
  s := s - 1;
  St[s] := ord(St[s] <> St[s + 1]);
  p := p + 1
end;

procedure NotLess;
begin
  s := s - 1;
  St[s] := ord(St[s] >= St[s + 1]);
  p := p + 1
end;

{ IOStatement =
    VariableAccess "Read" ¦
    Expression "Write" . }

procedure Readx;
begin
  ReadInt(St[St[s]]);
  s := s - 1; p := p + 1
end;

procedure Writex;
begin
  WriteInt(St[s], 6); Write(NL);
  s := s - 1; p := p + 1
end;

{ ProcedureStatement = IOStatement ¦
    [ ActualParameterList ] "ProcCall" .
  ActualParameterList =
    ActualParameter { ActualParameter } .
  ActualParameter =
    Expression ¦ VariableAccess . }

procedure ProcCall(Level, Displ: integer);
var x: integer;
begin
  s := s + 1;
  x := b;
  while Level > 0 do
    begin
      x := St[x];
      Level := Level - 1
```

```
    end;
  St[s] := x;
  St[s + 1] := b;
  St[s + 2] := p + 3;
  b := s;
  s := b + 2;
  p := p + Displ
end;

{ AssignmentStatement =
    VariableAccess Expression "Assign" . }

procedure Assign(Length: integer);
var x, y, i: integer;
begin
  s := s - Length - 1;
  x := St[s + 1];
  y := s + 2;
  i := 0;
  while i < Length do
    begin
      St[x + i] := St[y + i];
      i := i + 1
    end;
  p := p + 2
end;

{ IfStatement = Expression "Do" Statement
    [ "Goto" Statement ] .
  WhileStatement =
    Expression "Do" Statement "Goto" . }

procedure Dox(Displ: integer);
begin
  if St[s] = ord(true)
    then p := p + 2
    else p := p + Displ;
  s := s - 1
end;

procedure Gotox(Displ: integer);
begin p := p + Displ end;

{ Statement =
    AssignmentStatement | ProcedureStatement |
    IfStatement | WhileStatement |
    CompoundStatement | Empty .
  CompoundStatement = Statement { Statement } .
  BlockBody =
    { ProcedureDefinition } CompoundStatement .
  ProcedureDefinition =
```

```
    "Procedure" BlockBody "EndProc" . }

procedure Procedurex(VarLength, TempLength,
  Displ, LineNo: integer);
begin
  s := s + VarLength;
  if s + TempLength > Max then
    Error(LineNo, 'Stack Limit')
  else
    p := p + Displ
end;

procedure EndProc(ParamLength: integer);
begin
  s := b - ParamLength - 1;
  p := St[b + 2];
  b := St[b + 1]
end;

{ Program = "Program" BlockBody "EndProg" . }

procedure Programx(VarLength, TempLength,
  Displ, Lineno: integer);
begin
  b := StackBottom;
  s := b + 2 + VarLength;
  if s + TempLength > Max then
    Error(LineNo, 'Stack Limit')
  else
    p := p + Displ
end;

procedure EndProg;
begin Running := false end;

{ LocalVar(Displ) = Variable(0, Displ) . }

procedure LocalVar(Displ: integer);
begin
  s := s + 1; St[s] := b + Displ;
  p := p + 2
end;

{ LocalValue(Displ) = LocalVar(Displ) Value(1) . }

procedure LocalValue(Displ: integer);
begin
  s := s + 1; St[s] := St[b + Displ];
  p := p + 2
end;
```

```
{ GlobalVar(Displ) = Variable(1, Displ) . }

procedure GlobalVar(Displ: integer);
begin
  s := s + 1; St[s] := St[b] + Displ;
  p := p + 2
end;

{ GlobalValue(Displ) = GlobalVar(Displ) Value(1) . }

procedure GlobalValue(Displ: integer);
begin
  s := s + 1; St[s] := St[St[b] + Displ];
  p := p + 2
end;

{ SimpleValue = Value(1) . }

procedure SimpleValue;
begin St[s] := St[St[s]]; p := p + 1 end;

{ SimpleAssign = Assign(1) . }

procedure SimpleAssign;
begin
  St[St[s - 1]] := St[s];
  s := s - 2; p := p + 1
end;

{ GlobalCall(Displ) = ProcCall(1, Displ) . }

procedure GlobalCall(Displ: integer);
begin
  St[s + 1] := St[b];
  St[s + 2] := b;
  St[s + 3] := p + 2;
  b := s + 1;
  s := b + 2;
  p := p + Displ
end;

procedure LoadProgram(Name: String);
var x: integer;
begin
  Reset(Name);
  x := Min;
  while not EOF do
    begin
      Read(St[x]:char);
      x := x + 1
    end;
```

```
  StackBottom := x
end;

procedure RunProgram;
var op: OperationPart;
begin
  Running := true; p := Min;
  while Running do
    begin
      op := St[p]:OperationPart;
      if op <= Do2 then
        if op = Add2 then
          Add
        else if op = And2 then
          Andx
        else if op = Assign2 then
          Assign(St[p + 1])
        else if op = Constant2 then
          Constant(St[p + 1])
        else if op = Divide2 then
          Divide
        else  { op = Do2 }
          Dox(St[p + 1])
      else if op <= Greater2 then
        if op = EndProc2 then
          EndProc(St[p + 1])
        else if op = EndProg2 then
          EndProg
        else if op = Equal2 then
          Equal
        else if op = Field2 then
          Field(St[p + 1])
        else if op = Goto2 then
          Gotox(St[p + 1])
        else  { op = Greater2 }
          Greater
      else if op <= Not2 then
        if op = Index2 then
          Index(St[p + 1], St[p + 2],
            St[p + 3], St[p + 4])
        else if op = Less2 then
          Less
        else if op = Minus2 then
          Minus
        else if op = Modulo2 then
          Modulo
        else if op = Multiply2 then
          Multiply
        else  { op = Not2 }
          Notx
      else if op <= Procedure2 then
```

```
        if op = NotEqual2 then
          NotEqual
        else if op = NotGreater2 then
          NotGreater
        else if op = NotLess2 then
          NotLess
        else if op = Or2 then
          Orx
        else if op = ProcCall2 then
          ProcCall(St[p + 1], St[p + 2])
        else  { op = Procedure2 }
          Procedurex(St[p + 1], St[p + 2],
            St[p + 3], St[p + 4])
      else if op <= Read2 then
        if op = Program2 then
          Programx(St[p + 1], St[p + 2],
            St[p + 3], St[p + 4])
        else if op = Subtract2 then
          Subtract
        else if op = Value2 then
          Value(St[p + 1])
        else if op = Variable2 then
          Variable(St[p + 1], St[p + 2])
        else if op = VarParam2 then
          VarParam(St[p + 1], St[p + 2])
        else { op = Read2 }
          Readx
      else if op <= LocalVar2 then
        if op = Write2 then
          Writex
        else if op = GlobalCall2 then
          GlobalCall(St[p + 1])
        else if op = GlobalValue2 then
          GlobalValue(St[p + 1])
        else if op = GlobalVar2 then
          GlobalVar(St[p + 1])
        else if op = LocalValue2 then
          LocalValue(St[p + 1])
        else { op = LocalVar2 }
          LocalVar(St[p + 1])
       else if op = SimpleAssign2 then
          SimpleAssign
       else { op = SimpleValue2 }
          SimpleValue
    end
end;

procedure OpenFiles;
var Code, Input, Output: String;
begin
  WriteStr('  Program = ');
```

```
  ReadStr(Code);
  WriteStr('  Input = ');
  ReadStr(Input);
  WriteStr('  Output = ');
  ReadStr(Output);
  LoadProgram(Code);
  Reset(Input);
  Rewrite(Output)
end;

begin OpenFiles; RunProgram; Close end.
```

A.6 TEST PROGRAMS

```
{ Pascal- Test 1: Correct Symbols }

{abcdefghijklmnopqrstuvwxyz
{ABCDEFGHIJKLMNOPQRSTUVWXYZ
 1234567890} !"#$%&'()*+,-.
 /:;<=>?@[\]_~`}

+   -   *   <   =   >   <=   <>   >=   :=
(   )   [   ]   ,   .   :    ;    ..

0  32767

And  array  begin  const  div  do  else
end  if  mod  not  of  or  procedure
program  record  then  type  var  while

Integer  boolean  false  true  read  write
abcdefghijklmnopqrstuvwxyz0123456789
ABCDEFGHIJKLMNOPQRSTUVWXYZ0123456789
DNA  a12  ac  DNA  a12  ac
```

```
{ Pascal- Test 2: Syntax Analysis }

program Test2;
const
  a = 1; b = a;
type
  T = array [1..2] of integer;
  U = record f, g: integer; h: boolean end;
  V = record f: integer end;
var
  x, y: T; z: U;

procedure P(var x: integer; y: boolean);
const a = 1;

  procedure Q(x: integer);
  type T = array [1..2] of integer;
  begin
    x := - 1;
    x := x;
    x := (2 - 1) * (2 + 1) div 2 mod 2;
    if x < x then
      while x = x do Q(x);
    if x > x then
      while x <= x do P(x, false)
    else
      if not (x <> x) then {Empty}
  end;

begin if x >= x then y := true end;

procedure R;
var x: T;
begin x[1] := 5 end;

begin z.f := 6 end.
```

```
{ Pascal- Test 3: Syntax Errors }

program Test3;
const
  a := 1;
  b = 2;
  c =  ;
  d = 4;
type
  S = recrod f, g: integer end;
  T = array [1..2] of integer;
var
  x: integer;
begin
  if = 2 then
    x := 1
end.
```

```
{ Pascal- Test 4: Scope Analysis }

program Test4;
  type S = record f, g: boolean end;
  var v: S;

  procedure P(x: integer);
    const n = 10;
    type T = array [1..n] of integer;
    var y, z: T;

    procedure Q;
    begin read(x); v.g := false end;

  begin
    y := z;
    Q; P(5);
    write(x)
  end;

begin v.f := true; P(5) end.
```

```
{ Pascal- Test 5: Scope Errors }

program Test5;
const
  {a} = 1;
   b  = b;
type
   T = array [1..10] of T;
   U = record f, g: U end;
var
  x, y, x: integer;
begin
  x := a;
  y := a
end.
```

```
{ Pascal- Test 6: Type Analysis }

program Test6;
const
  a = 10; b = false;
type
  T1 = array [a..a] of integer;
  T2 = record f, g: integer; h : Boolean end;
var
  x, y: integer; z: Boolean;

procedure Q(var x: T1; z: T2);
begin
  x[10] := 1;
  z.f := 1;
  Q(x, z)
end;

procedure P;
begin Read(x); Write(x + 1) end;

begin
  P;
  x := 1;
  x := a;
  x := y;
  x := - (x + 1) * (y - 1) div 9 mod 9;
  z := not b;
  z := z or z and z;
  if x <> y then
    while x < y do {Empty}
end.
```

```
{ Pascal- Test 7: Type Errors }

program Test7;
type T = array [1..10] of integer;
var x: integer; y: Boolean; z: T;

procedure P(x: integer);
begin end;

begin
  y := not 1 and 2
    and 3;
  y := false * true div
    false;
  z := z mod z;
  x := 1 or 2 or
    3;
  y := false + true -
    true;
  z := z - z;
  if z <> z then
    P(true)
end.
```

```
{ Pascal- Test 8: Kind Errors etc. }

program Test8;
const
  a = integer;
type
  T = array [2..1] of integer;
  U = record f: integer end;
var x: integer; y: U;
  z: false;

procedure P(var x: integer;
  y: true);
begin end;

begin
  x[1] := 1;
  x.f := 1;
  P(false,
    true);
  x := P;
  false := true;
  y.g := 1
end.
```

```
{ Pascal- Test 9: Code Generation
          Correct output:
  0 1 2 3 4 5 6 7 -8 9 10 11 12 13
  1 0 1 1 0 0 1 1 0 14 15 16 17 }

program Test9;
const two = 2;
type
  S = array [1..10] of integer;
  T = record f, g: integer end;
var a: integer; b, c: S; d, e: T;

procedure WriteBool(x: Boolean);
begin if x then Write(1) else Write(0) end;

procedure EchoOne;
begin Read(a); Write(a) end;

procedure P(u: integer; var v: integer);
var x: integer;
begin {u = 2, v is bound to a}
  EchoOne;
  Write(u);
  v := 3; Write(a);
  x := 4; Write(x)
end;

procedure Q;
begin Write(5) end;

begin
  Write(0);
  P(two, a);
  Q;
  b[10] := 6; c := b; Write(c[10]);
  d.g := 7;  e := d; Write(e.g);
  Write(- 8); Write(8 + 1);
  Write(11 - 1); Write(22 div 2);
  Write(6 * 2); Write(27 mod 14);
  WriteBool(not false);
  WriteBool(false and true);
  WriteBool(false or true);
  WriteBool(1 < 2); WriteBool(1 = 2);
  WriteBool(1 > 2); WriteBool(1 <= 2);
  WriteBool(1 <> 2); WriteBool(1 >= 2);
  if true then Write(14);
  if false then Write(0) else Write(15);
  a := 16;
  while a <= 17 do
    begin Write(a); a := a + 1 end
end.
```

```
{ Pascal- Test 10: Program Example }

program Test10;
const max = 10;
type T = array [1..max] of integer;
var A: T; k: integer;

  procedure Quicksort(m, n: integer);
  var i, j: integer;

    procedure Partition;
    var r, w: integer;
    begin
      r := A[(m + n) div 2];
      i := m; j := n;
      while i <= j do
        begin
          while A[i] < r do i := i + 1;
          while r < A[j] do j := j - 1;
          if i <= j then
            begin
              w := A[i]; A[i] := A[j];
              A[j] := w; i := i + 1;
              j := j - 1
            end
        end
    end;

  begin
    if m < n then
      begin
        Partition;
        Quicksort(m, j);
        Quicksort(i, n)
      end
  end;

begin
  k := 1;
  while k <= max do
    begin Read(A[k]); k := k + 1 end;
  Quicksort(1, max);
  k := 1;
  while k <= max do
    begin Write(A[k]); k := k + 1 end
end.
```

B

A COMPILER PROJECT

This appendix describes a compiler project for a small programming language called PL ("The Project Language"). The project is divided into phases that correspond to the previous chapters. After reading a chapter you are ready to program the corresponding part of the project. You can use any Pascal compiler for the project.

The following is a weekly *project schedule* for a one-semester course on compilers based on this book:

Week	*Reading*	*Project Phase*
1	Chapters 1–3	
2	Chapter 4	
3	Chapter 4	Lexical Analysis
4	Chapter 5	Lexical Analysis
5	Chapter 5	Syntax Analysis
6	Chapter 6	Syntax Analysis
7	Chapter 7	Syntax Analysis
8	Chapter 7	Error Recovery

Week	*Reading*	*Project Phase*
9	Chapter 8	Scope Analysis
10	Chapter 8	Type Analysis
11	Chapter 9	Type Analysis
12	Chapter 9	Code Generation
13	Chapter 10	Code Generation
14		

To follow this schedule you must program about 100 lines of the compiler every week (including testing and documentation).

B.1 THE PL LANGUAGE

The programming language PL is a Pascal-like language with parallel assignments and guarded commands. Algorithm B.1 illustrates the features of PL.

A *program* is a block followed by a period. A *block* consists of definition part DP followed by a statement part SP:

begin DP SP **end**

A block describes operations on named entities called *objects*. An object is either a constant, a variable, or a procedure. (Types are denoted by word symbols instead of names.) Every object is introduced by a definition. There are no standard objects. The scope rules are the same as in Pascal—. Every activation of a block creates a new instance of the variables defined in the block.

The definition part of a block is a sequence of definitions followed by semicolons:

D1; D2; . . . Dm;

A *constant definition* introduces the name of a constant; for example,

const n = 10

A *variable definition* introduces the names of variables of the same type; for example,

integer x, i

The simple types of PL are denoted **integer** and **Boolean**. (The words **integer** and **Boolean** are not names but word symbols.)

```
$ PL Program: Linear Search
begin
  const n = 10; integer array A[n];
  integer x, i; Boolean found;

  proc Search
  begin integer m;
    i, m := 1, n;
    do i < m ->
      if A[i] = x -> m := i; []
        ~ (A[i] = x) -> i := i + 1;
      fi;
    od;
    found := A[i] = x;
  end;

  $ Input Table:
  i := 1;
  do ~ (i > n) -> read A[i]; i := i + 1; od;
  $ Test Search:
  read x;
  do ~ (x = 0) ->
    call Search;
    if found -> write x, i; []
      ~ found -> write x;
    fi;
    read x;
  od;
end.
```

Algorithm B.1

The variable definition

integer array A[n]

introduces an *array variable* with elements of type integer. Array elements can only be of simple types, and the indices must be natural numbers 1, 2, . . . , n. The number n is called the *length* of the array.

A *procedure definition* introduces the name of a block without parameters; for example,

proc Search
begin . . . **end**

The statement part of a block is a sequence of statements followed by semicolons:

S1; S2; . . . Sn;

An *empty statement* is denoted

skip

A *read statement* inputs one or more integers and assigns them to variables; for example,

read A[i]

A *write statement* outputs one or more integers defined by expressions; for example,

write x, i

The operands of read and write statements must be of type integer.

A *procedure statement* activates a procedure block; for example,

call Search

An *assignment statement* consists of a variable access list followed by an expression list; for example,

i, m := 1, n

Every variable access on the left side corresponds to an expression on the right side: The variable i corresponds to the expression 1, and the variable m corresponds to the expression n. The variable accesses must denote different variables (but the compiler cannot check that). The variable accesses and expressions must all be of the same simple type.

An assignment statement is executed in three steps:

(1) The variable accesses are evaluated from left to right to obtain a set of addresses.

(2) The expressions are evaluated from left to right to obtain a set of values.

(3) The values are assigned to the corresponding variables in arbitrary order.

This is known as a "parallel assignment."

An *if statement* has the form

```
if B1 -> SP1 [] B2 -> SP2 [] ... [] Bn -> SPn fi
```

For example,

```
if found -> write x, i; []
   ~found -> write x;
fi
```

The operator ~ denotes a **not** operation.

An if statement consists of *guarded commands* of the form

```
B -> SP
```

where B is a Boolean expression (called "a guard") while SP is a statement part; for example,

```
~found -> write x;
```

If one or more guards have the value **true**, the computer arbitrarily selects one of them and executes the corresponding statement part. The order in which the guards are evaluated is undefined. (The compiler writer can therefore choose the most convenient order.) If all the guards are **false**, the program execution is stopped with an error message.

A *do statement* also consists of guarded commands:

```
do B1 -> SP1 [] B2 -> SP2 [] ... [] Bn -> SPn od
```

For example,

```
do ~(i > n) -> read A[i]; i := i + 1; od
```

If one or more guards are **true**, the computer arbitrarily picks one of them and executes the corresponding statement part. The computer continues to look for true guards and execute statement parts until all the guards are false. At that point, the execution of the do statement ends.

The *relational operators*

```
<   =   >
```

apply to operands of the same simple type. The results are of type Boolean.

The *arithmetic operators*

```
+   -   *   /   \
```

apply to operands of type integer and yield integer results. The operators "/" and "\" denote the "**div**" and "**mod**" operations of Pascal.

The *Boolean operators*

& | ~

denote the operations **and**, **or**, and **not**.

The operators fall into four classes, shown below in order of increasing *precedence*:

Primary operators:	&	|	
Relational operators:	<	=	>
Adding operators:	+	−	
Multiplying operators:	*	/	\
Not operator:	~		

The PL grammar at the end of this section reflects these precedence rules. (Notice that Pascal uses different precedence rules.)

The Boolean values are denoted by the word symbols

false **true**

Capital letters and small letters are considered different. Only the first 10 characters of a name are significant. The word symbols cannot be used as names.

Two adjacent word symbols, names, or numerals must be separated by at least one separator. The *separators* are spaces, newline characters, and comments. There may be any number of separators before and after a symbol.

A *comment* extends from a "$" sign to the end of a line; for example,

$ Input Table:

Here is the *PL grammar*:

Program = Block "." .
Block = "**begin**" DefinitionPart StatementPart "**end**" .
DefinitionPart = { Definition ";" } .
Definition = ConstantDefinition | VariableDefinition |
  ProcedureDefinition .
ConstantDefinition =
  "**const**" ConstantName "=" Constant .

```
VariableDefinition = TypeSymbol VariableList |
  TypeSymbol "array" VariableList "[" Constant "]" .
TypeSymbol = "integer" | "Boolean" .
VariableList = VariableName { "," VariableName } .
ProcedureDefinition = "proc" ProcedureName Block .
StatementPart = { Statement ";" } .
Statement =
  EmptyStatement | ReadStatement | WriteStatement |
  AssignmentStatement | ProcedureStatement |
  IfStatement | DoStatement .
EmptyStatement = "skip" .
ReadStatement = "read" VariableAccessList .
VariableAccessList =
  VariableAccess { "," VariableAccess } .
WriteStatement = "write" ExpressionList .
ExpressionList = Expression { "," Expression } .
AssignmentStatement =
  VariableAccessList ":=" ExpressionList .
ProcedureStatement = "call" ProcedureName .
IfStatement = "if" GuardedCommandList "fi" .
DoStatement = "do" GuardedCommandList "od" .
GuardedCommandList =
  GuardedCommand { "[]" GuardedCommand } .
GuardedCommand = Expression "->" StatementPart .
Expression = PrimaryExpression
  { PrimaryOperator PrimaryExpression } .
PrimaryOperator = "&" | "|" .
PrimaryExpression = SimpleExpression
  [ RelationalOperator SimpleExpression ] .
RelationalOperator = "<" | "=" | ">" .
SimpleExpression =
  [ "-" ] Term { AddingOperator Term } .
AddingOperator = "+" | "-" .
Term = Factor { MultiplyingOperator Factor } .
MultiplyingOperator = "*" | "/" | "\" .
Factor = Constant | VariableAccess |
  "(" Expression ")" | "~" Factor .
VariableAccess = VariableName [ IndexedSelector ] .
IndexedSelector = "[" Expression "]" .
Constant = Numeral | BooleanSymbol | ConstantName .
Numeral = Digit { Digit } .
BooleanSymbol = "false" | "true" .
Name = Letter { Letter | Digit | "_" } .
```

B.2 PROJECT PHASES

Write a single-pass compiler for PL in the stepwise manner outlined in the following. The compiler should be able to translate a PL program of 300 lines with 100 names.

The project, which involves programming about 1200 lines, is divided into 6 phases.

Lexical Analysis

(1) Make a list of the word symbols and special symbols of PL and define an enumerated type that represents these symbols.

(2) Program the scanner as a procedure that inputs the next symbol of a PL program and assigns the corresponding enumeration value to a global variable. Use linear searching to recognize word symbols and names.

(3) Write a PL program (Test 1) to test the scanner systematically. Make the scanner analyze this program and print the ordinal values of the symbols.

Programming effort: 250 lines (2 weeks).

Syntax Analysis

(4) Make a list of the First and Follow symbols of each BNF rule of PL. Find the BNF rules that do not satisfy Grammar Restrictions 1 and 2 and rewrite those rules.

(5) Extend the compiler with parsing procedures *without* error recovery.

(6) Write a PL program (Test 2) to test the parsing of correct PL sentences. Use this program to test the parser.

Programming effort: 350 lines (3 weeks).

Error Recovery

(7) Extend the parsing procedures with recovery actions for syntax errors.

(8) Write a PL program (Test 3) to test the detection of syntax errors and the error recovery. Use Tests 2 and 3 to test the final parser.

Programming effort: 100 lines (1 week).

Scope Analysis

(9) Extend the compiler with scope analysis. *Hint*: Remember that the symbols **integer, Boolean, false,** and **true** are word symbols, not names.

(10) Write two PL programs (Tests 4 and 5) to test scope analysis of programs without and with scope errors. Use these programs to test the scope analysis.

Programming effort: 100 lines (1 week).

Type Analysis

(11) Extend the compiler with type analysis. *Hint*: The data types of PL are denoted by word symbols instead of names. Since types are not named objects they cannot be described by object records. They must be described by variant records of another type.

(12) Write two test programs (Tests 6 and 7) to test type analysis of programs without and with type errors. Use these programs to test the type analysis.

Program effort: 200 lines (2 weeks).

Code Generation

(13) Extend the compiler to make it generate code for the PL Interpreter listed in Section B.3. The program text of the interpreter includes the code rules of PL.

The interpreter checks for stack overflow. Consequently, the compiler does *not* have to estimate the extent of the temporaries used in blocks.

The interpreter loads the code of a compiled program at the beginning of the store (starting at address 1) and uses *absolute* addresses in jump instructions.

The compiler stores the code in a table and outputs it at the end of the compilation. Find a method for handling the forward references in jump instructions. (The basic idea is to go back and modify jump instructions in the code table whenever the compiler reaches a point where a jump address is known.)

In Pascal, the local variables of a block are introduced by a single variable definition part. In PL, a block may contain variable definitions in several different places. This syntactic freedom requires a slight modification of the method used to compile variable addresses.

(14) Write a PL program (Test 8) to test the code generation and make the compiler print the absolute addresses and ordinal values of the operation parts and arguments of the code.

(15) As a final demonstration, compile and interpret the sample program (Algorithm B.1).

Programming effort: 200 lines (2 weeks).

B.3 THE PL INTERPRETER

```
        {           THE PL INTERPRETER
                      20 April 1984
           Copyright (c) 1984 Per Brinch Hansen }

program PLInterpreter;
const Min = 1; Max = 4000;
type
  OperationPart = (Add2, And2, Arrow2, Assign2,
    Bar2, Call2, Constant2, Divide2, EndProc2,
    EndProg2, Equal2, Fi2, Greater2, Index2,
    Less2, Minus2, Modulo2, Multiply2, Not2,
    Or2, Proc2, Prog2, Read2, Subtract2,
    Value2, Variable2, Write2);

  Store = array [Min..Max] of integer;
var
  St: Store; p, b, s: integer;
  StackBottom: integer;
  Running: Boolean;

procedure Error(LineNo: integer; Text: String);
begin
  WriteStr('LineNo'); WriteInt(LineNo, 5);
  Write(SP); WriteStr(Text); Write(NL);
  Running := false
end;

procedure Allocate(Words: integer);
begin s := s + Words;
  if s > Max then
    begin WriteStr('Stack Overflow');
      Write(NL); Running := false
    end
end;

{ VariableAccess =
    "Variable" [ Expresion "Index" ] . }

procedure Variable(Level, Displ: integer);
var x: integer;
begin Allocate(1); x := b;
  while Level > 0 do
    begin x := St[x];
      Level := Level - 1
    end;
  St[s] := x + Displ;
  p := p + 3
```

```
end;

procedure Index(Bound, LineNo: integer);
var i: integer;
begin i := St[s]; s := s - 1;
  if (i < 1) or (i > Bound) then
    Error(LineNo, 'Range Error')
  else
    St[s] := St[s] + i - 1;
  p := p + 3
end;

{ Factor = "Constant" | VariableAccess "Value" |
    Expression | Factor "Not" . }

procedure Constant(Value: integer);
begin Allocate(1); St[s] := Value; p := p + 2 end;

procedure Value;
begin St[s] := St[St[s]]; p := p + 1 end;

procedure Notx;
begin St[s] := 1 - St[s]; p := p + 1 end;

{ Term = Factor { Factor MultiplyingOperator } .
  MultiplyingOperator =
    "Multiply" | "Divide" | "Modulo" . }

procedure Multiply;
begin p := p + 1; s := s - 1;
  St[s] := St[s] * St[s + 1]
end;

procedure Divide;
begin p := p + 1; s := s - 1;
  St[s] := St[s] div St[s + 1]
end;

procedure Modulo;
begin p := p + 1; s := s - 1;
  St[s] := St[s] mod St[s + 1]
end;

{ SimpleExpression =
    Term [ "Minus" ] { Term AddingOperator } .
  AddingOperator = "Add" | "Subtract" . }

procedure Minus;
begin St[s] := - St[s]; p := p + 1 end;

procedure Add;
```

```
begin p := p + 1; s := s - 1;
  St[s] := St[s] + St[s + 1]
end;

procedure Subtract;
begin p := p + 1; s := s - 1;
  St[s] := St[s] - St[s + 1]
end;

{ PrimaryExpression = SimpleExpression
    [ SimpleExpression RelationalOperator ] .
  RelationalOperator =
    "Less" | "Equal" | "Greater" . }

procedure Less;
begin p := p + 1; s := s - 1;
  St[s] := ord(St[s] < St[s + 1])
end;

procedure Equal;
begin p := p + 1; s := s - 1;
  St[s] := ord(St[s] = St[s + 1])
end;

procedure Greater;
begin p := p + 1; s := s - 1;
  St[s] := ord(St[s] > St[s + 1])
end;

{ Expression = PrimaryExpression
    { PrimaryExpression PrimaryOperator } .
  PrimaryOperator = "And" | "Or" . }

procedure Andx;
begin p := p + 1; s := s - 1;
  if St[s] = ord(true) then
    St[s] := St[s + 1]
end;

procedure Orx;
begin p := p + 1; s := s - 1;
  if St[s] = ord(false) then
    St[s] := St[s + 1]
end;

{ ReadStatement = VariableList "Read" .
  VariableList =
    VariableAccess { VariableAccess } . }

procedure Readx(No: integer);
var x: integer;
```

```
begin p := p + 2;
   s := s - No; x := s;
   while x < s + No do
    begin x := x + 1;
      ReadInt(St[St[x]])
    end
end;

{ WriteStatement = ExpressionList "Write" .
  Expression = Expression { Expression } . }

procedure Writex(No: integer);
var x: integer;
begin p := p + 2;
  s := s - No; x := s;
  while x < s + No do
    begin x := x + 1;
      WriteInt(St[x], 6); Write(NL)
    end
end;

{ AssignmentStatement =
    VariableList ExpressionList . }

procedure Assign(No: integer);
var x: integer;
begin p := p + 2;
  s := s - 2 * No; x := s;
  while x < s + No do
    begin x := x + 1;
      St[St[x]] := St[x + No]
    end
end;

{ ProcedureStatement = "Call" . }

procedure Callx(Level, Addr: integer);
var x: integer;
begin
  Allocate(3); x := b;
  while Level > 0 do
    begin x := St[x];
      Level := Level - 1
    end;
  St[s - 2] := x;
  St[s - 1] := b;
  St[s] := p + 3;
  b := s - 2;
  p := Addr
end;
```

```
{ IfStatement = GuardedCommandList "Fi" .
  DoStatement = GuardedCommandList .
  GuardedCommandList =
    GuardedCommand { GuardedCommand } .
  GuardedCommand =
    Expression "Arrow" StatementPart "Bar" . }

procedure Arrow(Addr: integer);
begin
  if St[s] = ord(true) then p := p + 2
  else p := Addr;
  s := s - 1
end;

procedure Bar(Addr: integer);
begin p := Addr end;

procedure Fi(LineNo: integer);
begin Error(LineNo, 'If Statement Fails') end;

{ ProcedureDefinition = "Proc" Block "EndProc" .
  Block =
    { ProcedureDefinition } StatementPart .
  StatementPart = { Statement } .
  Statement =
    Empty ¦ ReadStatement ¦ WriteStatement ¦
    AssignmentStatement ¦ ProcedureStatement ¦
    IfStatement ¦ DoStatement . }

procedure Proc(Varlength, Addr: integer);
begin Allocate(VarLength); p := Addr end;

procedure EndProc;
begin s := b - 1;
  p := St[b + 2]; b := St[b + 1]
end;

{ Program = "Prog" Block "EndProg" . }

procedure Prog(VarLength, Addr: integer);
begin b := StackBottom; s := b;
  Allocate(VarLength + 2); p := Addr
end;

procedure EndProg;
begin Running := false end;

procedure LoadProgram(Name: String);
var x: integer;
begin Reset(Name); x := Min;
  while not EOF do
```

```
    begin Read(St[x]:char); x := x + 1 end;
  StackBottom := x
end;

procedure RunProgram;
var op: OperationPart;
begin Running := true; p := Min;
  while Running do
    begin op := St[p]:OperationPart;
      if op <= Bar2 then
        if op = Add2 then Add
        else if op = And2 then Andx
        else if op = Arrow2 then Arrow(St[p + 1])
        else if op = Assign2 then Assign(St[p + 1])
        else { op = Bar2 } Bar(St[p + 1])
      else if op <= EndProg2 then
        if op = Call2 then
          Callx(St[p + 1], St[p + 2])
        else if op = Constant2 then
          Constant(St[p + 1])
        else if op = Divide2 then Divide
        else if op = EndProc2 then EndProc
        else { op = EndProg2 } EndProg
      else if op <= Less2 then
        if op = Equal2 then Equal
        else if op = Fi2 then Fi(St[p + 1])
        else if op = Greater2 then Greater
        else if op = Index2 then
          Index(St[p + 1], St[p + 2])
        else { op = Less2 } Less
      else if op <= Or2 then
        if op = Minus2 then Minus
        else if op = Modulo2 then Modulo
        else if op = Multiply2 then Multiply
        else if op = Not2 then Notx
        else { op = Or2 } Orx
      else if op <= Value2 then
        if op = Proc2 then
          Proc(St[p + 1], St[p + 2])
        else if op = Prog2 then
          Prog(St[p + 1], St[p + 2])
        else if op = Read2 then Readx(St[p + 1])
        else if op = Subtract2 then Subtract
        else { op = Value2 } Value
      else if op = Variable2 then
        Variable(St[p + 1], St[p + 2])
      else {op = Write2 } Writex(St[p + 1])
    end
end;

procedure OpenFiles;
```

```
var Code, Input, Output: String;
begin
  WriteStr('  Program = ');
  ReadStr(Code);
  WriteStr('  Input = ');
  ReadStr(Input);
  WriteStr('  Output = ');
  ReadStr(Output);
  LoadProgram(Code);
  Reset(Input);
  Rewrite(Output)
end;

begin OpenFiles; RunProgram; Close end.
```

REFERENCES

The textbooks by Gries [1971] and Aho and Ullman [1977] cover a variety of compilation methods from a somewhat theoretical point of view. Among other topics, they discuss finite automata and lexical analysis, context-free grammars, parse trees, top-down versus bottom-up parsing, and code optimization for traditional computers. Rosen [1967] includes reprints of some of the early papers on compilers.

Findlay and Watt [1978] is a good introduction to Pascal which also explains variant records, sets, and pointers. Wirth [1976] summarizes the data structures of Pascal and illustrates their use in the design of algorithms. The original Pascal Report is included in Jensen and Wirth [1974]. Welsh et al. [1977] discuss the ambiguities in Pascal. As Backhouse [1979] puts it: "The scope rules in Pascal are ambiguous because their definition in the Report is virtually non-existent!" Many of the problems of Pascal have been corrected in the IEEE Pascal Standard [1983]. Brinch Hansen [1985] defines the programming language Pascal* that was used to develop the Pascal— compiler.

The Algol 60 Report [Naur, 1963a] was the first use of the BNF notation to define a programming language. In addition, it defines the semantics of the language more concisely than any other language report I know.

Edison is an example of a programming language in which record fields follow the same scope rules as other kinds of objects [Brinch Hansen, 1983].

Wirth [1971] describes the first Pascal compiler which was developed for the CDC 6000 computers. Ammann [1974] summarizes a single-pass Pascal compiler that was developed in the stepwise manner recommended for the compiler project. Wirth [1975] describes a portable compiler for a Pascal subset which generates interpreted code for an ideal computer.

Knuth's volume 3 [1973] contains a comprehensive discussion and analysis of hashing.

The testing methods used here are mostly due to Naur [1963b, 1974].

Backhouse [1979] includes a thorough discussion of recursive-descent parsing with error recovery. Wirth [1976], Hartmann [1977], and Welsh and McKeag [1980] discuss variations of the error recovery method used here.

Dijkstra [1960] introduced the use of a stack to implement recursive procedures. In his version, the current context is represented by a table (called the "display") instead of a chain of static links. The Burroughs B5000 computer was one of the first language-based computers [Barton, 1961]. Organick [1973] is a detailed description of two later versions of the B5000 (the B5700 and the B6700 computers). Brinch Hansen [1983] introduces the idea of defining compiled code by a context-free grammar. Shimasaki et al. [1980] includes measurements of the frequency with which Pascal compilers refer to their local and global variables. Wirth [1971] comments on the difficulty of compiling code for a traditional computer (the CDC 6000). Wulf et al. [1975] describes the design of an optimizing BLISS compiler for the PDP 11 computers.

The parallel assignments and guarded comments of PL are due to Dijkstra [1976].

AHO, A. V., and ULLMAN, J. D., *Principles of Compiler Design.* Addison-Wesley, Reading, MA, 1977.

AMMANN, U., "The Method of Structured Programming Applied to the Development of a Compiler." *International Computing Symposium 1973.* North-Holland, Amsterdam, The Netherlands, 1974.

BACKHOUSE, R. C., *Syntax of Programming Languages: Theory and Practice.* Prentice-Hall, Englewood Cliffs, NJ, 1979.

BARTON, R. S., "A New Approach to the Functional Design of a Computer." *Proceedings of the Western Joint Computer Conference*, pp. 393–396, 1961.

BRINCH HANSEN, P., *The Architecture of Concurrent Programs.* Prentice-Hall, Englewood Cliffs, NJ, 1977.

BRINCH HANSEN, P., *Programming a Personal Computer.* Prentice-Hall, Englewood Cliffs, NJ, 1983.

BRINCH HANSEN, P., *The Pascal* Handbook for IBM Personal Computers.* 1985.

DIJKSTRA, E. W., "Recursive Programming." *Numerische Mathematik 2,* pp. 312–318, 1960. (Reprinted in Rosen, 1967).

DIJKSTRA, E. W., *A Discipline of Programming.* Prentice-Hall, Englewood Cliffs, NJ, 1976.

FINDLAY, W., and WATT, D. A., *Pascal—An Introduction to Methodical Programming.* Computer Science Press, Potomac, MD, 1978.

GRIES, D., *Compiler Construction for Digital Computers.* Wiley, New York, 1971.

HARTMANN, A. C., "A Concurrent Pascal Compiler for MiniComputers." *Lecture Notes in Computer Science 50,* Springer-Verlag, New York, 1977.

IEEE Standard Pascal Computer Programming Language. IEEE, New York, 1983.

IFIP Guide to Concepts and Terms in Data Processing. North-Holland, Amsterdam, The Netherlands, 1971.

INTEL, *MCS-86 User's Manual.* Santa Clara, CA, July 1978.

JENSEN, K., and WIRTH, N., "Pascal User Manual and Report." *Lecture Notes in Computer Science 18,* Springer-Verlag, New York, 1974.

KNUTH, D. E., *The Art of Computer Programming*: Vol. 3: *Sorting and Searching.* Addison-Wesley, Reading, MA, 1973.

NAUR, P., "Revised Report on the Algorithmic Language Algol 60." *Communications of the ACM 6* (1), pp. 1–17, Jan. 1963a. (Reprinted in Rosen, 1967.)

NAUR, P., "The Design of the Gier Algol Compiler." *BIT 3* (2–3), pp. 124–143 and 145–166, 1963b.

NAUR, P., *Concise Survey of Computer Methods.* Studentlitteratur, Lund, Sweden, 1974.

ORGANICK, E. I., *Computer System Organization: The B5700/B6700 Series.* Academic Press, New York, 1973.

ROSEN, S., *Programming Systems and Languages.* McGraw-Hill, New York, 1967.

SHIMASAKI, M., et al., "An Analysis of Pascal Programs in Compiler Writing." *Software—Practice and Experience 10,* pp. 149–157, 1980.

WEAVER, W., *Lady Luck. The Theory of Probability.* Doubleday, Garden City, NY, 1963.

WELSH, J., SNEERINGER, W., and HOARE, C. A. R., "Ambiguities and Insecurities in Pascal." *Software—Practice and Experience 7,* pp. 685–696, 1977.

WELSH, J., and McKEAG, M., *Structured System Programming.* Prentice-Hall, Englewood Cliffs, NJ, 1980.

WIRTH, N., "The Design of a Pascal Compiler." *Software—Practice and Experience 1,* pp. 309–333, 1971.

WIRTH, N., *Pascal-S: A Subset and Its Implementation.* ETH, Zurich, Switzerland, June 1975.

WIRTH, N., *Algorithms + Data Structures = Programs.* Prentice-Hall, Englewood Cliffs, NJ, 1976.

WULF, W., et al., *The Design of an Optimizing Compiler.* American Elsevier, New York, 1975.

SOFTWARE DISTRIBUTION

The Pascal* System is an educational software system for IBM Personal Computers written by Per Brinch Hansen. The system can be used to edit, compile, execute, and print programs written in Pascal*—a Pascal subset extended with

Concurrency
Modules
Library procedures
External procedures

Pascal* does not support reals, nested procedures, procedures as parameters, case, for, goto, repeat, and with statements.

The Pascal* System can be used for programming projects in computer science courses on

Introductory Programming
Data Structures and Algorithms
Compilers
Concurrent Programming
Operating Systems

The object code of the Pascal* System is stored on a 5 1/4″ double-sided diskette for IBM Personal Computers. To use the Pascal* Diskette, you need one of these personal computers

IBM Personal Computer
IBM Portable Computer
IBM Personal Computer jr.
Compaq Portable Computer

with

64 K bytes memory
Keyboard
Monochrome display (with adapter)
Printer (with parallel adapter)
Single (or dual) drive for
5 1/4″ double-sided diskettes

The Pascal* System can read text files written by Per Brinch Hansen's Edison-PC System (and vice versa) on double-sided diskettes.

Please use the reverse side of this form to obtain information on how to order the Pascal* Handbook and Diskette.

Karl V. Karlstrom
Computer Science Editor
Prentice-Hall, Inc.
Englewood Cliffs, New Jersey 07632
U.S.A.

INFORMATION REQUEST

Please send me information on how to order Per Brinch Hansen's Pascal* Handbook and Diskette for IBM Personal Computers.

Name ____

Address ____

____

____

____

____

INDEX

A

B

O

P